Learn to Program with Assembly

Foundational Learning for New Programmers

Jonathan Bartlett

Apress®

Learn to Program with Assembly: Foundational Learning for New Programmers

Jonathan Bartlett
Tulsa, OK, USA

ISBN-13 (pbk): 978-1-4842-7436-1   ISBN-13 (electronic): 978-1-4842-7437-8
https://doi.org/10.1007/978-1-4842-7437-8

Managing Director, Apress Media LLC: Welmoed Spahr
Acquisitions Editor: Steve Anglin
Development Editor: Matthew Moodie
Coordinating Editor: Mark Powers

Cover designed by eStudioCalamar

Cover image by Sitraka Rakotoarivelo on Unsplash (www.unsplash.com)

Distributed to the book trade worldwide by Apress Media, LLC, 1 New York Plaza, New York, NY 10004, U.S.A. Phone 1-800-SPRINGER, fax (201) 348-4505, e-mail orders-ny@springer-sbm.com, or visit www. springeronline.com. Apress Media, LLC is a California LLC and the sole member (owner) is Springer Science + Business Media Finance Inc (SSBM Finance Inc). SSBM Finance Inc is a **Delaware** corporation.

For information on translations, please e-mail booktranslations@springernature.com; for reprint, paperback, or audio rights, please e-mail bookpermissions@springernature.com.

Apress titles may be purchased in bulk for academic, corporate, or promotional use. eBook versions and licenses are also available for most titles. For more information, reference our Print and eBook Bulk Sales web page at http://www.apress.com/bulk-sales.

Any source code or other supplementary material referenced by the author in this book is available to readers on GitHub. For more detailed information, please visit http://www.apress.com/source-code.

Printed on acid-free paper

Dedicated to Dale and Cindy Hanchey. Learning from their wisdom set me up for a career full of success.

Table of Contents

About the Author

Jonathan Bartlett is a software developer, researcher, and writer. His first book, *Programming from the Ground Up*, has been required reading in computer science programs from DeVry to Princeton. He has been the sole or lead author for eight books on topics ranging from computer programming to calculus. He is a Senior Software Research and Development Engineer for Specialized Bicycle Components with a focus on cross-team and cross-platform integration work.

About the Technical Reviewer

Paul Cohen joined Intel Corporation during the very early days of the x86 architecture, starting with the 8086, and retired from Intel after 26 years in sales/marketing/management. He is currently partnered with Douglas Technology Group, focusing on the creation of technology books on behalf of Intel and other corporations. Paul also teaches a class that transforms middle- and high-school students into real, confident entrepreneurs, in conjunction with the Young Entrepreneurs Academy (YEA), and is a traffic commissioner for the city of Beaverton, Oregon, and on the board of directors of multiple nonprofit organizations.

CHAPTER 1

Introduction

1.1 The Purpose of the Book

Have you ever wondered how your computer works? I mean, how it *really* works, underneath the hood? I've found that many people, including professional computer programmers, actually have no idea how computers operate at their most fundamental level.

You need to read this book whether or not you ever plan on writing assembly language code. If you plan on programming computers, you need to read this book in order to demystify the operation of your most basic tool—the processor itself. I've worked with a lot of programmers over the years. While you can do good work only knowing high-level languages, I have found that there is a glass ceiling of effectiveness that awaits programmers who haven't learned the machine's own language.

Learning assembly language is about learning how the processor itself thinks about your code. It is about gaining the mind of the machine. Even if you never use assembly language in practice, the depth of understanding you will receive by learning assembly language will make your time and effort worthwhile. You will understand at a more visceral level the various trade-offs that are made with different programming languages and why certain high-level operations may be faster than others and get an overall sense of what your computer is really doing.

Additionally, while the practical uses of assembly language are getting fewer and further between, there are still many places where assembly language knowledge is needed. Compiler writers, kernel developers, and high-performance library implementers all utilize assembly language to some degree and probably always will. Additionally, embedded developers, because of resource constraints, often program in assembly language as well.

© Jonathan Bartlett 2021
J. Bartlett, *Learn to Program with Assembly*, https://doi.org/10.1007/978-1-4842-7437-8_1

1.2 Who Is This Book For?

This book is for programmers at any level. This book should work as your first or your fortieth programming book. Some later chapters will assume some familiarity with various programming languages, but the core content is written so that anyone can pick it up and read it.

I generally assume some working knowledge of Linux and the command line. However, if you haven't used the command line, Appendix B will give a brief introduction.

If you don't use Linux as your primary operating system, that's okay, too. I've built a Docker image that is customized to work with this book, and Appendix A will help you get started using it.

You only need to know the basics—how to run programs on the command line, how to edit text files, etc. If you have done any work at all on the command line (or have read and worked through Appendix B), you probably know everything that you need to get started. If you haven't, there are numerous tutorials on the Internet about getting started on the command line. You don't need to be an advanced systems administrator. If you know how to change location, edit files, and create directories, that's all the skills you actually need.

1.3 Why Learn Assembly Language?

In the modern age of modern programming languages where a single line of code can replace hundreds of lines of assembly language, why bother to study assembly language at all? The fact is assembly language is how your computer runs. Any good craftsman knows how their tools work, and computer programming is no different. Knowing your tools helps you get the most out of them.

The biggest advantage is one that is hard to point to concretely—it is simply understanding how the pieces fit together. Some people are perfectly happy not knowing how the tools that they work with actually function. However, those people often wind up being mystified by certain problems and then have to go to someone who actually knows how these tools function to figure it out. Knowing assembly language makes *you* the guru who understands how everything fits together.

Of course, there are also more practical reasons I can point to. Understanding how many security exploits work relies on understanding how the computer is actually operating. So, if your goal is to do computer security work, in order to actually understand how hackers are manipulating the system, you have to know how the system works in general.

Some people learn assembly language so that they can make faster programs. While modern optimizing compilers are really great at making fast assembly language, since they are computer programs, they can only operate according to fixed rules and axioms. Human creativity, however, allows for the creation of new ideas which go beyond what computers are programmed to do.[1]

There are other cases where assembly language is actually simpler for programming. For many embedded processors and applications, programming in a high-level language is actually *harder* than just programming in assembly language directly. If you are doing low-level work with hardware working with individual bits and bytes, then assembly language oftentimes winds up being *more* straightforward and easy to program in than a high-level language.[2]

There are also many areas of modern programming on standard computers which *must* happen in assembly language, or at least require a background knowledge of it. Compilers, new programming languages, operating system code, drivers, and other system-level features all require either direct assembly language programming or a background knowledge of it.

Again, I will say that, for me, the greatest benefit of learning assembly language programming is simply gaining a better mental model for what is happening in the computer when I'm programming. When people describe security exploits, I can understand what they are talking about. When people describe why some programming feature "costs" too much in terms of execution speed, I have a mental framework to understand why. When low-level issues arise, I have a feel for what sorts of things might be causing problems.

---

[1] The optimal methodology is actually to combine both humans and computers and let the computer apply the fixed rules and let human creativity see where they can improve upon them.

[2] Note that most embedded processors will use a *different* assembly language than the one in this book. Nevertheless, I think that you will find learning the assembly language that is on your own computer beneficial and that most of the *ideas* transfer easily to other processors, even if the instructions are a little different. Embedded processors come with a whole host of their own difficulties, so having mastery of assembly language *in general* before trying to program an embedded processor is definitely worthwhile.

1.4 A Note to New Programmers

If you are reading this book and you are new to programming, I want to offer a special word to you. While I think you have made a good choice using this book to learn programming, I want you to know that it may not be as exciting as other programming languages. Reading this book will help you to gain the understanding of the processor to make you great at programming. Because you know all the things the computer is doing under the hood, you will have insights when doing more exciting types of programming that others won't have.

However, assembly language itself is not incredibly exciting to write. You are literally doing everything by hand, so even doing simple things tends to take a long time. The purpose of higher-level programming languages is to speed up the process of writing code. What I don't want you to do is to read this book and then think, "Oh my! Programming takes so much work!" Remember, most of us got into this business to automate things, and that includes automating the task of programming. Many experienced programmers can pack a lot of juice into even a single line of code in a high-level language.

If you don't know, programming languages are generally grouped into "high-level" and "low-level" languages. Higher-level languages are focused more on making code that matches more closely the problem you are trying to solve, while lower-level languages are focused on making code that more closely follows the computer's own mode of operation. Assembly language is the almost-lowest-level language there is. The instructions in assembly language exactly match the instructions that the processor executes. The only thing lower than assembly language is writing machine opcodes (see Appendix K if that is of interest to you). As you will see, computers translate *everything* into numbers. That includes your programs. However, it would be hard to read and manipulate a program if it were just numbers. Therefore, almost everyone writes the actual code in assembly language and then uses a program (called an assembler) to translate that into machine code. Assembly language is basically human-readable machine code.

That is why I say that learning assembly language will give you insight into the operation of the computer. Unlike other programming languages, when you learn assembly language, you are learning to program the computer on its own level. I've generally found that it is somewhat dangerous to automate a process you don't understand, especially for someone who is trying to be an expert. An expert mathematician will certainly use software to aid their thinking, but only because they know what the software is automating. An expert race car driver will certainly use their car's steering system to maneuver, but they will still know how the car is operating underneath. This helps them understand how decisions they make at the wheel will affect various system components such as the tread on the tires or gasoline usage. As a casual driver, these things aren't important to me, so my understanding generally stops at the steering wheel and the gas tank. However, if I planned on being a performance race car driver, even if I never maintained the car myself, even if I had a whole crew that did that for me, I would still be well served to understand the car at its deepest level in order to get the most out of it at critical junctures.

Different people have different ideas, but, if you are willing, I definitely suggest starting with assembly language. It will cause you to think differently about problems and computers and ultimately will shape your thinking to more closely match what is required for effective computer programming.

1.5   Types of Assembly Language

Note that there is not a single type of machine language for all computers, although most PCs share the same machine language. Machine languages are usually divided up by **instruction set architecture (ISA)**. The ISA refers to the set of instructions that are allowed by the computer. Many, many different computers share the same ISA, even when built by different manufacturers. Almost all modern PCs use the **x86-64** ISA (sometimes referred to as **AMD64**). Older PCs use the **x86** ISA (this is the 32-bit version of x86-64). Many cell phones use a variation of the **ARM** ISA. Finally, some older game consoles (and really old Macs) use the **PowerPC** ISA. Many other ISAs exist, but are usually restricted to chips that have very specialized uses, such as in embedded devices.

The ISA covered in this book is the x86-64 ISA. This was developed by AMD as a 64-bit extension to the 32-bit x86 ISA developed by Intel. It is now standard in PC-based systems and most servers.

In addition, since assembly language uses human-readable symbols that translate into machine code, different groups have implemented assembly language using different syntaxes. There is no difference in the final machine code, but the different syntaxes have different looks. The two main syntaxes are NASM syntax (sometimes called Intel syntax) and AT&T (sometimes called GAS) syntax. Again, there is no difference in functionality, only in look. We will use AT&T syntax here, because this is the syntax used both in the Linux kernel and as the default syntax by the GNU Compiler

Collection (GCC) toolchain. If you need to use NASM syntax for some reason, a quick translation guide between the two syntaxes is available in Appendix D.

Finally, different operating systems utilize the chips in different ways. The focus here will be on 64-bit Linux-based operating systems. You will need to be running a 64-bit Linux-based operating system to use this book. However, as noted, if you are not on Linux, you can use the Docker setup in Appendix A to run a compatible Linux instance inside a 64-bit Mac or a 64-bit PC.

1.6 Structure of This Book

This book is arranged into three basic parts. This chapter and the next are introductory material before the main parts of the book. They are here to get you started, but are not really about how to program in assembly language.

Part I of the book focuses on the basics of assembly language itself. The programs are not very exciting, because assembly language itself doesn't do much except move data around and process it. Because we are limiting ourselves to assembly language itself, the results of these programs are always numbers. However, the simple nature of the programs will help you get a good feel for assembly language and how it works before trying more complicated things such as input/output. New instructions will still be provided in subsequent parts of the book, but you should have a pretty good feel for assembly language by the time you finish this part of the book. Additionally, most of what you learn in this part is transferable to any other operating system running on a CPU with the x86-64 instruction set.

Part II of the book goes into detail on how programs interact with the operating system. This includes things like displaying to the screen, reading and writing files, and even a bit of user input. It also includes some system management features, such as how to interact with system libraries and how to request more memory from the operating system. This part is very specific to the Linux operating system. While most operating systems provide similar facilities, the specifics of how to use them are unique to the particular operating system you are using.

Part III of the book discusses how programming languages get implemented at the lowest level. Being an introductory book, the goal here isn't to teach you the *best* way to implement programming languages, but rather to give you a feel for the kinds of things that the computer is doing under the hood in various programming languages. How would someone implement feature X, Y, or Z? If modern programming languages amaze and mystify you, Part III should help to make them less enigmatic. Part III is not about a particular programming language, but will guide you through various types of language features that you may find in any number of programming languages.

If this is your first book on computer programming, my recommendation is to stop after Part II and then come back and read Part III after you have gained some experience with other programming languages. This will provide the needed context for understanding Part III of the book.

Part IV of the book has several appendixes that cover various topics that are important to know, but don't quite fit anywhere within the main text. As you are interested, take a look at the appendixes to find short introductions to various topics.

The best way to learn programming is by doing. I would suggest programming every example written in the text yourself to make sure that you fully understand what is occurring. Additionally, every chapter ends with a list of exercises. Those exercises are intended to help you make practical use of what you know and give you experience in thinking about programming on the assembly language level.

CHAPTER 2

The Truth About Computers

I'm going to now share with you the shocking truth about computers—computers are really, really stupid. Many people get enamored with these devices and start to believe things about computers that just aren't true. They may see some amazing graphics, some fantastic data manipulation, and some outstanding artificial intelligence and assume that there is something amazing happening inside the computer. In truth, there *is* something amazing, but it isn't the intelligence of the computer.

2.1 What Computers Can Do

Computers can actually do very few things. Now, the modern computer instruction set is fairly rich, but even as the number of instructions that a computer knows increases in abundance, these are all primarily either (a) faster versions of something you could already do, (b) computer security related, or (c) hardware interface related. Ultimately, as far as computational power goes, all computers boil down to the same basic instructions.

In fact, one computer architecture, invented by Farhad Mavaddat and Behrooz Parham, only has one instruction, yet can still do any computation that any other computer can do.[1]

So what is it that computers can do computationally? Computers can

- Do basic integer arithmetic
- Do memory access

---

[1] For those curious, the instruction is "subtract and branch if negative." If you don't know what that means, it will make a lot more sense by the time you finish this book. If you want to know more about this computer, the paper is "URISC: The Ultimate Reduced Instruction Set Computer" in the *Journal of Electrical Engineering Education*, volume 25. These sorts of computers are known today as OISC systems ("one instruction set computers").

9

© Jonathan Bartlett 2021
J. Bartlett, *Learn to Program with Assembly*, https://doi.org/10.1007/978-1-4842-7437-8_2

- Compare values

- Change the order of instruction execution based on a previous comparison

If computers are this limited, then how are they able to do the amazing things that they do? The reason that computers can accomplish such spectacular feats is that these limitations allow hardware makers to make the operations very fast. Most modern desktop computers can process over a *billion* instructions *every second*. Therefore, what programmers do is leverage this massive pipeline of computation in order to combine simplistic computations into a masterpiece.

However, at the end of the day, all that a computer is really doing is really fast arithmetic. In the movie *Short Circuit*, two of the main characters have this to say about computers—"It's a machine... It doesn't get happy. It doesn't get sad. It doesn't laugh at your jokes. It just runs programs." This is true of even the most advanced artificial intelligence. In fact, the failure to understand this concept lies at the core of the present misunderstanding about the present and future of artificial intelligence.[2]

2.2 Instructing a Computer

The key to programming is to learn to rethink problems in such simple terms that they can be expressed with simple arithmetic. It is like teaching someone to do a task, but they only understand the most literal, exact instructions and can only do arithmetic.

There is an old joke about an engineer whose wife told him to go to the store. She said, "Buy a gallon of milk. If they have eggs, get a dozen." The engineer returned with 12 gallons of milk. His wife asked, "Why 12 gallons?" The engineer responded, "They had eggs." The punchline of the joke is that the engineer had over-literalized his wife's statements. Obviously, she meant that he should get a dozen *eggs*, but that requires context to understand.

The same thing happens in computer programming. The computer *will* hyper-literalize every single thing you type. You must expect this. Most bugs in computer programs come from programmers not paying enough attention to the literal meaning of what they are asking the computer to do. The computer can't do anything except the literal meaning.

---

[2] For more information about this issue, see Erik Larson's book, *The Myth of Artificial Intelligence: Why Computers Can't Think the Way We Do*. I've also written about this some—see my article "Why I Doubt That AI Can Match the Human Mind," available at https://mindmatters. ai/2019/02/why-i-doubt-that-ai-can-match-the-human-mind/.

Learning to program in assembly is helpful because it is more obvious to the programmer the hyper-literalness of how the computer will interpret the program. Nonetheless, when tracking down bugs in any program, the most important thing to do is to track what the code is actually saying, not what we meant by it.

Similarly, when programming, the programmer has to specify *all* of the possible contingencies, how to check for them, and what should be done about them. Imagine we were programming a robot to shop for us. Let us say that we gave it the following program:

1. Go to the store.

2. If the store has corn, buy the corn and return home.

3. If the store doesn't have corn, choose a store that you haven't visited yet and repeat the process.

That sounds pretty specific. The problem is, what happens if no one has corn? We haven't specified to the robot any other way to finish the process. Therefore, if there was a corn famine or a corn recall, the robot will continue searching for a new store *forever* (or until it runs out of electricity).

When doing low-level programming, the consequences that you have to prepare for multiply. If you want to open a file, what happens if the file isn't there? What happens if the file is there, but you don't have access to it? What if you can read it but can't write to it? What if the file is across a network, and there is a network failure while trying to read it?

The computer will only do exactly what you tell it to. Nothing more, nothing less. That proposition is equally freeing and terrifying. The computer doesn't know or care if you programmed it correctly, but will simply do what you actually told it to do.

2.3 Basic Computer Organization

Before we go further, I want to be sure you have a basic awareness of how a computer is organized conceptually. Computers consist of the following basic parts:

- The CPU (also referred to as the processor or microprocessor)

- Working memory

- Permanent storage

- Peripherals

- System bus

Let's look at each of these in turn.

The **CPU** (central processing unit) is the computational workhorse of your computer. The CPU itself is divided into components, but we will deal with that in Section 2.7. The CPU handles all computation and essentially coordinates all of the tasks that occur in a computer. Many computers have more than one CPU, or they have one CPU that has multiple "cores," each of which is more or less acting like a distinct CPU. Additionally, each core may be hyperthreaded, which means the core itself to some extent acts as more than one core. The **permanent storage** is your hard drive(s), whether internal or external, plus USB sticks, or whatever else you store files on. This is distinct from the **working memory**, which is usually referred to as **RAM**, which stands for "random access memory."[3] The working memory is usually wiped out when the computer gets turned off.

Everything else connected to your computer gets classified as a **peripheral**. Technically, permanent storage devices are peripherals, too, but they are sufficiently foundational to how computers work I treated them as their own category. Peripherals are how the computer communicates with the world. This includes the graphics card, which transmits data to the screen; the network card, which transmits data across the network; the sound card, which translates data into sound waves; the keyboard and mouse, which allow you to send input to the computer; etc.

Everything that is connected to the CPU connects through a **bus**, or **system bus**. Buses handle communication between the various components of the computer, usually between the CPU and other peripherals and between the CPU and main memory. The speed and engineering of the various computer buses is actually critical to the computer's performance, but their operation is sufficiently technical and behind the scenes that most people don't think about it. The main memory often gets its own bus (known as the front-side bus) to make sure that communication is fast and unhindered.

Physically, most of these components are present on a computer's motherboard, which is the big board inside your desktop or laptop. The motherboard often has other functions as well, such as controlling fans, interfacing with the power button, etc.

---

[3] It's called random access memory because you can easily access any given part of the memory. This was in comparison to disks or tape, in which you had to physically move the read/write head to the right spot before you could read the data. Modern solid state drives are essentially random access as well, but we still use the term RAM to refer to the main memory, not the disks.

2.4 How Computers See Data

As mentioned in the introduction, computers translate everything into numbers. To understand why, remember that computers are just electronic devices. That is, everything that happens in a computer is ultimately reducible to the flow of electricity. In order to make that happen, engineers had to come up with a way to represent things with flows of electricity.

What they came up with is to have different voltages represent different symbols. Now, you could do this in a lot of ways. You could have 1 volt represent the number 1, 2 volts represent the number 2, etc. However, devices have a fixed voltage, so we would have to decide ahead of time how many digits we want to allow on the signal and be sure sufficient voltage is available.

To simplify things, engineers ultimately decided to only make two symbols. These can be thought of as "on" (voltage present) and "off" (no voltage present), "true" and "false," or "1" and "0." Limiting to just two symbols greatly simplifies the task of engineering computers.

You may be wondering how these limited symbols add up to all the things we store in computers. First, let's start with ordinary numbers. You may be thinking, if you only have "0" and "1," how will we represent numbers with other digits, like 23? The interesting thing is that you can build numbers with any number of digits. We use ten digits (0–9), but we didn't have to. The Ndom language uses six digits. Some use as many as 27.

Since the computer uses two digits, the system is known as **binary**. Each digit in the binary system is called a **bit**, which simply means "binary digit." To understand how to count in binary, let's think a little about how we count in our own system, **decimal**. We start with 0, and then we progress through each symbol until we hit the end of our list of symbols (i.e., 9). Then what happens? The next digit to the left increments by one, and the ones place goes back to zero. As we continue counting, we increment the rightmost digit over and over, and, when it goes past the last symbol, we keep flipping it back to zero and incrementing the next one to the left. If that one flips, we again increment the one to the left of that digit, and so forth.

Counting in binary is exactly the same, except we just run up against the end of our symbol list much more quickly. It starts at 0, then goes to 1, and then, hey, we are at the end of our symbols! So that means that the number to the left gets incremented (there is always imaginary zeroes to the left of the digits we have) and our rightmost digit flips back to zero. So that means that after 0 and 1 is 10! So, counting in binary looks like this (the numbers on the left are the equivalent decimal numbers):

0. 0

1. 1

2. 10 (we overflowed the ones position, so we increment the next digit to the left and the ones position starts over at zero)

3. 11

4. 100 (we overflowed the ones position, so we increment the next digit to the left, but that flips that one to zero, so we increment the next one over)

5. 101

6. 110

7. 111

8. 1000

9. 1001

10. 1010

11. 1011

12. 1100

As you can see, the *procedure* is the same. We are just working with fewer symbols.

Now, in computing, these values have to be stored somewhere. And, while in our imagination, we can imagine any number of zeroes to the left (and therefore our system can accommodate an infinite number of values), in physical computers, all of these numbers have to be stored in circuits somewhere. Therefore, the computer engineers group together bits into fixed sizes.

A **byte** is a grouping of 8 bits together. A byte can store a number between 0 and 255. Why 255? Because that is the value of 8 bits all set to "1": 11111111.

Single bytes are pretty limiting. However, for historic reasons, this is the way that computers are organized, at least conceptually. When we talk about how many gigabytes of RAM a computer has, we are asking how many billions (giga-) of bytes (groups of 8 bits together) the computer has in its working memory (which is what **RAM** is).

Most computers, however, fundamentally use larger groupings. When we talk about a 32-bit or a 64-bit computer, we are talking about how the number of bits that the computer naturally groups together when dealing with numbers. A 64-bit computer, then, can naturally handle numbers as large as 64 bits. This is a number between 0 and 18,446,744,073,709,551,615.

Now, ultimately, you can choose any size of number you want. You can have bigger numbers, but, generally, the processor is not predisposed to working with the numbers in that way. What it means to have a 64-bit computer is that the computer can, in a single instruction, add together two 64-bit numbers. You can still add 64-bit numbers with a 32-bit or even an 8-bit computer; it just takes more instructions. For instance, on a 32-bit computer, you could split the 64-bit number up into two pieces. You then add the rightmost 32 bits and then add the leftmost 32 bits (and account for any carrying between them).

Note that even though computers store numbers as bits, we rarely refer to the numbers in binary form unless we have a specific reason. However, knowing that they are bits arranged into bytes (or larger groupings) helps us understand certain limitations of computers. Oftentimes, you will find values in computing that are restricted to the values 0–255. If you see this happen, you can think, "Oh, that probably means they are storing the value in a single byte."

2.5 It's Not What You Have, It's How You Use It

So, hopefully by now you see how computers store numbers. But don't computers store all sorts of other types of data, too? Aren't computers storing and processing words, images, sounds, and, for that matter, negative or even non-integer numbers?

This is true, but it is storing all of these things *as numbers*. For instance, to store letters, the letters are actually converted into numbers using ASCII (American Standard Code for Information Interchange) or Unicode codes (which we will discuss more later). Each character gets a value, and words are stored as consecutive values.

Images are also values. Each pixel on your screen is represented by a number indicating the color to display. Sound waves are stored as a series of numbers.

So how does the computer know which numbers are which? Fundamentally, the *computer* doesn't. All of these values look exactly the same when stored in your computer—they are just numbers.

What makes them letters or numbers or images or sounds is how they are *used*. If I send a number to the graphics card, then it is a color. If I add two numbers, then they are numbers. If I store what you type, then those numbers are letters. If I send a number to the speaker, then it is a sound. It is the burden of the programmer to keep track of which numbers mean which things and to treat them accordingly.

This is why files have extensions like `.docx`, `.png`, `.mov`, or `.xlsx`. These extensions tell the computer how to interpret what is in the file. These files are themselves just long strings of numbers. Programs simply read the filename, look at the extension, and use that to know how to use the numbers stored inside.

There's nothing preventing someone from writing a program that takes a word processing file and treating the numbers as pixel colors and sending them to the screen (it usually looks like static) or sending them to the speakers (it usually sounds like static or buzzing). But, ultimately, what makes computer programs useful is that they recognize how the numbers are organized and treat them in an appropriate manner.

If this sounds complicated, don't worry about it. We will start off with very simple examples in the next chapter.

What's even more amazing, though, is that the computer's instructions are themselves just numbers as well. This is why your computer's memory can be used to store both your files and your programs. Both are just special sequences of numbers, so we can store them all using the same type of hardware. Just like the numbers in the file are written in a way that our software can interpret them, the numbers in our programs are written in a special way so that the computer hardware can interpret them properly.

2.6 Referring to Memory

Since a computer has billions of bytes of memory (or more), how do we figure out *which* specific piece of memory we are referring to? This is a harder question than it sounds like. For the moment, I will give you a simplified understanding which we will build upon later on.

Have you ever been to a post office and seen an array of post-office boxes? Or been to a bank and seen a whole wall of safety deposit boxes? What do they look like?

Usually, each box is the same size, and each one has a number on it. These numbers are arranged sequentially. Therefore, box 2345 is right next to box 2344. I can easily find any box by knowing the number on the outside of the box.

This is how memory is usually organized. You can think of memory as boxes, where each box is 1 byte big. Each memory box has an **address**, which tells the computer how to find it. I can ask for the byte that is at address 279,935 or at address 2,341,338. If I know the address, I can go find the value in that location. Because they are bytes, each value will be between 0 and 255. Figure 2-1 gives a visual for what this looks like.

Now, since we are on 64-bit computers, we can actually load bigger values. We will typically be loading 8 bytes at a time. So, instead of asking for a single byte, we will be asking for 8 bytes, starting with the one at the given address. So if we load from address 279,935, we will get all of the bytes from address 279,935 to 279,942.

Different size values have various names on the x86-64 platform. These names come from the fact that the ancestor of the x86-64 was a 16-bit processor. Typical sizes include

- **1 byte (8 bits)**: Typically just referred to as a byte

- **2 bytes (16 bits)**: Known as a "word" or a "short"

- **4 bytes (32 bits)**: Known as a "double-word" or an "int"

- **8 bytes (64 bits)**: Known as a "quadword"[4]

Looking again at Figure 2-1, the memory itself doesn't have any knowledge of whether or not a value is a single byte or multiple bytes. For the memory, it is all stored a byte at a time. However, if you were to access a memory location as a quadword (i.e., 8 bytes), it would treat the memory at that address *and the next seven locations after* as a single unit. So, accessing a quadword from memory address 0014 in the figure would actually use all of the values from 0014 to 0021 as one giant value. However, Chapter 7 has some additional important information on how these bytes are stitched together.

---

[4] A quadword is sometimes referred to as a "long" or a "long long," but these usages are sufficiently inconsistent that we will generally avoid using them. For instance, "long" will sometimes refer to 4-byte values.

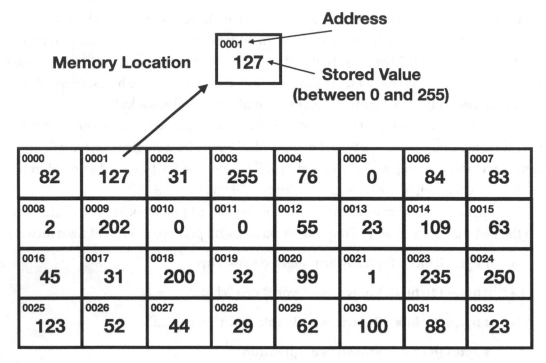

Figure 2-1. *Conceptual View of Memory*

This figure shows the conceptual layout of 32 bytes of memory. Each location contains a value between 0 and 255 (which is 1 byte) and is labeled by an address, which is how the computer knows where to find it. The actual values here do not have any particular meaning, just shown to give examples of byte values.

2.7 The Structure of the CPU

The CPU itself has an organization worth considering. Modern CPUs are actually extremely complex, but they maintain a general conceptual architecture that has generally remained stable over time.

The common conceptual parts of a CPU are

- Registers
- Control unit
- Arithmetic and logic unit

- Memory management unit

- Caches

Registers are tiny blocks of memory inside the processor itself. These are bits of data that the processor can access directly without waiting. Most registers can be used for any purpose the programmer wishes. Essentially what happens is that programs load data from memory into the registers, then process the data in the registers using various instructions, and then write the contents of those registers back out to memory.

Some registers also have special purposes, such as pointing to the next instruction to be carried out, holding some sort of processor status, or being able to be used for some special processor function. Registers are standardized—that is, the available registers is defined by the CPU architecture, so you won't get a different set of registers if you use an AMD chip or an Intel chip, as long as they are both implementing the x86-64 instruction set architecture.

Programming in assembly language involves a lot of register access.

The **control unit** sets the pacing for the chip. It handles the coordination of all the different parts of the chip. It handles the **clock**, which doesn't tell time, but is more like a drum beat or a pacemaker—it makes sure that everything operates at the same speed.

The **arithmetic and logic unit** (**ALU**) is where the actual processing takes place. It does the additions, subtractions, comparisons, etc. The ALU is normally wired so that basic operations can be done with registers extremely quickly (typically in a single clock cycle).

The memory management unit is a little more complex, and we will deal with it further in Chapter 14. However, in a simple fashion, it manages the way that the processor sees and understands memory addresses.

Finally, CPUs usually have a lot of different **caches**. A cache is a piece of memory that holds other memory closer to the CPU. For instance, instructions are usually carried out in the same order that they are stored in memory. Therefore, rather than wait for the control unit to request the next instruction and then wait for the instruction to arrive from main memory, the CPU can preload a segment of memory that it thinks will be useful into a cache. That way, when the CPU asks for the next instruction, it doesn't have to wait on the system bus to deliver the instruction from memory—it can just read it directly from the cache. CPUs implement all sorts of caches, each of which cache different things for different reasons, and even have different access speeds.

They key to understanding CPU architecture is to realize that the goal is to make maximal use of the CPU within the limits of computer chip engineering.

2.8 The Fetch-Execute Cycle

The way that the processor runs programs is through the **fetch-execute cycle**. The computer operates by reading your program one instruction at a time. It knows which instruction to read through a special register known as the **instruction pointer** (or **IP**), which is also known as the **program counter** (or **PC**).

The computer essentially runs an endless cycle of the following operations:

1. Read the instruction from the memory address specified by the instruction pointer.

2. Decode the instruction (i.e., figure out what the instruction means).

3. Advance the instruction pointer to the next instruction.[5]

4. Perform the operation indicated by the instruction.

Each instruction is extremely limited in its operation. Available instructions do operations like the following:

*   Load a value from memory into a register.

*   Store a value from a register into memory.

*   Do a single arithmetic operation.

*   Compare two values.

*   Go to a different location in the code (i.e., modify the instruction pointer) based on the result of a previous comparison.

You might be surprised, but those are pretty much all the instructions you really need in a computer.

You may be wondering how you get from instructions like that to doing things like displaying graphics in a computer. Well, graphics are composed of individual dots called pixels. Each pixel has a certain amount of red, green, and blue in them. You can represent these amounts with numbers. The graphics card has memory locations

---

[5] The reason why step 2 is before step 3 is because different instructions are of different lengths and it has to decode the instruction before it knows how much to advance the instruction pointer. Step 3 occurs before step 4, because step 4 could itself include a modification of the instruction pointer and we don't want to get in the way of any modification done there.

available for each pixel on your screen. Therefore, to display a graphic onscreen, you need only to move the color values to the correct places in memory.

Likewise, let's think about input. When someone moves their mouse, this modifies a value in memory. This memory location can be loaded into a register, compared to other values, and then the appropriate code can be executed based on those movements.

Now, these are somewhat simplified explanations (in real computers, these operations are all mediated by the operating system), but they serve to give you a feel for how simply moving, storing, comparing, and manipulating numbers can bring you all of the things that computers offer.

2.9 Adding CPU Cores

Most modern computers have more than one CPU core. A **CPU core** is like a CPU, but more than one of them may exist on a single chip, and while each core is largely independent of the other cores on the same chip, the cores may share a certain amount of circuitry, such as caches.

Additional hardware has been developed to keep the different CPU cores synchronized with each other. For example, imagine if one core had a piece of memory stored in one of its caches and another core modified that same data. Getting that change communicated to the other cores can be a challenging prospect for hardware engineers. This is known as the **cache coherence** problem. It is usually solved by having the CPUs and caches implement what is known as the **MESI protocol**, which basically allows caches to tell other caches they need to update their values.

Thankfully, caching issues are handled almost entirely in hardware, so programmers rarely have to worry about them. There are a few instructions that we can use to do a minor amount of cache manipulation, such as flushing the cache, requesting that the cache load certain areas of memory, etc. However, for the most part, the complexity of modern CPUs (and the wide variety of implementations of that CPU architecture) usually means that the CPU will be much better at handling its cache than you could possibly be.

2.10 A Note About Memory Visualizations

One thing to note is that visualizations of computer memory is made difficult because sometimes we think of memory in terms of their addresses, in which case it seems obvious to put the higher addresses on the top and the lower addresses on the bottom, because we naturally arrange numbers that way. However, sometimes it is more natural to visualize something as "starting" at the top and "finishing" at the bottom, and, in those cases, we oftentimes put the lower memory addresses on the top and the higher ones on the bottom. All of this to say, the drawings of memory in this book will each indicate whether they are drawn with the lower addresses at the top of the drawing or at the bottom. So, when looking at memory visualizations in this book, please be sure to note which way the visualization is oriented.

PART I

Assembly Language Basics

CHAPTER 3

Your First Program

We have talked enough *about* programming—it is time to actually get started! This chapter will start out with an extremely simple assembly language program just to show the basics of how to convert an assembly language program into a program you can execute. Then, we will move on and add some extremely basic functionality to our program. After that, we will have enough background knowledge to go into more depth about assembly language programming.

If your computer is not running the Linux operating system (i.e., it is a Mac or is running Windows), you will need to use the directions in Appendix A in order to get a suitable environment up and running using Docker (don't worry—this will not adversely impact your computer). This setup has all of the tools you will need preinstalled. If you have never used the command line before, be sure to check out Appendix B for a basic tutorial.

If you are already running Linux, be sure that the developer tools (especially GCC) are installed on your computer. How to do this will vary depending on your specific Linux distribution. Alternatively, you can also run the Docker setup mentioned in Appendix A.

3.1 Building a Simple Assembly Language Program

The first program we will program will do nothing but exit with a status code. For this program, don't worry yet about how it works. The goal is to just get something entered and worked through the process. The process for getting your code converted into a program is outlined in Figure 3-1.

The code for this first program is as follows. Type it in as the file `myexit.s` using an editor. Type it in exactly as written. We will discuss it line by line in the next section.

myexit.s

```
# My first program.  This is a comment.
```

© Jonathan Bartlett 2021
J. Bartlett, *Learn to Program with Assembly*, https://doi.org/10.1007/978-1-4842-7437-8_3

```
.globl _start

.section .text

_start:
    movq $60, %rax
    movq $3, %rdi
    syscall
```

This is known as the **source code**. Source code is the code that a human writes for a computer to do. The source code gets **assembled** into **machine language** using the **assembler** (we are using the GNU Assembler). Machine language has the same *meaning* as the source code, but it transformed into a format that the computer is better able to process.[1] To run the assembler, enter the following command in the command line (not in the file):

```
as myexit.s -o myexit.o
```

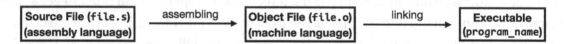

***Figure 3-1.** How a Program Is Built from Source Code*

This takes your source code, converts it to machine code, and places it in an **object file** called myexit.o. An object file contains code, but it is not yet runnable. On larger programs, lots of object files are generated and then linked together using the **linker**. Even though we only have one file, we still need to link it in order to make it runnable. The following command will link the file:

```
ld myexit.o -o myexit
```

This will produce the executable file myexit in your current directory. To run it, just run

```
./myexit
```

You may notice that it does nothing except, well, exit. That's not quite true, though. It did leave an **exit status code**, which you can access through the command line like this:

```
echo $?
```

---

[1] Appendix K has some basic information on what this looks like, but you probably shouldn't worry about that at this point.

If all went well, this should print out a 3 on your screen. Why 3? Just because it is an unusual status, and therefore you will know that the status is from your program. To get a different status, you can modify the original code. Replace $3 with any number between 0 and 255 (be sure to prefix it with a dollar sign), reassemble, relink, and rerun your program, and it will show that value when you do echo $?.

3.2 Line-by-Line Analysis

To begin with, the first line is a comment:

```
# My first program.   This is a comment.
```

If this is your first programming language, comments are notes to yourself and other programmers about the program. Remember that programs spend more time being *maintained* than being written for the first time. This means that what you can keep in your head today you will forget about a year from now when trying to update your program. It's even more difficult if someone *else* has to modify your program. Comments help you and others navigate your code and tell what is going on, but they don't change anything about what the computer will do. In assembly language, comments start with the hashtag mark, #. Everything on the same line after that point is ignored by the assembler.

If you are being super lazy, you can skip entering the comments in your code. However, I think it's best to leave them in. Typing the comments will help you to think more clearly about the program you are writing.

The next line is

```
.globl _start
```

Anything that starts with a dot (.) is an instruction to the assembler (known as a **directive**) and doesn't usually generate code on its own. What .globl does is tell the assembler that the symbol _start (and its corresponding value) should not be discarded after the assembly process is over. Normally, all of our own names for things get discarded by the assembler. The .globl directive tells the assembler not to do this, usually because it is going to be referred to by something else. Here, the _start symbol is a special symbol used by the linker to know where the program should start running when the user runs the program, known as the **entry point** of the program.

The next line is another command to the assembler:

```
.section .text
```

The .section directive tells the assembler that the next part of the listing should be placed in the code section of the program, historically known as the text of the program (even though it isn't actually readable *text*). The other section we will spend a lot of time dealing with in this book is the .data section, which will handle predefined memory storage in our program.

In assembly language, you can freely switch between .data and .text sections, and the assembler and linker will group all of the data and code sections together in the final executable.

The next line is

```
_start:
```

This is called a **label**, and it *defines* the value of the _start symbol. This tells the assembler that _start refers to (i.e., it *labels*) the address in memory that the code (or data) that follows it resides in. Note that you don't have to know where the code will live when it is running—the linker will take care of that. Instead, you simply *label* the location using _start:, and from that point on, the symbol _start will refer to that location in the code. Think of it as kind of like a bookmark.

As mentioned previously, _start is a special symbol which is used by the linker to know where to start the program executing. However, you will often want to create your own symbols to refer to various parts of your code.

So far, though, we don't have any actual instructions for the computer to execute. However, the next line is the first real instruction:

```
movq $60, %rax
```

The name of the instruction is movq, which stands for "move quadword." As mentioned in Chapter 2, a quadword is a 64-bit (8-byte) value. In this book, the quadword is the typical value size we will be dealing with.

This instruction moves the value 60 into the register named %rax, which is a 64-bit register. Remember that a register is a storage location within the CPU itself, not inside main memory. The register name looks funny, and we will discuss these names in a later section. The dollar sign before the 60 means that we are treating 60 as a value, not an address, or anything else. If we had left off the dollar sign, it would try to load a value from memory address 60 into the register, which is not what we want (and will likely trigger an error).

The number 60 refers to the **system call number** of the command we want the operating system to run (which will be the exit system call). Each operating system function is assigned a system call number, and 60 is the one for exit. Note that we will cover system calls in quite a bit of detail in Chapter 10.

Note that moving this value into %rax does not *make* the call (that comes in a later instruction); it is just preparing to do so.

The next line is similar:

```
movq $3, %rdi
```

This has the same basic meaning as the previous line (move a 64-bit value into a register), just using a different value (3) and a different register (%rdi). In the exit system call, the %rdi register holds the exit status of the program. Therefore, whatever value we load into %rdi will be available when the user does echo $?.

The final line is simply

```
syscall
```

This instruction actually performs the system call. It tells the processor to transfer control to the operating system to perform a task. The requested task, as mentioned earlier, is known as the system call number and is stored in %rax (60 in our case for the exit system call). If the system call uses additional data (the exit system call takes a value for the exit status), this is placed in %rdi. Other system calls require even more data, and each piece of data has a defined register that it should be in.

If these register names look funny, that's okay. We will go into more detail about the available registers in Chapter 4.

That is your first program—congratulations!

3.3 The Meaning of the Code

As you can see, assembly language is really a step-by-step process. You tell the processor each and every thing you want it to do. Each step in the process is its very own line.

Each instruction is fairly straightforward, although the acronyms sometimes throw people for a loop. The movq instruction tells the processor to move data around in 64-bit chunks (8 bytes at a time). Other instructions exist for other sized chunks: movl for 32-bit chunks (4 bytes), movw for 16-bit chunks (2 bytes), and movb for 8-bit chunks (1 byte).

The movq instruction has two **operands**—the first is the "source" and the second is the "destination." The two operands are separated by a comma. Operands are essentially "options" that give additional detail to the instruction about what to do.[2] Operands can also be called **arguments** or **parameters**, though those terms are usually used in relation to function calls (covered in Chapter 11).

In the movq instruction, the source can be any number of things. It can be a register. It can be a memory address. It can be other things as well. In this program, we used an actual number as the source. The $ is what told the assembler that the number we were using was just a number and did not have some other meaning.

The destination is similar and has similar meanings. In our case, the destination was a register. In the first instruction, it used the register %rax, and in the second instruction, it used the register %rdi.

Therefore, these instructions told the computer to move specific numbers into these registers. I always like to read instructions as sentences. If you take the instruction movq $3, %rdi, you can read it as saying, "move the number three into the %rdi register."

There are a lot of variations on this instruction. You could, for instance, move information from one register to another. For example, doing movq %rax, %rdi would move data from the %rax register to the %rdi register. We will learn many other variations in the coming chapters.

The last instruction is the syscall (system call) instruction. This instruction is a special instruction that causes the Linux kernel (the core operating system) to take over. System calls are used when you need more than just computation power—when you need access to system resources such as files, the network, the display, other processes, etc. In this case, we are telling the operating system that we are done executing. The operating system will then clean up any resources it has allocated for us, stop our code from running any further, and return our exit status code back to the command that called us (usually our shell).[3]

---

[2] In terms of language, you can think about the instruction as being the verb, and operands, if they are needed, are acting as the other parts of speech, such as the indirect object, the direct object, or any adjectives or adverbs.

[3] If you have programmed in 32-bit assembly, you may wonder what happened to the int 0x80 instruction or the Linux 2.6 sysenter instruction. There are a lot of behind-the-scenes implementation details that make the syscall run much faster than int 0x80. Therefore, on x86-64 systems, Linux operates using the syscall instruction. Additionally, the new interface gave the kernel team a chance to optimize several details about which registers are used, how the system call numbers are assigned, etc., giving x86-64 several considerable speed advantages when interfacing with the kernel.

Note that `syscall` instruction does not care in what order the registers were set. We could have set `%rdi` first and `%rax` second, and it would not have changed the meaning of the program. It only matters what the values are at the time that the `syscall` instruction is issued. Later, we will talk about what each of the registers means and how they are used in the system call interface. But, for now, just realize that, generally, the `syscall` instruction works by giving special jobs to different registers that have to be set up before the instruction is issued, and then the operating system will make use of the values in those registers.

Always keep in mind that instructions in your program are executed one at a time in sequential order.[4] The code will start at the location marked by `_start` and then execute the first instruction, then move to the next instruction, then move to the next instruction, etc. Operating a single step at a time is what allows computers to be implemented in electronics. Remember, in order for an instruction to be available in assembly language, that instruction has to be implemented by a circuit on the CPU. Therefore, the instructions that we encounter will only have a limited scope in what they can do, because they are limited by what can be encoded into the chip's circuits.

You may be wondering about the spacing we are using in our program. Spacing is largely ignored in assembly language, except as needed to separate the instructions from its operands. As a matter of style, I usually put labels, most assembler instructions (such as `.section` or `.globl`), and top-level comments in the leftmost column. I usually indent the actual instructions themselves. Comments within the code are usually put to the right of the instructions or above the instructions and are indented to match the instructions. I also leave a blank line between logically distinct sections of code to help readers recognize which pieces of code belong together.

The main thing is to make your code readable not only by yourself but by others. Whatever makes the code easiest to follow/understand is what is best.

---

[4] Modern processors are smart enough that they can sometimes reorder instructions or execute more than one at a time if it makes your code faster. However, it will only do this if the reordering or simultaneous execution *has the same effect* as running your program in the written order. Thus, as a programmer, you don't have to worry about it. Just know that if your processor supports "out-of-order execution," you don't have to worry about what order the process will execute your code—the processor will make sure that it runs as you wrote it, just faster. See Appendix I for more details on this.

3.4 Stepping Through Your Program

If you are having trouble seeing what your program is doing, it is often helpful to run it using a **debugger**. A debugger is a program that will run your program a step at a time and let you see exactly what is happening inside the program as it runs.

Personally, I think running through a program with a pen and paper and writing out the values of each register at each point in time is the best way to analyze a program. Doing so helps you really think about what it is you are doing and what the computer looks like at each step. However, it is also good to know how to use a debugger to step through your program for you and show you what is happening.

While it can be useful at any stage of development, it is especially instructive for beginners to see what their code is actually doing to the computer. For information on debugging your programs, see Appendix C. Note that some of the information there we won't get to until later chapters, but nonetheless, if you want to watch your program unfold a step at a time, Appendix C will show you how.

Exercises

1. Take the program given in this chapter and change the value to be returned (the one stored in %rdi). Be sure you get back the right value when your program exits. Don't forget to assemble and link your program before running it again.

2. Make a mistake! Misspell one of the instructions and see what the assembler does.

3. Make another mistake! Leave off the syscall instruction and see what happens.

4. Read through Appendix C. See if you can run your program a step at a time under the debugger.

CHAPTER 4

Registers and Simple Arithmetic

In the last chapter, we learned the basic structure of an assembly language program and how to assemble, link, and run it and display the exit status code. This chapter will focus on getting to know the register set of the x86-64 ISA as well as learning a few new instructions to make the code a little more interesting. We will start by looking at a few arithmetic instructions so we can expand beyond just moving data around.

4.1 Simple Arithmetic Instructions

So far, we have learned two instructions: movq (and its cousins) and syscall. However, there are many other instructions available. In this section, we are going to expand our knowledge of instructions by focusing on simple arithmetic. Note that, for right now, we are only dealing with nonnegative integers. We will eventually get to negative numbers and decimals, but we will start with nonnegative integers because they are easier to understand.

On x86-64, arithmetic instructions only have two operands. The second operand has two functions—it operates as both part of the arithmetic and is also the destination where the result is stored.

For instance, let's say that we wanted to add the contents of %rax and %rdi. The instruction for this is

```
addq %rax, %rdi
```

What this does is take the value in %rax, add it to the value in %rdi, and store the resulting value in %rdi, erasing whatever was there before. The two operands are still usually considered the "source" and the "destination" even though they both are used as sources of the value.

© Jonathan Bartlett 2021
J. Bartlett, *Learn to Program with Assembly*, https://doi.org/10.1007/978-1-4842-7437-8_4

If you insert this line into the previous program immediately before the syscall, then the resulting value will be 63 instead of 3 (since %rax had 60 in it). The first operand can also be a plain number, such as $25. addq $25, %rdi will add 25 to whatever is currently in %rdi and then store the result in %rdi.

Some simple arithmetic instructions include

> **addq**: Adds the source and the destination together.

> **subq**: Subtracts the source from the destination.

In computer programming, adding and subtracting one are so common that there is even specific instructions for them. These instructions only take a destination, which is whatever you wanted to add or subtract one to/from.

> **incq**: Increments (adds one to) the destination.

> **decq**: Decrements (subtracts one from) the destination.

Multiplication and division are more complex. With these instructions, the destination is assumed to be %rax. You never list %rax in the instruction, because it is there implicitly with the instruction. The simplest forms of multiplication and division instructions include

> **mulq**: Multiplies the source by %rax. %rax is the destination. A number cannot be used as the source—it must be a register or memory location.

> **divq**: Divides %rax by the source. %rax is the destination. A number cannot be used as the source—it must be a register or memory location. The remainder is stored in another register, %rdx, which should be set to zero before the instruction occurs.

Don't forget that, for mulq and divq, the destination is *implicit* in the instruction. That is, we never write %rax, it is implied by the instruction itself.

As an example, if you performed the instruction mulq %rbx, this would take %rbx, multiply it by %rax, and then store the result in %rax. That's because the usage of %rax is *implicit* in the instruction. That is the only register that mulq can use as a destination, so you don't need to write it out. Likewise, if you issued the instruction divq %rcx, this would take %rax, divide it by %rcx, and then store the result in %rax and the remainder in %rdx.

Many instructions use other registers implicitly as well. The names of registers are often assigned based on which types of operations they are used implicitly on. %rax is sometimes known as the "accumulator" since it is often the implicit target of mathematics instructions (and thus *accumulates* the results). Also, don't forget that while we can specify specific numeric values as the source in movq, addq, and subq, these are not allowed for mulq and divq.

One other note—all these instructions, but especially mulq and divq, are actually more complicated than we have presented here. We are taking baby steps. More details about these are given in Chapters 5 and 8.

The following is a simple arithmetic program. See if you can figure out the final result of the program.

arithmetic.s

```
.globl _start
.section .text
_start:
    # Perform various arithmetic functions
    movq $3, %rdi
    movq %rdi, %rax
    addq %rdi, %rax
    mulq %rdi
    movq $2, %rdi
    addq %rdi, %rax
    movq $4, %rdi
    mulq %rdi
    movq %rax, %rdi

    # Set the exit system call number
    movq $60, %rax

    # Perform the system call
    syscall
```

Remember to follow each line, one after the other. If it helps, use a piece of paper, and write down the value of each register after each instruction. After following the program yourself, enter it in the file `arithmetic.s` and assemble it, link it, run it, and check the output using the following commands:

```
as arithmetic.s -o arithmetic.o
ld arithmetic.o -o arithmetic
./arithmetic
echo $?
```

Did you get the correct result? If not, go back through and see if you can figure out where you went wrong. After that, play with the program. Do a variety of additions, subtractions, and multiplications. Just remember that the final result has to be (a) 255 or less and (b) stored in `%rdi`, or it won't be properly returned as the exit status.

4.2 Register Layouts

So far, we have introduced three registers—`%rax`, `%rdi`, and `%rdx`. You may be wondering where these names come from, as they are a little strange. First, there is also quite a bit about it that we haven't gotten to yet, and that accounts for the strangeness of some of the names. Additionally, however, this instruction set architecture has gone through quite a history, and much of the naming is the result of this history. The instruction set architecture was first established as a 16-bit ISA, then extended into a 32-bit ISA, and finally extended into what it is now.

You can see this history in the naming of the registers. Originally, the accumulator was just called `%ax` and held 16 bits. When the architecture was extended to 32 bits, the 32-bit version of `%ax` was called `%eax` (i.e., "extended" `%ax`). When the architecture was further extended to 64 bits, the name of the 64-bit version became `%rax`.

All of these register names are still available and still operate just as they did before. The way it is implemented is that `%rax` contains all 64 bits of the register, `%eax` simply refers to the least significant 32 bits of the `%rax` register, and `%ax` refers to the least significant 16 bits of the `%rax` register. Additionally, `%ax` can be further divided into bytes, with `%ah` referring to the most significant 8 bits of `%ax` (called the "high byte") and `%al` referring to the least significant 8 bits of `%ax` (called the "low byte"). The diagram in Figure 4-1 shows this in more detail.

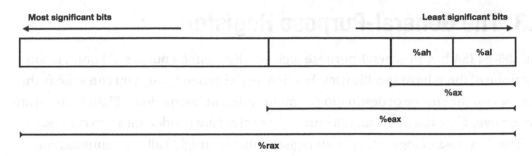

Figure 4-1. *Register Layout of* `%rax`

The preceding register layout shows how `%rax` has embedded within it the smaller registers `%eax` (32 bits), `%ax` (16 bits), `%ah` (8 bits), and `%al` (8 bits). The least significant bits are shown in this diagram on the rightmost side. Also note that anytime that bits are labeled, bit 0 is the least significant bit (furthest right) and bit 63 is the most significant bit (furthest left).

Let's talk for a moment about the terms "most significant bits" and "least significant bits." Think of the decimal number 23,415. Which digits play the most significant roles in this number? The leftmost digits do. If we changed the "2" for another digit, it would make a much more significant impact than if we changed any other digit in the number. If we changed the "2" to a "1," it would drop the value of the number by 10,000. The "5" is the least significant digit. If we dropped the "5" to a "1" it would only drop the value of the number by 4.

Remember, then, that "bit" just means "binary digit." So, if I have a number in binary which is 1011001101111, the digits to the left are the most significant, and the digits to the right are the least significant. Note, however, that sometimes the significance in numeric terms doesn't always tell you how the number is physically stored. But that is another topic for a later chapter (see Chapter 7).

The important thing to note is that in Figure 4-1, the older registers always occupy the least significant positions of the newer, larger versions of the register. The reason for that is simple. Let's say we start with the whole of `%rax` set to zero. Next, we load in the value $9 (0000000000001001) into `%ax`. Because this is also the least significant bits of `%eax` and `%rax`, that means that this number will continue to have the same meaning for those registers as well. For `%eax`, it will just mean 00000000000000000000000000001001, and for `%rax`, it will mean 0000000000000000000000000000000000000000000000000 000000001001. Since the 1001 part is in the least significant bits, it will continue to have the same numeric meaning for all of them.

4.3 The General-Purpose Registers

The x86-64 ISA has 16 general-purpose registers. By "general purpose," I don't mean that none of them have specific uses, but that, in the general case, you can specify these registers for the source or destination of many different instructions. Eight of those are carried over from the 32-bit architecture. These eight are divided into two classes.

The first class of registers are four registers that we might call the computational registers. These registers are %rax, %rbx, %rcx, and %rdx. These registers are divided up just like %rax as shown in Figure 4-1. For instance, %rbx has a 32-bit version called %ebx embedded in it, which has the original %bx embedded in that, whose individual high and low bytes can be referred to by %bh and %bl. These registers are normally used for general computation. Additionally, the ability to access individual bytes of the registers can come in handy, as a lot of data is organized around individual bytes.

However, these registers also have specific purposes, which have one or more instructions tailored to their function:

> **%rax:** This is the accumulator. It is the most widely used general-purpose register for computation.
>
> **%rbx:** This is known as the "base register." This is often used for indexed addressing, which is covered in Chapter 6.
>
> **%rcx:** This is known as the "counter register." It is historically used for counts when doing repetitive code (loops). See Chapter 5 for more information.
>
> **%rdx:** This is known as the "data register." It has some special significance in certain arithmetic operations and input/output operations and is also sometimes used in some instructions in coordination with %rax, such as with the divq instruction.

The next four registers are still considered "general purpose" because they can be used in computation, but they are actually focused on specific tasks. The first two (%rsi and %rdi) can be safely for general purposes, but it is best to leave the others for their special purpose. Note that, while each of these has a 32-bit and 16-bit version, you cannot access any individual bytes in these registers. For instance, the %rdi register has a 32-bit version (%edi) and a 16-bit version (%di), but there is no register that will give me any individual bytes from this register. This is because they are largely intended to be **pointers**, which means they will store the memory address of other values. These registers are

> **%rsi**: This is the "source index" register. It has special uses for working with longer spans of memory (see Chapter 9).

> **%rdi**: This is the "destination index" register. It is often used in conjunction with %rsi for working with longer spans of memory (see Chapter 9).

> **%rbp**: This is the "base pointer." We will discuss the usage of the base pointer in Chapter 11.

> **%rsp**: This is the "stack pointer." We will discuss the stack and the stack pointer in Chapter 11.

Finally, while the previous registers can trace their history back to the original 8086 chip that started it all, the x86-64 ISA gives us eight new general-purpose registers. These are simply labeled as %r8 through %r15. You may wonder why the counting starts at 8 instead of 9. This is because, in low-level programming, counting almost always starts at zero instead of one. Therefore, the first eight registers can be considered 0–7 (though you can't refer to them that way in assembly language), and these new registers are 8–15.

Even though these registers didn't exist in previous versions of the ISA, these registers also have 32-bit, 16-bit, and individual-byte versions. For instance, %r11 refers to the whole 64-bit version of the register. However, you can refer to the 32-bit version by specifying %r11d, the 16-bit version by specifying %r11w, and the least significant (low) byte by specifying %r11b. Each of the new general-purpose registers can be accessed in this way.

Additionally, several of these registers have special instructions that operate with them, but their usage is sufficiently obscure that we will not cover them in this book.

4.4 Writing Binary Numbers

Now, so far, when writing explicit values, we have been writing the numbers in decimal. However, the machine actually thinks in binary. If you wish, you can actually write numbers directly in binary. The assembler, though, needs to know that the number is a binary number; otherwise, it couldn't distinguish between 10 meaning "ten" and 10 as a binary number, which means "two" in decimal. Therefore, when writing in binary, we prefix the number with 0b (that's a zero and then a lowercase "b"). So, in assembly language, $10 refers to the decimal number ten, and $0b10 refers to the binary number 10, which in decimal is two.

So, if I want to see what a number in binary looks like in decimal, I can simply write a program like the one as follows. Because echo $? always prints the number in decimal, then I will get to see what the value is in decimal. Remember, under the hood, *everything* is in binary.

binaryexit.s

```
.section .text
.globl _start
_start:
    movq $0b1101, %rdi
    movq $60, %rax
    syscall
```

To assemble and run the program, you can do

```
as binaryexit.s -o binaryexit.o
ld binaryexit.o -o binaryexit
./binaryexit
echo $?
```

You can modify the binary value in binaryexit.s and see the different results. Remember, though, if the value goes beyond 255, only the least significant 8 bits will be returned.

4.5 Playing with the Registers

Now we have a lot more registers we can play with. In addition to having more registers, we have also learned that the 64-bit registers have 32-bit, 16-bit, and sometimes 8-bit registers embedded within them. How do we access those in instructions?

Have you noticed that many of our instructions have a q after them? We have movq, addq, etc. The reason for this is that the instruction is including the size of operand it is dealing with. This may be obvious now, since the register name also implies a size, but, when we deal with main memory later on, it will sometimes not be implicitly obvious.

The q suffix refers to **quadwords**. This is a bit of a misnomer, but I'll explain the meaning. The original x86 ISA was actually a 16-bit architecture prior to 1985. This meant that the "standard" size of operations was 16 bits. The standard size of a value in an architecture is known as the **word** size.

When the architecture expanded to 32 bits, technically the word size changed to 32 bits. However, to maintain continuity with previous terminology and documentation (which had the word size as 16 bits), 32-bit values and registers are referred to as being "double-word" size (these are also referred to as "long" values). When the architecture expanded again to 64 bits, even though the word size is technically 64 bits, 64-bit values are considered in the documentation as "quadword" size.

In the GNU Assembler, you use the q suffix on instructions to indicate quadwords, the l suffix to indicate double-words (longs), the w suffix to indicate words, and the b suffix to indicate individual bytes.

So, to move a single byte (say the number 5) into the %ah register, you would use the following instruction:

```
movb $5, %ah
```

To move the %ax register into the %dx register, you would use the following instruction:

```
movw %ax, %dx
```

The following code will play around with different register sizes. It starts by loading a 16-bit value into %bx, and then it accesses the high and low bytes (%bh and %bl) individually.

valuesize.s

```
.section .text
.globl _start
_start:
    movw $0b0000000100000010, %bx
    addb %bh, %bl
    movb $0, %bh

    movq %rbx, %rdi

    movq $60, %rax
    syscall
```

To assemble, link, and run the program, do the following:[1]

```
as valuesize.s -o valuesize.o
ld valuesize.o -o valuesize
./valuesize
echo $?
```

To understand this program, let's look at this initial value that is loaded into %bx: $0b0000000100000010. This is a 16-bit value that is being stored in a 16-bit register. However, the %bx register can be accessed by individual bytes—%bh and %bl. If we break up this value into two pieces, we can see that the high 8 bits is 00000001 (which is 1 in decimal) and the low 8 bits is 00000010 (which is 2 in decimal).

Then, these two values are added together and then stored in %bl. However, we need them in %rdi so that it will be put into the exit status code. We cleared out the high byte (%bh) of %bx and then moved the whole of %rbx (which includes %bx) into %rdi to be the status code.

We then set %rax to 60 (the exit system call number). Now, with our registers properly set up, we issued the syscall instruction to send our exit status code back to the command line environment.

So why didn't we do this operation directly in %di or %rdi? Why start with %bx and then move the result? If you remember, %rdi does not have the ability to access individual bytes. Therefore, we used register %bx to do individual-byte manipulation and then moved the result to the place it needed to go to be used in the system call. A lot of assembly language winds up being shuffling between registers that have different functions or special instructions associated with them.

While this may seem like a contrived example, the fact is that this is actually a faster way to load values. Notice that we were able to essentially load two registers (%bh and %bl) with a single instruction, because they are both part of %bx. The ability to conceptualize a value broken down into bits and then separated, or, alternatively, a series of small values joined together in a larger one, is actually key to being able to understand a lot of low-level code. Sometimes we will want to even treat a number as if it were a collection of individual, unconnected bits, where each bit has its own individual meaning.

---

[1] Note that this is the last time I will show how a simple program is assembled, linked, and run. I'm going to assume that you can determine the procedure in simple cases going forward.

Exercises

1. Rewrite the first program in this chapter (`arithmetic.s`), but use different registers to hold the intermediate values.

2. Write your own sequence of arithmetic operations. Walk through the code by hand before running it so you know how it should work. Then, run the code using the debugger (Appendix C) to verify that you were correct. Be sure to check the contents of the registers at every step.

3. Make a mistake! Use the wrong `mov` instruction for a given register (i.e., `movq $5, %rax`). What does the assembler say when this happens?

4. Rewrite the `binaryexit.s` program in this chapter to output different values. See if you can figure out the decimal number that will be output from your binary representation.

5. Write a program (even if it is a nonsense program) that utilizes byte, word, long (double-word), and quadword instructions.

CHAPTER 5

Comparison, Branching, and Looping

In this chapter, we are going to look at how the computer makes comparisons and decisions.

5.1 The `%rip` Register and the `jmp` Instruction

In Chapter 4, we learned about the general-purpose registers. These registers are general purpose because they can be used for most arithmetic instructions. However, there are a few registers which are not usable in this way, but have a specific function that is maintained by the CPU itself. These are the **special-purpose registers**.

The first register I want to talk about you will probably never need to refer to directly, and that is the instruction pointer, or `%rip` (it is prefixed with an r because it is a 64-bit register). The instruction pointer simply points to the next memory location that the processor is going to process an instruction from. This lets the CPU know where to pull the next instruction from when the next clock cycle runs. During each instruction, the CPU will increment the instruction pointer to point to the next instruction—the one immediately after the current instruction.

This register can be manipulated through **jump** instructions. A jump instruction tells the computer to alter the flow of the program by setting the instruction pointer to a value that is different from where the CPU was going to set it to. The most basic form of this instruction is simply `jmp`, which tells the processor the address of the next instruction you want to execute.

© Jonathan Bartlett 2021
J. Bartlett, *Learn to Program with Assembly*, https://doi.org/10.1007/978-1-4842-7437-8_5

To give you a simple example, the next program will skip over several instructions using the jmp instruction:

jmpexample.s

.globl _start

.section .text
_start:
```
    movq $7, %rdi
    jmp nextplace

    # These two instructions are skipped
    movq $8, %rbx
    addq %rbx, %rdi
```

nextplace:
```
    movq $60, %rax
    syscall
```

As you can see, just as _start is a label which marked a place in the code where the code begins, in this code, nextplace also marks a location in the code. However, unlike _start, I made up the name nextplace and could call it anything I wanted. _start has a special meaning (it is where the code begins executing), but I can add additional labels anywhere in the code I wish.

Here, nextplace bookmarks the memory location that contains the instruction that follows the label. So, when I issued the instruction jmp nextplace, that tells the CPU to alter its instruction pointer so that the next instruction to execute will be the one at the memory address labeled by nextplace, skipping the two instructions in the middle.

Figure 5-1 gives a conceptual model of what is occurring.

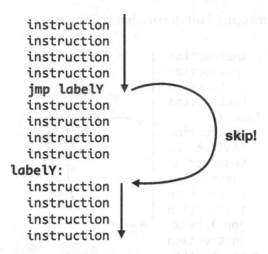

Figure 5-1. *Skipping Instructions Using the Jump Instruction*

Here, the instruction flow skips several instructions because of a jmp instruction to the label labelY which is further down in the code.

Not only can you use jmp to skip instructions, you can use it to repeat them as well. Think about it this way, we can jump to a *previous* section of code which will cause us to repeat it. The following code will cause an **infinite loop**, which means it will simply repeat itself forever until you stop it (if you aren't familiar with Linux, simply pressing Ctrl+C will stop the program):

infiniteloop.s

```
.globl _start

.section .text
_start:
    movq $60, %rax

another_location:
    movq $8, %rdi

    jmp another_location

    # This never gets executed
    syscall
```

In this program, the label another_location marks a location within the code. Later in the program, we jump back to that location. Then the program will execute again from that location and eventually hit our jump instruction again, in which case it will go back to another_location yet again.

Figure 5-2 gives a conceptual model of what is occurring.

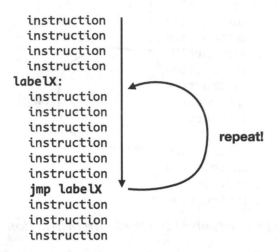

Figure 5-2. *Repeating Instructions Using the Jump Instruction*

Here, the instruction flow repeats several instructions because of a `jmp` instruction to the label `labelX` which had already occurred previously in the code.

As we have seen, jumps can occur to any location within your code. The next example is a confused nest of jumps. See if you can follow the code and guess what it does before running it:

followthejump.s

.globl _start

.section .text
_start:
```
    movq $25, %rax
    jmp thelabel
```

somewhere:
```
    movq %rax, %rdi
    jmp anotherlabel
```

label1:
```
    addq %rbx, %rax
    movq $5, %rbx
    jmp here
```

labellabel:
    syscall

anotherlabel:
    movq $60, %rax
    jmp labellabel

thelabel:
    movq %rax, %rbx
    jmp there

here:
    divq %rbx
    jmp somewhere

there:
    addq $5, %rbx
    jmp label1

anywhere:
    jmp thelabel

If you got the result wrong, you should try stepping through the program with a debugger as outlined in Appendix C.

5.2 Conditional Jumping and the %eflags Register

The jmp instruction is known as an **unconditional jump**. That is because it always jumps no matter what. It can be useful, but what ultimately makes a computer powerful is the ability to branch *conditionally*. A **conditional jump** is a variant of the jmp instruction that only jumps based on certain conditions.

Unlike higher-level languages, the conditions that are available for a conditional jump instruction are very limited. To understand the conditions that are available for a jump instruction, we have to introduce a new special-purpose register, the %eflags register.[1] Rather than thinking about %eflags as holding a single value, you usually think

---

[1] The %eflags register begins with e and not r because it is a 32-bit register. Since its bits are defined by individual statuses, there were not additional status flags needed to extend it to be 64 bits.

49

about the different bits of %eflags separately. Each bit holds a true/false status of a previous operation.

Most of the bits of the %eflags register are for operating system usage and aren't of extreme concern to us. However, there are two flags that come in useful continually:

ZF: The **zero flag** is set to 1 if the result of the last arithmetic operation was zero, or 0 if it was not.

CF: The **carry flag** is set to 1 if the result of the last arithmetic operation resulted in a "carry"—that is, the result was bigger than could be held in the destination register.

There are two more flags that we will deal with in Chapter 8 when we deal with signed numbers.

What happens is that at the end of each arithmetic instruction (instructions like addX, mulX, but not movX), the processor sets the value of these status bits in the %eflags register.

The typical way to make use of these flags is with a conditional jump statement. A conditional jump statement will jump based on the configuration of particular flags. If the condition matches, the jump will occur. Otherwise, the processor will just go to the next instruction as if nothing happened. Common jump instructions include

jz: "Jump if Zero" (jump if the zero flag is set to 1).

jnz: "Jump if Not Zero" (jump if the zero flag is set to 0).

jc: "Jump if Carry" (jump if the carry flag is set to 1).

jnc: "Jump if No Carry" (jump if the carry flag is set to 0).

Let us now consider a program which will raise a value to a given power. That is, given the values 2 and 3, it will raise 2 to the 3rd power (i.e., 2^3, or $2 \times 2 \times 2$, which results in 8). Another interesting feature of exponents is that anything raised to the zeroth power is 1. There's good reason for that mathematically, but if you're not a math guy, just trust me on that one.

How would we do this? What we want to do is to take the first value (the base) and multiply it by itself continually. We will use the second value (the exponent) and use it as a counter to keep track of our multiplication. We will run a loop that will continually multiply the current value by the base and decrease our exponent until it is zero, at which time we will leave the loop:

exponent.s

.globl _start

```
# This will calculate 2^3.
# You can modify %rbx and %rcx to calculate
# another exponential.
```

.section .text
_start:
```
    # %rbx will hold the base
    movq $2, %rbx

    # %rcx will hold the current exponent count
    movq $3, %rcx

    # Store the accumulated value in %rax
    movq $1, %rax
```

mainloop:
```
    # Adding zero will allow us to use the flags to
    # determine if %rcx has zero to begin with
    addq $0, %rcx

    # If the exponent is zero, we are done
    jz complete

    # Otherwise, multiply the accumulated value by our base
    mulq %rbx

    # Decrease the counter
    decq %rcx

    # Go back to the beginning of the loop and try again
    jmp mainloop
```

complete:
```
    # Move the accumulated value to %rdi so we can return it
    movq %rax, %rdi
```

```
# call the "exit" system call
movq $60, %rax
syscall
```

The program starts by loading the initial values into registers. It first loads the base (the number we will be multiplying by itself) into %rbx. Then, the exponent is loaded into %rcx. This will provide a countdown for the number of times we want to multiply %rbx by itself. Finally, a starting value is loaded into %rax. Since anything raised to the zero power is 1, and the base multiplied by 1 is our first number anyway, the program starts by loading a 1 into %rax.

The next instruction is labeled with the mainloop label. This is the point we will return to when repeating the multiplication over and over. The instruction itself may be surprising. The program adds 0 to %rcx. Why would we want to do this?

What we really want to know is whether or not %rcx is zero. However, the movq instruction doesn't set anything in %eflags. Therefore, by adding 0 to %rcx, this will set the zero flag on %eflags if the result is zero (i.e., if %rcx was zero to begin with).[2] Then, if %rcx is already zero (i.e., the program is given a zero exponent), the program jumps to the completion step. Otherwise, it keeps on going.

Next, we multiply by the base that is in %rbx. Remember, the multiply instruction always multiplies with %rax and stores the result there. So, the first time through, %rax will just be the base; the second time through, it will be the base squared; the third time through, it will be the base cubed; etc. Again, this is why %rax is known as the accumulator—many instructions implicitly use this particular register as storing the results of operations.

Next, we decrease %rcx. Here, we are using %rcx as a **counter**—a number which increases or decreases for every usage. We are using %rcx to keep track of where we are in the multiplying. It starts with the exponent, and every time through the loop we will decrease it by one. When %rcx becomes zero, we know that we have finished all of the multiplications and can stop.

---

[2] We will learn a better way to compare values in the next section.

After decrementing %rcx, we jump back to the start of the loop (which is designated in our code with the mainloop label).[3] So, if %rcx became zero when it was decremented, then jz instruction will cause it to exit the loop and go to the complete label.

At the complete label, we take %rax, which holds our result, and move it to %rdi in order to return it back to the user. We then do our normal exit system call routine to finish the program.

5.3 Comparisons

In the previous program, when we wanted to see if %rcx was zero, we added zero to it and checked the flags. There's nothing wrong with that per se, but it is somewhat unintuitive. As a matter of fact, there are a lot of interesting things you can do by just performing arithmetic and checking flags, but doing that makes the code hard to follow.

Thankfully, the instruction set gives us instructions to do explicit comparisons between numbers, as well as several jump instructions which look at the resulting flags and use them to tell the results of the comparison.

The cmpq instruction (and its relatives cmpb, cmpw, and cmpl) compares two numbers to tell which one is larger or if they are both equal. Internally, it performs the comparison by subtracting the numbers (but discarding the result rather than storing it) and then setting the flags accordingly. Then, there are special jump instructions that read the flags and know what that means in terms of which one was larger.

If we issued the command cmpq %rbx, %rax, then the CPU would actually subtract %rbx from %rax, but, rather than storing the result, it would just set the flags and discard the result. The flags will indicate that either %rbx and %rax are the same (the zero flag was set), %rax is greater than %rbx (flags were cleared), or %rax is less than %rbx (the flags set for this are complicated and will be covered in Chapter 8).

Note that the comparison can be of a register with a register, a register with a specific value, or, as we will see later, a register with a value from memory. However, if you are comparing a register with a specific value, the value needs to be placed first in the comparison.

---

[3] Interestingly, we could have moved the mainloop label to be *after* the addq instruction. This is because the result of decrementing %rcx will still set the zero flag. Additionally, jump instructions do not affect %eflags. Therefore, the zero flag will maintain its state across the jump, and we don't actually need to do the addition. However, that's a lot to follow if you are a new assembly language programmer, so I thought I would make it simpler and just repeat the addq instruction each time through the loop.

After the `cmpq` instruction sets the flags, there are corresponding jump instructions that will test one or more of these flags to see whether or not it should jump. Given the command `cmpq ARG1, ARG2`

> **je** will jump if ARG2 equals ARG1.
>
> **jne** will jump if ARG2 *does not* equal ARG1.
>
> **ja** will jump if ARG2 is above (greater than) ARG1.
>
> **jae** will jump if ARG2 is above (greater than) or equal to ARG1.
>
> **jb** will jump if ARG2 is below (less than) than ARG1.
>
> **jbe** will jump if ARG2 is below (less than) or equal to ARG1.

Note that the order of the arguments is backward than what you might expect. Other conditional jump instructions are available as well, based on a variety of flag configurations, but are not especially helpful for beginners.

5.4 Other Conditional Instructions

The suffixes on the jump instruction—e, ne, a, ae, b, be, and others—are known as **condition codes**. In addition to conditional jumps, the instruction set has other conditional instructions which utilize these condition codes.

The `cmov` family of instructions perform conditional moves. It works just like the `mov` family of instructions, but is based on the same kinds of conditions that the conditional jump instructions use. For instance, `cmovgq %rax, %rbx` will move the contents of `%rax` into `%rbx` if the previous comparison determined a "greater than" condition. Likewise, `cmovleq %rax, %rbx` will do the same move if it was a "less than or equal" condition.

The `loop` family of instructions combines several actions into one. What `loopq` does is the following:

1. Decrement `%rcx`.

2. Jump to the specified label if the result of the decrement is not zero.

The `%rcx` register is known as the "counter" register, because of instructions like `loopq` which use it to do special count-based actions.

To see the instruction in action, here is the same program again, but this time using a loopq instruction:

exponentloop.s

.globl _start

```
# This will calculate 2^3.
# You can modify %rbx and %rcx to calculate
# another exponential.

.section .text
_start:
    # %rbx will hold the base
    movq $2, %rbx

    # %rcx will hold the current exponent count
    movq $3, %rcx

    # Store the accumulated value in rax
    movq $1, %rax

    # If the exponent is equal to zero, we are done
    cmpq $0, %rcx
    je complete

mainloop:
    # Multiply the accumulated value by our base
    mulq %rbx

    # Decrement %rcx, go back to loop label if %rcx is
    # not yet zero
    loopq mainloop

complete:
    # Move the accumulated value to %rdi so we can return it
    movq %rax, %rdi
    # call the "exit" system call
    movq $60, %rax
    syscall
```

Note that the loopq instruction allows the loop to be extremely short. The instruction itself is doing most of the work. It is acting as a conditional control, managing the value of %rcx, and defining the boundaries of the loop. Therefore, the whole loop is just two instructions.

Note that the idea behind this instruction is that it jumps if it is *still in the loop* and doesn't jump if you exit the loop. Therefore, this instruction is usually at the tail end of a loop. If your loop requires a condition to enter the loop, that is usually done at the beginning. In our case, we check whether %rcx is zero at the very beginning.

There are also two variants, loopeq and loopneq. These read the %eflags register to give additional conditions to continue looping. loopeq will only continue the loop (i.e., perform a jump) if the previous comparison resulted in equality (i.e., if the zero flag is set). loopneq will only jump if the previous comparison resulted in inequality (i.e., the zero flag is not set).

5.5 A Note About Looping and Branching in Assembly Language

Branching and looping is one area that tends to confuse assembly language programmers who come to assembly language after using other programming languages first. The reason for this is that other programming languages tend to put fences around blocks of code. A for loop functions as a unit, with the start and end of the loop well defined and the control variables spelled out.

In assembly language, however, each instruction is an island unto itself. Many instructions, such as loopq, are built for the purpose of helping you write loops, but there is nothing in assembly language that forces you to use the instructions that way. You could use loopq to decrement %rcx and jump if %rcx is not zero for some non-loop-related reason if you wanted to.

The point is that there is nothing in the language itself that maintains the connection between parts of a loop. You have to maintain that connection by jumping to the right place in your jump, conditional jump, or loop instruction. There are no guardrails in assembly language that make sure you do the right thing.

Because of this, conditionals and loops in assembly language can indeed get messy. In fact, one of the main motivators of higher-level languages was to prevent the messiness of assembly language-style programming, with its proliferation of jump instructions. Historically, many programming languages had a GOTO statement which would perform similar to assembly language jumps. However, it caused code to get so messy that it was essentially taken out of most programming languages, and, for those languages that left it in, programmers were shunned who used it.[4]

Nonetheless, for assembly language, that's literally all that we have! The best solution for assembly language programming is to use spacing, labels, and comments in your code to make it clear what your code is doing and why.

Exercises

1. Create your own version of `followthejump.s`. Walk through the code yourself to be sure you know what it is going to do. Then step through it with the debugger to make sure it does what you expect.

2. Create a program that just loops a certain number of times and then exits. Approximately how many times does it have to loop before it takes a full second to run? This number will be very large. Can you estimate how many instructions the CPU executed in that time period?

3. Modify the program `exponentloop.s` several times, each time making it raise a different number to a different power.

4. Even though we have already learned about the `mulq` instruction, write a program that will multiply two numbers by repeatedly adding in a loop.

5. Write a program that starts with a value in a register and yields a 1 if that number is even and 0 if that number is odd (hint—think about the `divq` instruction and remainders).

6. Implement the previous program by counting down in a loop rather than using the `divq` instruction.

---

[4] The debate about the use of GOTO statements in computer programming stretches back to the 1960s, with Edsger Dijkstra's letter in *Communications of the ACM* titled "Go To Statement Considered Harmful." There are a many people who remain in favor of limited usage of GOTO statements, but only for a very limited set of circumstances where they make code clearer.

CHAPTER 6

Working with Data in Memory

While registers store the values that the CPU is actively processing, most of a program's data is in main memory, not in registers. In this chapter, we will learn the basics of how to access main memory in assembly language.

6.1 Adding Fixed-Length Data Sections to Programs

To begin with, we will look at adding fixed-length data sections to programs.

Data sections are marked in code with the command `.section .data`. This will allow you to add fixed-length data sections to your program. Within the data section, we name the memory storage for our data using labels (similar to our existing `_start` label) and then write the initial values that will be stored in that memory.

The following code will allocate and initialize three quadwords of data. It will add two of them together and store the result in the final location.

simpledata.s

```
.globl _start

.section .data
first_value:
    .quad 4
second_value:
    .quad 6
final_result:
    .quad 0
```

© Jonathan Bartlett 2021
J. Bartlett, *Learn to Program with Assembly*, https://doi.org/10.1007/978-1-4842-7437-8_6

```
.section .text
_start:
    # Load values into registers
    movq first_value, %rbx
    movq second_value, %rcx

    # Perform the computation
    addq %rbx, %rcx

    # Store results into memory
    movq %rcx, final_result

    # Return the value to the operating system
    movq $60, %rax
    movq final_result, %rdi
    syscall
```

After telling the assembler that we are in the data section, we then added the label first_value (followed by a colon). What that does is basically bookmark that location in memory. Whatever the memory address of the next line winds up being, that's what first_value will refer to.

So what is after first_value? The .quad directive tells the assembler that the values that follow will all be sized as quadwords (64 bits or 8 bytes). Other sizes are available, such as .byte for individual bytes (see Chapter 13 for more details). So, .quad 4 means that the assembler will allocate a single quadword and store the value 4 there. You can actually put any number of values after the .quad directive, and it will store them each as a separate quadword sequentially in memory. The address of where this is loaded can be referred to using the label first_value.

Using similar reasoning, you can see that second_value is the address of the next memory location, which will hold a 6. Finally, final_value is the address of the next memory location, which will start by holding a zero, but which we will modify in the program.

In order to manipulate the data, we have to move it into registers. In the x86-64 ISA, for the mov family of instructions (i.e., movb, movw, movl, and movq), one (but not both!) of the operands to the instructions can be a memory location. Therefore, if we want to manipulate first_value and second_value, the general process is to first load them into registers, then manipulate them, and then store them back into memory.

The instruction movq first_value, %rbx tells the assembler to move the data from the location specified by the address that first_value refers to and store it in %rbx. Note that there is no dollar sign in front of first_value. That's because first_value doesn't refer to the value 6 itself, but to the *address of the memory* where first_value is stored. If you use a number without a dollar sign in assembly language, it is treated as an address of memory, rather than a value. Even though first_value doesn't look like a number, underneath the covers, it actually is just a number. It's just that we don't care what the specific value of it is; we only care that it is tied to the memory location.

We then load the second value into %rcx with the command movq second_value, %rcx. Now that they are both in registers, we can manipulate them. The program simply adds them together. It then stores the result in the location specified by final_value.

After this, we are now ready to return to the operating system. We load the exit system call number into %rax and then load the final value from its memory location into %rdi. Finally, we call syscall to perform the exit.

One thing to note is that this program, like many programs in this book, is intentionally inefficient in order to demonstrate various features of assembly language. We are using toy programs, so I try to move data around a little bit more and be a little inefficient so that you have more to bite your teeth into.

In any case, see the following to see a shorter version of this same program (only four instructions rather than seven):

simpledatashort.s

```
.globl _start

# Program Data
.section .data
first_value:
    .quad 4
second_value:
    .quad 6

.section .text
_start:
    # Load values into registers
```

```
movq first_value, %rdi

# Perform the computation
addq second_value, %rdi

# Return the value to the operating system
movq $60, %rax
syscall
```

In this version, since the final register that everything needs to be in is %rdi, we will use that register to store the intermediate values as well. Therefore, the first instruction loads the memory directly into %rdi. On the second instruction, rather than loading the second addition operand to a register, we are simply directly adding it to %rdi.[1] Many instructions (not just the mov family) can work with one of the operands being a memory location. Therefore, we just accessed the memory directly and added it to %rdi, which also stored the result in %rdi. Now all that's left to do is load exit's system call number into %rax and issue the syscall instruction.

6.2 Memory Addressing Modes

Single values are all well and good, but usually data comes in bigger packages than that.

Let's look at a case where we need to access a whole set of numbers in sequence (known as an **array**). Let us say that we want to find the largest value of a set of numbers. To create the set of numbers in the data section, we would put the following in our code:

```
mynumbers:
    .quad 5, 20, 33, 80, 52, 10, 1
```

This creates storage for seven numbers and initializes their values. It also creates a label for the address of the first value: mynumbers. There's just one problem—there is no way for the program to tell where the numbers stop. Remember that memory is just one

---

[1] The question of whether to access memory values directly or load them into registers first is a tricky decision. Generally, if you are going to do more than one thing with them, it is better to load it into a register first, because every memory access takes additional time. However, if you are only doing a single operation with the value, skipping the register removes an extraneous instruction from the process. There are also additional considerations in Appendix I that you can take into account.

memory address after another. The CPU doesn't know where things start and end, so our code has to *tell* it when to stop.

There are three common ways for telling the computer where the stopping point is:

1. Have a special value (called a **sentinel** value) that means "stop."

2. Have a memory location before the actual start of the data that tells the number of elements of the array.

3. Mark the end of the array with another label.

The first way is usually the easiest to program, but comes at the cost of having a value that can't be used in the normal way (i.e., your sentinel value can't actually be a data value that you could hit). The second way is the most flexible, because, when we get to functions, it allows for variably sized arrays easier. The third way is slightly easier to program, but it is usually only workable in very limited circumstances (such as toy programs like the ones we are writing).

We will adopt choice number 2—we will have a memory location that tells the number of elements of the array. Therefore, our data section will look like this:

```
numberofnumbers:
    .quad 7
mynumbers:
    .quad 5, 20, 33, 80, 52, 10, 1
```

So, in this case, each value is quadword sized. numberofnumbers stores the number of elements in our array, and mynumbers marks the start of the array.

What we are going to do is create a loop which iterates through each element in the array and checks to see which one is the largest. However, so far, we have only learned how to access values that occur *at* a label. How will we access the ones beyond it? The answer is that assembly language contains multiple **addressing modes**. An addressing mode is essentially the way that the CPU finds a value for an instruction.

We have already been using addressing modes; we just didn't call them that. The addressing modes we have used so far include

> **Immediate mode**: This is when we put the value of interest directly in the instruction. For instance, in movq $5, %rax, the $ indicates that it should use immediate mode. That is, the value is contained within the instruction itself.

Register mode: This is when we are referring to a register to find or store a value. In movq $5, %rax, the %rax is a register.

Direct memory mode: This is when we are referring to a value by its address. The address itself is part of the instruction. When we did movq first_value, %rbx, first_value is a direct memory address.[2]

However, there are many more addressing modes available. The one we will look at in this section is known as **register indirect mode**. In this addressing mode, a register holds the value of the address to access. So, let's say that %rbx held a memory address, and we wanted to take the contents of that memory address and move it to %rax. The command for this is movq (%rbx), %rax. If %rbx contains an invalid memory address, you'll either wind up with junk in %rax, or if the memory location just doesn't exist at all, it will cause an error and the program will abort.

Figure 6-1 shows this addressing mode visually.

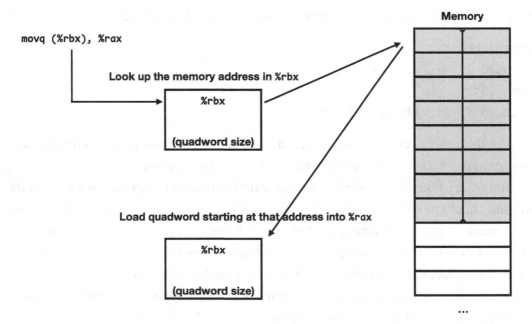

Figure 6-1. *A Visual Representation of Register Indirect Addressing Mode*

---

[2] Note that first_value just becomes a number when the assembler runs. It refers to the particular memory location, and we are treating it as an address. However, if we added a dollar sign in front of it, then it would be treated just as an immediate-mode number.

Note that in this drawing, lower memory addresses are drawn toward the top of the drawing.

So, to demonstrate the usage of the register indirect addressing mode, let's make use of it to find the largest value in our array. What we will do is load the value of the address of our array into a register and then use register indirect addressing to access the values themselves. When we want to access the next value, we simply add 8 to the register that contains the address (remember, quadwords are 8 bytes long, so the next value will be 8 bytes after the current one). We will use a counter to make sure we don't go beyond the end of the array.

largestvalue.s

```
.globl _start

.section .data
# How many data elements we have
numberofnumbers:
    .quad 7

# The data elements themselves
mynumbers:
    .quad 5, 20, 33, 80, 52, 10, 1

### This program will find the largest value in the array

.section .text
_start:
    ### Initialize Registers ###

    # Put the number of elements of the array in %rcx
    movq numberofnumbers, %rcx

    # Put the *address* of the first element in %rbx
    movq $mynumbers, %rbx

    # Use %rdi to hold the current-high value
    movq $0, %rdi

    ### Check Preconditions ###

    # If there are no numbers, stop
```

```
    cmp $0, %rcx
    je endloop

    ### Main Loop ###
myloop:
    # Get the next value (currently pointed to by %rbx)
    movq (%rbx), %rax

    # If it is not bigger, go to the end of the loop
    cmp %rdi, %rax
    jbe loopcontrol

    # Otherwise, store this as the biggest element so far
    movq %rax, %rdi

loopcontrol:
    # Change the address in %rbx to point to the next value
    addq $8, %rbx

    # Decrement %rcx and keep going until %rcx is zero
    loopq myloop

    ### Cleanup and Exit ###
endloop:
    # We're done - exit
    movq $60, %rax
    syscall
```

Notice these two instructions: movq numberofnumbers, %rcx and movq $mynumbers, %rbx. Both of these reference memory locations. However, the first one is using direct addressing mode. It is taking the *contents* of the memory at the memory address labeled by numberofnumbers and moving them into %rcx. The second one, however, is prefixed with a dollar sign. That means that the memory address *itself* is being used as an immediate-mode value. In other words, the address itself is being loaded into %rbx.

So, whatever address mynumbers referred to, that address is now in %rbx. Therefore, later on, we can use (%rbx) to refer to the contents of that memory address.

In the main program, what we are doing is (a) loading the next value into %rax, (b) comparing it with our current maximum value in %rdi, and then, if it is less than or equal to what is already there (i.e., it isn't bigger than the current maximum value), skipping the instruction that moves the %rax into %rdi.

The loopcontrol segment of code then does two things. First, it advances %rbx to point to the next value. It does this by adding 8 (the size of a quadword) to %rbx. Then, the loopq instruction decrements %rcx and then checks to see if we have gotten to the end (i.e., %rcx is zero). If we haven't, then it takes us back to myloop.

6.3 General Addressing Mode Syntax

Technically, you can do everything you need with register indirect addressing mode. Since you can store the address in a register, and you can do arithmetic on the register, that's all that's required. However, to make life easier (and programs faster), there are other addressing modes available.

However, all the memory addressing modes can be combined into a generalized addressing mode syntax. That is, they will all be written the same way, just with some parts left out for different modes. The general syntax for accessing memory is

```
VALUE(BASEREG, IDXREG, MULTIPLIER)
```

In this, VALUE is a fixed value, BASEREG and IDXREG are registers, and MULTIPLIER is a fixed multiplier, which can be 1, 2, 4, or 8 (it is 1 if left out).

The memory address that this refers to is calculated as follows:

```
address = VALUE + BASEREG + IDXREG * MULTIPLIER
```

Figure 6-2 shows how this works visually.

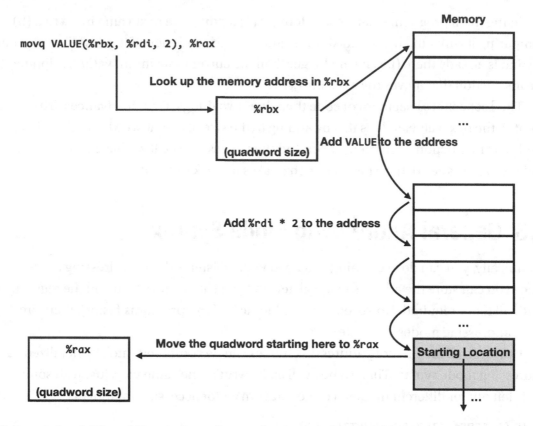

Figure 6-2. *A Visual Depiction of How the Generalized Addressing Mode Syntax Works*

Note that in this drawing, lower memory addresses are drawn toward the top of the drawing.

If a piece is left out, it is assumed to be zero (except for MULTIPLIER, which is assumed to be one). So, when we were doing direct addressing mode, the only part of this we used was VALUE. When we were using register indirect mode, the only part of this we used was (BASEREG).

To see this in action, we will show a variant of the program to find the largest value. This one will only use %rbx as an **index** into the array. An index simply tells *which* value in the array to access. So, if %rbx is 0, that is the first element (indexes start counting at zero). If %rbx is 1, that is the second element, and so on:

largestvalueindex.s

.globl _start

.section .data
How many data elements we have
numberofnumbers:
    .quad 7

The data elements themselves
mynumbers:
    .quad 5, 20, 33, 80, 52, 10, 1

This program will find the largest value in the array

.section .text
_start:
    ### Initialize Registers ###

    # Put the number of elements of the array in %rcx
    movq numberofnumbers, %rcx

    # Put the index of the first element in %rbx
    movq $0, %rbx

    # Use %rdi to hold the current-high value
    movq $0, %rdi

    ### Check Preconditions ###

    # If there are no numbers, stop
    cmp $0, %rcx
    je endloop

    ### Main Loop ###
myloop:
    # Get the next value of mynumbers indexed by %rbx
    movq mynumbers(,%rbx,8), %rax

    # If it is not bigger, go to the end of the loop
    cmp %rdi, %rax
    jbe loopcontrol

```
    # Otherwise, store this as the biggest element so far
    movq %rax, %rdi
```

loopcontrol:
```
    # Move %rbx to the next index
    incq %rbx

    # Decrement %rcx and keep going until %rcx is zero
    loopq myloop

    ### Cleanup and Exit ###
```
endloop:
```
    # We're done - exit
    movq $60, %rax
    syscall
```

The memory lookup in this program is movq mynumbers(,%rbx,8), %rax. According to the preceding formula, this will take %rbx (the index); multiply it by the multiplier, which is 8 (because each value is 8 bytes long); and add it to mynumbers. This will be the address that it uses to access the memory. BASEREG in the preceding formula is missing, so it is assumed to be zero.

While this is a fairly straightforward modification of the original program, assembly language allows us to think about programs differently and optimize them so that the program follows the thinking patterns of the computer. The instruction set we are working with likes to count *down* to zero (because of the loop family of instructions). We normally think about going from the start of the array to the end, but what if we went the other way? What if we went from the end of the array back to the beginning?

In this case, %rcx could do double duty as both the counter and the index! This removes two instructions from the code, one of which is in our loop.

The only problem with this is that %rcx would be an index from 1 to 7, while our previous index (%rbx) was from 0 to 6. Therefore, we will have to subtract 8 (one quadword) from the value (mynumbers) to account for this. That's okay, because the assembler knows how to do this and will do it for us.

The code for this is as follows:

largestvaluercx.s

.globl _start

.section .data
How many data elements we have
numberofnumbers:
    .quad 7

The data elements themselves
mynumbers:
    .quad 5, 20, 33, 80, 52, 10, 1

This program will find the largest value in the array

.section .text
_start:
    ### Initialize Registers ###

    # Put the number of elements of the array in %rcx
    movq numberofnumbers, %rcx

    # Use %rdi to hold the current-high value
    movq $0, %rdi

    ### Check Preconditions ###

    # If there are no numbers, stop
    cmp $0, %rcx
    je endloop

    ### Main Loop ###
myloop:
    # Get the next value of mynumbers indexed by %rbx
    movq mynumbers-8(,%rcx,8), %rax

    # If it is not bigger, go to the end of the loop
    cmp %rdi, %rax

```
    jbe loopcontrol

    # Otherwise, store this as the biggest element so far
    movq %rax, %rdi

loopcontrol:
    # Decrement %rcx and keep going until %rcx is zero
    loopq myloop

    ### Cleanup and Exit ###
endloop:
    # We're done - exit
    movq $60, %rax
    syscall
```

As mentioned, the address lookup was modified to be movq mynumbers-8(,%rcx,8), %rax. So, since mynumbers is known by the assembler (it is whatever address the assembler assigns to that data), the assembler can also subtract 8 and encode that number into the instruction. The subtraction here is not done by the CPU when it runs, it is done at the time of assembly. Again, the reason for this is that, unlike the previous program, %rcx is going to be 1 through 7, not 0 through 6. Therefore, if we didn't adjust it, it would start at the second element and run past the end of the array.

6.4 More Addressing Modes

While the general formula VALUE(BASEREG, IDXREG, MULTIPLIER) covers all of the bases technically, many of the ways that this is used have specific names. As we've already mentioned, using just VALUE alone is the direct addressing mode, and using (BASEREG) is the register indirect addressing mode. Other common modes include

> **Indexed mode**: This is the mode we used in the previous program. Here, VALUE represents the address of an array, and IDXREG represents the index to the array, with MULTIPLIER representing the size of each array element. BASEREG is left out.

> **Base pointer mode**: This is also referred to as **displacement mode**. In this mode, BASEREG is known as the base pointer, and VALUE, rather than being an address, is a fixed offset from BASEREG

(either positive or negative—negative values are fully supported here). This is a very common mode which we will get into shortly, but we don't quite know enough to understand its usage.

Base pointer indexed mode: This mode makes use of all of the different components of the general formula. BASEREG is a register that points to a location; the location is offset by VALUE and then indexed by IDXREG, which is multiplied by MULTIPLIER. This is illustrated in Figure 6-2.

Program counter (PC)–relative addressing mode: This mode will be discussed in Chapter 15. It is just listed here for completeness.

One other instruction I want to leave you with in this section is the leaq instruction. This instruction means "load effective address." What it does is this—given a general formula for memory as given earlier, leaq, rather than load the contents of the memory at this location, will calculate the final address and store the address itself into the destination register.

This can be useful for a variety of reasons. You may need to do more than one calculation on the address of a piece of memory. Alternatively, you may do it just for easier to read code. In the first version of the largestvalue.s program, we loaded the pointer to our array into %rbx like this: movq $mynumbers, %rbx. There's nothing wrong with that, but someone may not see the dollar sign and therefore may not realize that you are loading the address into %rbx, not the value at the address. Using leaq makes this more obvious. If you issued the instruction leaq mynumbers, %rbx, then it is more obvious from the instruction itself that you are trying to load an address into %rbx. After all, that's what leaq actually stands for.

Important Note   There is one important limitation to keep in mind about all of these instructions. While memory references can be used as the source or destination of *many* different instructions, they cannot be used for *both* the source and the destination. One of those has to be a register or an immediate-mode value.

Exercises

1. Play with the values that you are looking through. Modify them, add more values, remove values, etc. Be sure to set the value in numberofnumbers to be the correct number of elements.

2. Make a mistake! Modify the value in numberofnumbers to be 3. What happens? Why?

3. Make a mistake! Modify the value in numberofnumbers to be greater than 1000. What happens? Why?

4. Rewrite each of the programs in this chapter to look for the *smallest* value, not the largest value.

5. Write a new program to search an array for a value. In addition to having values in memory like numberofnumbers and mynumbers, have another value that is the number you are searching for. Write a program to give back 1 if the value is found and 0 if it is not found. Test it with several values.

6. Rewrite the previous program so that it gives back the *index* of the value, if found.

CHAPTER 7

Data Records

7.1 Laying Out Data Records

Now that we know some data access techniques, we can now learn about how to store **records** (also known as **structs** or **structures**). A record is just a well-defined segment of data. Remember, everything in the computer is just numbers. Therefore, if we want to store multiple things about an entity, we need to know where these bits of data are. Because of this, we define how the data will be laid out in memory, and that is the record format.

Let's say that we want to store records about people. Character data is harder, so we will address that later. However, let's say that we want to store each person's age, height, weight, and hair color. We would define a record layout for this.

But first, how do we store hair color? Remember, everything in the computer is a number. Therefore, we will just define a number to represent each color. We will say that red is 1, brown is 2, blonde is 3, black is 4, and white is 5 (if I've left your hair color out, you have my apologies, but feel free to define your own values!). I assigned those values arbitrarily—you can have the numbers mean whatever you wish. The point is that since everything is a number, we have to assign *some* number to represent those values.

Now, we have to define what this record will look like in memory. Because our experience is limited to integers, and it is easiest dealing with quadwords, we will lay out the record as follows:

1. One quadword for the person's weight (in pounds)

2. One quadword for the person's hair color

3. One quadword for the person's height (in inches)

4. One quadword for the person's age (in years)

© Jonathan Bartlett 2021
J. Bartlett, *Learn to Program with Assembly*, https://doi.org/10.1007/978-1-4842-7437-8_7

So, for instance, to represent myself, I would be .quad 280, 2, 72, 44 (280 pounds, brown hair, 72 inches tall, and 44 years old). Again, the computer has no way of knowing what these numbers mean; it only knows how your code uses them. Therefore, you have to define ahead of time what the values mean and how they are laid out in memory so you can know how to use them.

Figure 7-1 shows how this looks in memory.

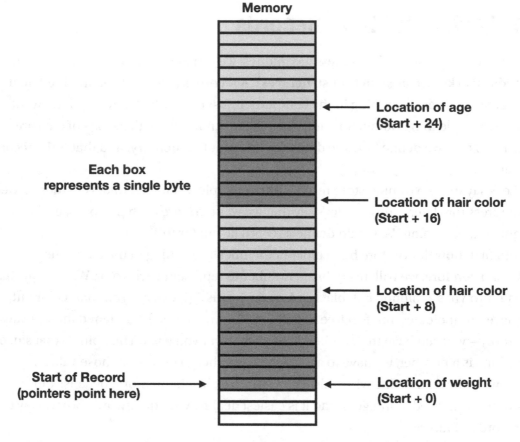

Figure 7-1. *How Our Person Data Record Is Laid Out in Memory*

Note that in this drawing, lower memory addresses are drawn toward the bottom of the drawing.

7.2 Creating Constants with .equ

In order to simplify your life, it is helpful to create **constants** which can be used as offsets into the record to make loads and stores easier. A constant is a value that never changes. It is a number that is defined once, and then you can reference that constant by name. The labels we are using are themselves constants. They are just constants where the assembler decides what value they will refer to. You can also make constants where *you* decide what value they will refer to.

Constants are declared using the .equ directive. This defines a constant for the assembler. For instance, if I wrote the line .equ MYCONSTANT, 5, then, anywhere I wrote MYCONSTANT, the assembler would substitute the value 5. In the GNU Assembler, you can define a constant before or after it is used. In fact, as we will see shortly, you can even define it in another file, as long as the constant is marked as global (using the .globl directive), and the files are linked together.

In our case, it will be useful to define constants that tell how far each field is from the start of the record. For instance, since the person's weight is the first value, the offset from the start of the record is zero. Therefore, we might define a constant like HEIGHT_ OFFSET and set it to 0. The person's hair color is a quadword (8 bytes) into the record. Therefore, we might define a constant like HAIR_OFFSET and set it to 8. Likewise, HEIGHT_ OFFSET would be 16 and AGE_OFFSET would be 24.

In code, this would look like the following:

```
.equ WEIGHT_OFFSET, 0
.equ HAIR_OFFSET, 8
.equ HEIGHT_OFFSET, 16
.equ AGE_OFFSET, 24
```

If we want to share all of these constants with other files, we can mark them all global at once like this:

```
.globl WEIGHT_OFFSET, HAIR_OFFSET, HEIGHT_OFFSET, AGE_OFFSET
```

You may be wondering how we will use these. Well, let's say that we have the address of our record stored in %rbx, and we want to get the value of the person's age and put it in %rax. We could do that with the command movq AGE_OFFSET(%rbx), %rax. Since we are using VALUE and BASEREG from the general addressing mode syntax, the final address is VALUE + BASEREG, which is the address of the age field of our record.

Interestingly, when you make constants, you can also include some basic calculations in them—even involving other constants! As long as the calculation is simple (add, subtract, multiply, divide), the assembler will handle the computation for you. So, for instance, I could have defined my offsets like this:

```
.equ WEIGHT_OFFSET, 0
.equ HAIR_OFFSET, WEIGHT_OFFSET + 8
.equ HEIGHT_OFFSET, HAIR_OFFSET + 8
.equ AGE_OFFSET, HEIGHT_OFFSET + 8
```

Which way you choose to declare your offsets—either explicitly (as in the first case) or having the assembler calculate the offset in comparison to the previous offset (as in the second case)—depends on your own style. The assembler doesn't care at all.

A really neat trick you can do with this is to calculate the number of bytes between two labels in your program. Since the labels are themselves constants, and the assembler can do arithmetic with constants, if you subtract two memory address labels, it will give you the number of bytes between them. If the labels are of the start and end of a set of records, you can then divide this number by the record size and have the assembler auto-calculate the number of records you have. This way, rather than having to keep count of your records, the assembler will do it for you.

Here's an example:

```
.equ PERSON_RECORD_SIZE, 32
numpeople:
    # Calculate the number of people in array
    .quad (endpeople - people)/PERSON_RECORD_SIZE
people:
    # Array of people
    .quad 250, 3, 75, 24
    .quad 250, 4, 70, 11
    .quad 180, 5, 69, 65
endpeople:
```

So, in this snippet, you can see that the people label marks the starting memory address of the data and the endpeople label marks the memory address that immediately follows. Therefore, subtracting them will give the total number of bytes. If we divide it by the record size (which we defined in PERSON_RECORD_SIZE), that tells us the total number of records between those two markers. Here, we store that value in a memory location marked with the label numpeople.

7.3 Splitting Up Your Program

We are going to write several programs that operate on the same pieces of data. In order to avoid having to retype all of the data sections (and other parts of the code), we are going to have to split our programs up into multiple files.

The first file we will code will simply be the data records themselves. We will call this file persondata.s, and it will just contain the records of the people and information about how to access different parts of the record. Many pieces of this file should seem familiar from previous sections of this chapter.

persondata.s

```
.section .data

.globl people, numpeople
numpeople:
    # Calculate the number of people in array
    .quad (endpeople - people)/PERSON_RECORD_SIZE
people:
    # Array of people
    .quad 200, 2, 74, 20
    .quad 280, 2, 72, 44 # me!
    .quad 150, 1, 68, 30
    .quad 250, 3, 75, 24
    .quad 250, 2, 70, 11
    .quad 180, 5, 69, 65
endpeople: # Marks the end of the array for calculation purposes

# Describe the components of the struct
.globl WEIGHT_OFFSET, HAIR_OFFSET, HEIGHT_OFFSET, AGE_OFFSET
.equ WEIGHT_OFFSET, 0
.equ HAIR_OFFSET, 8
.equ HEIGHT_OFFSET, 16
.equ AGE_OFFSET, 24
```

```
# Total size of the struct
.globl PERSON_RECORD_SIZE
.equ PERSON_RECORD_SIZE, 32
```

This file will only need to be assembled once:

```
as persondata.s -o persondata.o
```

This will create an object file that contains the data records and the constants, but nothing else. We will combine this with our code when we later link the files together. So far, we have only had one file to link, so the link stage may have seemed superfluous. However, when we start incorporating multiple files, the link stage starts to make more sense. Each assembly listing gets assembled into its own object file, and all the object files get linked together at the end to make a final executable.

Notice that we declared the label people as being global with .globl people. This means that it will be available to other object files during the linking stage. So, if I refer to people in another assembly language file, it will **resolve** the meaning of that when it links the files together.

Now, let's write a simple program which finds the tallest person in the file and exits with their age. Note that this file doesn't include any of the data, or even the constants that we defined previously.

tallest.s

```
.globl _start
.section .text
_start:
    ### Initialize Registers ###

    # Pointer to first record
    leaq people, %rbx

    # Record count
    movq numpeople, %rcx

    # Tallest value found
    movq $0, %rdi

    ### Check Preconditions ###
```

```
# If there are no records, finish
cmpq $0, %rcx
je finish

### Main Loop ###
```
mainloop:
```
# %rbx is the pointer to the whole struct
# This instruction grabs the height field
# and stores it in %rax
movq HEIGHT_OFFSET(%rbx), %rax

# If it is less than or equal to our current
# tallest, go to the next one.
cmpq %rdi, %rax
jbe endloop

# Copy this value as the tallest value
movq %rax, %rdi
```
endloop:
```
# Move %rbx to point to the next record
addq $PERSON_RECORD_SIZE, %rbx

# Decrement %rcx and do it again
loopq mainloop

### Finish it off ###
```
finish:
```
movq $60, %rax
syscall
```

We can now assemble this into an object file as follows:

```
as tallest.s -o tallest.o
```

We now have *two* object files—persondata.o and tallest.o. We can use the linker to combine them together like this:

```
ld persondata.o tallest.o -o tallest
```

This creates the executable file `tallest` from the previous two files. This executable can be run just as before:

```
./tallest
echo $?
```

If you did everything correctly, it should give 75.

7.4 Sharing Data with Another Program

The next program will do something a little different. It will count the number of brown-haired people in our data. The code for this is as follows:

browncount.s

```
.globl _start
.section .text
_start:
    ### Initialize Registers ###

    # Pointer to first record
    leaq people, %rbx

    # Total record count
    movq numpeople, %rcx

    # Brown-hair count
    movq $0, %rdi

    ### Check Preconditions ###

    # if there are no records, finish
    cmpq $0, %rcx
    je finish

    ### Main Loop ###
mainloop:
    # Is the hair color brown (2)?
    cmpq $2, HAIR_OFFSET(%rbx)
```

```
    # No?  Go to next record
    jne endloop

    # Yes?  Increment the count
    incq %rdi
endloop:
    addq $PERSON_RECORD_SIZE, %rbx
    loopq mainloop
finish:
    movq $60, %rax
    syscall
```

We can then assemble it and link it with the persondata.o file that we already have:

```
as browncount.s -o browncount.o
ld persondata.o browncount.o -o browncount
```

You can now run the program.

7.5 Changing the Data Record Layout

One of the great things about using constants for your offsets is that if you ever want to change your data layout, it is easy to do so without breaking your program. Let's say, for instance, that we wanted to add a new field to our data—the person's shoe size. Let's also say that we want this to be the second field in the record.

Now, if we had just hard-coded offsets into our programs instead of using constants, doing this would require that we go and find these offsets and rewrite them based on the new record format. This would be especially hard, because we would have to think if each occurrence of 16 referred to the HEIGHT_OFFSET or something else. By naming your constants, it is clear what their function is in the program.

The following is a modification of persondata.s, now called persondataexpanded.s. This file adds the shoe size field to the data records and modifies the constants to reflect the new record layout. However, we will *not* have to change our actual program code, tallest.s and browncount.s. They will just need to be relinked to the new data object file, and they will function perfectly well!

persondataexpanded.s

.section .data

.globl people, numpeople
numpeople:
    # Calculate the number of people in array
    .quad (endpeople - people)/PERSON_RECORD_SIZE
people:
    # Array of people
    .quad 200, 10, 2, 74, 20
    .quad 280, 12, 2, 72, 44 # me!
    .quad 150, 8, 1, 68, 30
    .quad 250, 14, 3, 75, 24
    .quad 250, 10, 4, 70, 11
    .quad 180, 11, 5, 69, 65
endpeople: # Marks the end of the array for calculation purposes

Describe the components of the struct
.globl WEIGHT_OFFSET, SHOE_OFFSET, HAIR_OFFSET, HEIGHT_OFFSET, AGE_OFFSET
.equ WEIGHT_OFFSET, 0
.equ SHOE_OFFSET, 8
.equ HAIR_OFFSET, 16
.equ HEIGHT_OFFSET, 24
.equ AGE_OFFSET, 32

Total size of the struct
.globl PERSON_RECORD_SIZE
.equ PERSON_RECORD_SIZE, 40

To assemble, link, and run, just do

```
as persondataexpanded.s -o persondataexpanded.o
ld persondataexpanded.o tallest.o -o tallest
./tallest
echo $?
```

Try this with both the tallest example and the browncount example.

7.6 Storing Character Data

In this section, I wanted to talk about character data. A lot of what we store and display is *text*, so knowing how the computer deals with text is important. Now, unfortunately, we still aren't at the point where we can read or display text, but since we are talking about data, and so much data is textual data, I did want to give you a little bit of insight and practice with how it is stored and manipulated.

Data in computers, as we have seen, is entirely numbers. Sometimes the numbers represent values for data, such as height. Other times, values signify something, such as hair color. One thing that computers often must store are strings of letters. In programming, however, we rarely refer to "letters," but rather to **characters**. Letters really only refer to the alphabetic letters. However, most users want to type more than letters—they want spaces, numbers, punctuation marks, glyphs, etc. All of these ideas are unified in the concept of a character—a single, discrete glyph that can be written (or, in the case of spaces, not written).

Characters are represented by numbers. For instance, the letter "A" is typically represented by the number 65, the letter "B" is represented by the number 66, etc. However, remember that uppercase and lowercase letters are different characters, so they have their own codes, starting with "a" being represented by the number 97. This list of which characters are represented by which numbers is known as the ASCII code.[1]

ASCII was developed when 8-bit computers were prevalent and storage was limited. Because of this, ASCII is itself limited to single bytes. When ASCII is stored, each character gets a byte. This, however, limits the characters available to basically English characters.

As computers have internationalized, ASCII has become fairly limiting. In fact, even the notion of a "character" stretches the boundaries of some written languages. When you add in all these different languages, numbers, symbols, emojis, etc., 255 characters just isn't enough. This need for more characters prompted the development of **Unicode**, which is a standardized system for representing characters. Unicode has a lot of complications, and we certainly don't want to take the time to address them now. If you're interested, you can see Appendix H for more information. ASCII is much easier to deal with for beginners.

---

[1] ASCII stands for American Standard Code for Information Interchange. There's nothing special about it, except that the fact that everyone agrees on it makes it more useful for moving data. For instance, there's an older standard called EBCDIC, where, for instance, "a" is 129, but nobody uses this anymore.

Thankfully, ASCII is also compatible with the most common form of Unicode, called **UTF-8**, which was specifically built to be ASCII compatible. Therefore, your knowledge of ASCII will roughly transfer to working with Unicode later on. As long as you stick with basic English characters and punctuation, ASCII and UTF-8 are identical.

Now, since ASCII characters are single bytes, we can't just deal with them like we did with quadwords and just load them into a 64-bit register. The assembler will store characters as bytes, and we will need to use the movb in order to get them to the right place. Additionally, we will need to move the characters into the byte-sized registers—%ah, %al, %bh, %bl, %ch, %cl, %dh, and %dl.

Just like we can declare data of various sizes in assembly language, we can also declare textual data. To declare a bit of data as ASCII text, you use the .ascii directive.

```
mytext:
    .ascii "This is a string of characters.\0"
```

As you probably guessed, mytext is a label that refers to the memory address of the first character in the **string** (a string is a consecutive stretch of characters that belong together). The double quotation marks show the computer where the string starts and ends. However, you may be wondering what the \0 is doing.

As we mentioned in Chapter 6, when you have arrays of values, you need to know where the endpoint is. In that chapter, we opted to have a separate value tell us the length. That can work with character data, too. However, another common way to mark the ending of a string is with the **null** character. The null character has a literal value of 0 in ASCII, and it specifically means "the end of the string." Therefore, if your string is a **null-terminated string** (has a null character at the end), then all you need to know is the address of the first character. You can just process the string until you get to the null. The backslash tells the assembler that you are inserting a special character. \0 is the null character, \n is a newline, \t is a tab character, and \\ gives you a backslash itself. There are others as well, but those are the ones you are likely to run into.

Going back to the string, this .ascii directive is essentially the same as a .byte directive. If you know the ASCII codes for each letter, you can represent the preceding data with a .byte directive as follows:

```
mytext:
    .byte 84, 104, 105, 115, 32, 105, 115, 32, 97, 32, 115
    .byte 116, 114, 105, 110, 103, 32, 111, 102, 32, 99
    .byte 104, 97, 114, 97, 99, 116, 101, 114, 115, 46, 0
```

While this is ugly looking, it actually is the exact same data as before. If you recognize that capital letters start at 65, lowercase letters start at 97, and spaces are represented by the code 32, you can see that these are identical. In fact, as an exercise, you should go through and verify that the preceding text matches the bytes just presented.

One thing that may be surprising is that digits themselves have their own codes. A digit is itself a written character and so, itself, has character codes, *and those codes have little to do with the value of the numbers themselves.* So, for instance, the *character* 0 has an ASCII code of 48, 1 has a code of 49, etc. As you can see, when treated as characters, there's not a lot you can do mathematically with these!

One other note—you can actually write a character as a value in an assembly listing using single quotes. So, for instance, if I want to load the ASCII code for the letter a into %al, I can do it with the instruction movb $'a', %al. Don't forget the dollar sign so the assembler knows to use immediate mode—otherwise, the assembler will think you are referring to the memory location at address 97!

The following is a program that will count the number of lowercase letters in our string. A lowercase letter is one that is between 97 (a) and 122 (z), inclusive.

lowercasecount.s

```
.globl _start

.section .data
mytext:
    .ascii "This is a string of characters.\0"

.section .text
_start:
    ### Initialization

    # Move a pointer to the string into %rbx
    movq $mytext, %rbx

    # Count starts at zero
    movq $0, %rdi

mainloop:
    # Get the next byte
    movb (%rbx), %al
```

```
    # Quit if we hit the null terminator
    cmpb $0, %al
    je finish

    # Go to the next byte if the value isn't between a and z
    cmpb $'a', %al
    jb loopcontrol

    cmpb $'z', %al
    ja loopcontrol

    # It's lower-case! Add one to %rdi
    incq %rdi

loopcontrol:
    # Next byte
    incq %rbx

    # Repeat
    jmp mainloop

finish:
    movq $60, %rax
    syscall
```

As you can see, our loop is using the null character to know when to stop. So, if you left out the null character from the string, the program would continue until either it found a null character by chance or if it ran past the memory allocated to your program (in which case the program would crash).

Some variations you may try to this program include

1. Count the uppercase characters.

2. Count the non-letter characters.

3. Count the total number of characters.

7.7 Endianness

Technically, we could move the data into our registers in larger chunks. That is, we could literally move words, longs (double-words), or quadwords into our registers, thus cutting out a large number of memory accesses. However, to do that successfully, we have to know how the bytes of our registers are stored into memory. This may seem like it should be intuitively obvious, but intuitions differ, and, in different instruction set architectures, this is done in various ways.

Let's say that we have a quadword in the following bits:

1000000011000000111000001111000011111000111111001111111011111111

Some people think that the digits should be stored such that the least significant digits are in the lowest numbered memory regions. However, if we did that, this would be stored in memory as the following byte sequence:

1. 11111111

2. 11111110

3. 11111100

4. 11111000

5. 11110000

6. 11100000

7. 11000000

8. 10000000

This is known as **little endian** format, because the "little end" (least significant byte) is stored first.

Other people think that since we think about the big end being first, we should put it first in memory. This is known as **big endian** format, because the "big end" (most significant byte) is stored first. This is also known as **network byte order** because of its predominance in networking protocols. Big endian is stored in memory in the following order:

1. 10000000

2. 11000000

3. 11100000

4. 11110000

5. 11111000

6. 11111100

7. 11111110

8. 11111111

The x86-64 instruction set architecture is a little endian instruction set.

Now, let's look at what would happen if we loaded the first quadword starting at mytext from the previous program into a quadword register, such a %rax. If we did movq mytext, %rax, then %rax would look like this after the instruction:

Now, moving the whole quadword at once to %rax makes fewer memory accesses. However, the only pieces of %rax that we can access as individual bytes are %al and %ah. What happens if we want to access the rest of the bytes individually?

The rol and ror instructions will *rotate* the register left and right, respectively, by the specified number of bits (the number bits can be specified either as an immediate-mode value or a value stored in a register). So, for instance, if we take the preceding value in %rax and issue the instruction ror $16, %rax, this will result in rotating the value 2 bytes (16 bits) to the right, yielding the contents of the register being as follows:

This allows for the next 2 bytes in the string to be accessible through %al and %ah. Continuing in this manner requires more code to be *written*, but the resulting code is faster because it makes fewer memory accesses. However, the code to do this is fairly tedious, because you have to separately code each byte access and check each individual byte to see if it is null and if it needs to be counted.

Because it is so tedious, I expect few will actually code this example, but you should at least look through this code and recognize how it is working with the different bytes. The resulting code is about 5% to 15% faster. There are a lot fewer comments in the code so the code listing doesn't get ridiculously long, but the labels should help you find your way in it:

multibytemov.s

```
.globl _start

.section .data
mytext:
    .ascii "This is a string of characters.\0"

.section .text
_start:
    ### Initialization

    # Move a pointer to the string into %rbx
    movq $mytext, %rbx

    # Count starts at zero
    movq $0, %rdi

mainloop:
    # Get the next quadword
    movq (%rbx), %rax

byte1:
    cmpb $0, %al
    je finish
    cmpb $'a', %al
    jb byte2
    cmpb $'z', %al
    ja byte2
    incq %rdi

byte2:
    cmpb $0, %ah
    je finish
```

```
    cmpb $'a', %ah
    jb byte3
    cmpb $'z', %ah
    ja byte3
    incq %rdi
```

byte3:

```
    # Shift the next bytes into position
    rorq $16, %rax
    cmpb $0, %al
    je finish
    cmpb $'a', %al
    jb byte4
    cmpb $'z', %al
    ja byte4
    incq %rdi
```

byte4:

```
    cmpb $0, %ah
    je finish
    cmpb $'a', %ah
    jb byte5
    cmpb $'z', %ah
    ja byte5
    incq %rdi
```

byte5:

```
    # Shift the next bytes into position
    rorq $16, %rax
    cmpb $0, %al
    je finish
    cmpb $'a', %al
    jb byte6
    cmpb $'z', %al
    ja byte6
    incq %rdi
```

byte6:

```
    cmpb $0, %ah
    je finish
    cmpb $'a', %ah
    jb byte7
    cmpb $'z', %ah
    ja byte7
    incq %rdi
```

byte7:

```
    # Shift the next bytes into position
    rorq $16, %rax
    cmpb $0, %al
    je finish
    cmpb $'a', %al
    jb byte8
    cmpb $'z', %al
    ja byte8
    incq %rdi
```

byte8:

```
    cmpb $0, %ah
    je finish
    cmpb $'a', %ah
    jb loopcontrol
    cmpb $'z', %ah
    ja loopcontrol
    incq %rdi
```

loopcontrol:

```
    addq $8, %rbx
    jmp mainloop
```

finish:

```
    movq $60, %rax
    syscall
```

There are several instruction families that can help with endianness and similar byte-oriented operations (each of them having a suffix indicating the word size being used):

> **xchg**: This instruction exchanges values of its two operands. It's like a mov instruction, except that the values are copied to each other, not just in one direction.

> **bswap**: This instruction reverses the order of bytes in the destination. bswapq %rax reverses the order of the bytes in %rax. Note that there isn't a version of this command that works on word-size (16-bit) registers. This is because instead of writing bswapw %ax, since the bytes of the 16-bit general-purpose registers are available individually, you can get the same effect just by using xchg and saying, for instance, xchgb %ax, %al.

> **ror**: This rotates a value right by the specified number of bits. rorq $16, %rcx rotates register %rcx to the right by 16 bits. In a rotation, anything rotated all the way off to the right comes back in on the left.

> **rol**: This is the same as ror but rotates to the left.

> **shr**: This shifts a value right by the specified number of bits. This is identical to ror, except that the bits that get shifted all the way off to the right do *not* come back in on the left, but instead zeroes get shifted in on the left-hand side.

> **shl**: This is the same as shr, but shifts to the left.

7.8 Including Strings in Data Records

There are a lot of ways to include a string in a data record. The easiest is probably to have a fixed-size segment for the string, but have the string be null-terminated at an earlier point.

For instance, we can add a name to our data record about a person. We could reserve 32 bytes of storage for the name. Here is a version of the person data that includes names:

persondataname.s

.section .data

.globl people, numpeople
numpeople:
    # Calculate the number of people in array
    .quad (endpeople - people)/PERSON_RECORD_SIZE
people:
    # Array of people
    .ascii "Gilbert Keith Chester\0"
    .quad 200, 10, 2, 74, 20
    .ascii "Jonathan Bartlett\0"
    .quad 280, 12, 2, 72, 44 # me!
    .ascii "Clive Silver Lewis\0"
    .quad 150, 8, 1, 68, 30
    .ascii "Tommy Aquinas\0"
    .quad 250, 14, 3, 75, 24
    .ascii "Isaac Newn\0"
    .quad 250, 10, 4, 70, 11
    .ascii "Gregory Mend\0"
    .quad 180, 11, 5, 69, 65
endpeople: # Marks the end of the array for calculation purposes

Describe the components of the struct
.globl NAME_OFFSET, WEIGHT_OFFSET, SHOE_OFFSET
.globl HAIR_OFFSET, HEIGHT_OFFSET, AGE_OFFSET
.equ NAME_OFFSET, 0
.equ WEIGHT_OFFSET, 32
.equ SHOE_OFFSET, 40
.equ HAIR_OFFSET, 48
.equ HEIGHT_OFFSET, 56
.equ AGE_OFFSET, 64

```
# Total size of the struct
.globl PERSON_RECORD_SIZE
.equ PERSON_RECORD_SIZE, 72
```

Notice that the names were **padded** with additional characters after the null character in order to use up the space. The specific character we put there is irrelevant, as our string processing will always stop at the null character. However, despite the fact that we have 32 bytes reserved, the maximum string length is actually 31 characters, because we have to reserve 1 byte for the null character. If this character isn't present, any code reading the strings won't know how to stop.

The way that individual characters are accessed here is by (a) having the address of the record in one register (we'll say %rbx), (b) having the index of the character you want to access (starting with 0) in another register (we'll say %rcx), and then issuing an instruction such as movb NAME_OFFSET(%rbx,%rcx,1), %al.

Now, having a fixed-length field has problems. First of all, it imposes a maximum size on the name. Here, we simply can't support names longer than 31 characters. Additionally, for short names, we are wasting space. If your name is "Jo Smit," we've wasted a lot of space holding your name.

To solve both of these problems, the alternative way of storing the names is to store them as **pointers**. That is, we will store the names themselves elsewhere, where we can allocate the *exact* amount of space we need, and then store in the record itself the memory address where that string lives. Example data records for that are as follows:

persondatanamepointer.s

```
.section .data

.globl people, numpeople
numpeople:
    # Calculate the number of people in array
    .quad (endpeople - people)/PERSON_RECORD_SIZE
people:
    # Array of people
    .quad $gkcname, 200, 10, 2, 74, 20
    .quad $jbname, 280, 12, 2, 72, 44 # me!
    .quad $cslname, 150, 8, 1, 68, 30
    .quad $taname, 250, 14, 3, 75, 24
    .quad $inname, 250, 10, 4, 70, 11
```

```
    .quad $gmname, 180, 11, 5, 69, 65
endpeople: # Marks the end of the array for calculation purposes
gkcname:
    .ascii "Gilbert Keith Chester\0"
jbname:
    .ascii "Jonathan Bartlett\0"
cslname:
    .ascii "Clist Silver Lewis\0"
taname:
    .ascii "Tommy Aquinas\0"
inname:
    .ascii "Isaac Newn\0"
gmname:
    .ascii "Gregory Mend\0"

# Describe the components of the struct
.globl NAME_PTR_OFFSET, WEIGHT_OFFSET, SHOE_OFFSET
.globl HAIR_OFFSET, HEIGHT_OFFSET, AGE_OFFSET
.equ NAME_PTR_OFFSET, 0
.equ WEIGHT_OFFSET, 8
.equ SHOE_OFFSET, 16
.equ HAIR_OFFSET, 24
.equ HEIGHT_OFFSET, 32
.equ AGE_OFFSET, 40

# Total size of the struct
.globl PERSON_RECORD_SIZE
.equ PERSON_RECORD_SIZE, 48
```

The drawback to this method is that it is a little more complex (and a little less efficient) to deal with. Rather than being able to load a character with a single instruction, we have to first load the address of the string into a register and then load the character offset. For instance, we could issue the instruction movq NAME_PTR_OFFSET(%rbx), %rdx to load the address of the string into %rdx and then do movb (%rdx,%rcx,1), %al to get the character at the index specified by %rcx into %al. Pointers in x86-64 are themselves quadwords.

Structuring records properly is both a science and an art. There are many, many ways that it can be done, each with their own benefits and drawbacks. In these days of large memories and fast computers, usually it is best to favor flexibility over speed or stinginess.

Exercises

1. Think about various things on the computer and how they would be represented as a data structure. How would the position of your cursor be represented? What about the pixels on your screen?

2. Open up a preferences dialog box on your computer. Think about how you might create a record that would hold the kind of data that the preferences box is asking for.

3. What other information might we add to our person record? Modify the record structure and add a field or two. Check to be sure the programs still run correctly.

4. Let us say that a person might have a mother and a father that is in the data. How might we structure the data so that a person's record links to their mother and father?

5. Modify the `browncount.s` program to count anybody who has brown OR blonde hair.

6. Create a program that finds the youngest age in the array.

7. Modify the previous program so that, after finding the youngest age in the array, it gives back the index of the record with that age, rather than the age itself.

8. Create a program that uses the data in `persondataname.s` and gives back the length of the longest name.

CHAPTER 8

Signed Numbers and Bitwise Operations

So far, we have only considered values that are nonnegative integers. Technically, this is really what all values are underneath the covers. However, using special instructions and flags of the %eflags register, the CPU can treat these values as if they were different kinds of numbers (such as signed integers or even decimal numbers). In this chapter, we will look at these instructions and flags and aim to understand how the processor deals with these values.

8.1 Decimal, Binary, Hexadecimal, and Octal Numbers

Before we get to how the computer itself stores numbers, I want to talk a bit about how we *write* the numbers we are going to use in programming. As we've already mentioned, while we tend to use decimal to write numbers, the computer is actually using binary for everything.

If we wanted, we could write our numbers in binary as well! However, how would the assembler distinguish between 10 meaning a decimal ten and 10 meaning a binary ten (decimal two)? The way it does this is by adding a prefix to the number telling the assembler what base you are using. The prefix for a binary number is 0b (that's a zero followed by the letter "b"). So, 10 means the decimal number ten, but 0b10 means a binary 10, which is 2 in decimal.

This can be extremely useful when you are interested in specific bit patterns. If you want a value that only has the fourth least significant bit set, that is easiest to write in

© Jonathan Bartlett 2021
J. Bartlett, *Learn to Program with Assembly*, https://doi.org/10.1007/978-1-4842-7437-8_8

binary: 0b1000. If you care about the bits but not about the decimal number, writing in binary is really helpful.

Another important base for computers is base 16, known as **hexadecimal**. Here, there are 16 separate digits per place value. You have 0–9 for the first ten digits and then a, b, c, d, e, and f (case does not matter—you can write hexadecimal numbers with uppercase or lowercase characters according to preference).[1] Since a follows 9, it means 10. f is another important one to memorize—it means 15. Then, in hexadecimal, when we move to the next place, instead of it being the "tens" place, it is the "sixteens" place. So, the number 20 in hexadecimal is $2 \times 16 = 32$ in decimal. The number 2C is $2 \times 16 + 12 = 44$ in decimal.

The next place is 16^2 or 256. So, if I have the hexadecimal number AC2, that is $10 \times 256 + 12 \times 16 + 2 = 2754$. The next place is 16^3, then the next place is 16^4, and so on.

Why do we care about hexadecimal numbers? Well, with decimal, it is hard to tell from the size of the number how many bytes it takes up. For instance, how many bytes does the number 124,000 use? It's 3 bytes, but it is hard to tell from the number itself. In hexadecimal, however, every hexadecimal digit is exactly 4 bits, and every two hexadecimal characters is exactly 1 byte!

Therefore, hexadecimal is often thought of as a "condensed binary." With practice, you can look at a hexadecimal number and "see" what it means in binary. To write hexadecimal in code, you use the prefix 0x at the beginning of your numbers (zero followed by the letter "x"). Therefore, 0x31 means hexadecimal 31, which is $3 \times 16 + 1 = 49$.

One other system which is less often used is octal (base 8). In octal, each digit represents 3 bits, which isn't all that useful. However, and this is the main reason I'm mentioning octal, in the GNU Assembler, *merely starting a number with zero switches to octal*! Therefore, if you accidentally write 053 instead of 53, the actual value will be computed as $5 \times 8 + 3 = 43$.

Now, also remember that any immediate-mode value will need to be prefixed with a $. So, if you want to load %rax with the hexadecimal number 7A, you would do it like this: movq $0x7A, %rax.

---

[1] Note that the hexadecimal system opens up the number system to corny jokes, especially in error codes. For instance, some common error codes in the history of computing have included 0xBBADBEEF, 0xDEADDEAD, 0xCAFEBABE, and 0x8BADF00D. Usually trying to write in "hexspeak" is considered a little unprofessional, but that doesn't mean it isn't sometimes done.

8.2 Representing Signed Integers

Having different ways of writing numbers is interesting, but, ultimately, they all get stored the same way—as bits in memory. Now we will get into more details on how the computer itself is storing and processing other types of numbers than just the nonnegative integers.

The first kind of number we will look at is signed integers—integers that can be positive or negative. If you think about it, there are several possible ways that a computer could store a signed value. For instance, it could reserve the first bit as the sign bit and then use the rest of the bits for the absolute value. The problem here is that it makes signed and unsigned arithmetic very different and creates a lot of special cases for the computer to handle.

Therefore, instead of just adding a sign bit, most instruction sets (including x86-64), use the **two's complement** mechanism for signed numbers. The way that two's complement works is that while positive integers count *up* from zero, negative integers count *back* from zero.

Let's say we were only working with a single-byte number, starting at zero (0b00000000). If we add one, we get 0b00000001. If we subtract one, we basically wrap all the way around to the other side, giving us 0b11111111. If treated as a signed byte, this value is -1 (it would be 255 if it were treated as an unsigned byte).[2] If we subtract one again, we get 0b11111110 (-2 as a signed byte). Subtracting one again yields 0b11111101 (-3 as a signed byte).

Now, ultimately, the positive and negative integers are sharing the same byte, so how do we know which is which? The answer is that we use the first bit to tell us if the value is positive or negative. If the first (i.e., most significant) bit is zero, then that means the value is positive, and if the first bit is one, then that means the value is negative. This first bit is known as the **sign flag**, because it marks whether or not the value is positive or negative. This means that roughly half of our numbers are reserved for positive numbers and half for negatives. For a single byte, the positive numbers are 1 through 127, and the

---

[2] I'm using the words "treated as" because the computer doesn't know or care what you are storing in its memory or registers. It only cares which instructions you use on them. If you use signed instructions one time and unsigned instructions another time, you will get a weird answer, but, ultimately, the computer doesn't care.

negatives are -1 through -128.[3] If you "wrap around" (i.e., adding 4 to 126 gives you 130, which is actually -126), this is called an **overflow** condition.

Two's complement arithmetic has several interesting properties:

- Addition and subtraction are identical except how the flags are set. If I add 0b00000001 (+1) to 0b11111111 (-1), the result, whether using signed or unsigned integers, is 0b00000000. The only difference is whether this should indicate an overflow condition or not.[4]

- It is easy to tell that a number is a negative number. If the most significant bit is set, it is negative.

- It is easy to increase the number of bits of a number through **sign extension**. Basically, if I have an 8-bit signed number and I want to make it 64 bits, I can simply take the sign bit and repeat it going leftward until I fill up the remaining bits.

- There is a unique value for zero. If we think to our first idea for a number system (that we just have a sign bit), we can see that we would have both a negative and positive zero, which can get confusing.

To obtain the negative of a particular value in the two's complement system, all you have to do is flip all the bits and then add one. So, if I want a -5, I first look at how 5 is written in binary, 0b00000101. To make it negative, I first flip all the bits, yielding 0b11111010. Finally, I add one, giving 0b11111011. This is -5 in binary.

Moving to 32-bit or 64-bit numbers is exactly the same, just with more digits. Negative 5 as a 64-bit number is

0b1111111111111111111111111111111111111111111111111111111111111011

The instruction to convert a positive value to a negative (and vice versa) is the neg family of instructions. neg instructions take a single operand which is both the source and destination of the operation. For instance, negq %rax will take the negative of %rax and store it back into %rax.

---

[3] There is always one more of the negative numbers than the positive numbers because zero doesn't have a sign flag.

[4] This property is true of subtraction and multiplication as well, but it would be a distraction to demonstrate them.

8.3 Additional Flags for Signed Integers

Now that *we* know how to work with negative numbers in binary, we need to look at how to get the processor to do it. For addition and subtraction, it is actually the exact same instruction families: add and sub. The difference is in which flags we might look at after the instructions. In addition to the carry flag (CF) and zero flag (ZF) which we introduced in Chapter 5, additional flags of interest include

OF: The **overflow flag** tells us that if we were intending the numbers to be used as signed numbers, we overflowed the values and now the sign is wrong.

SF: The **sign flag** tells us whether the sign flag (the most significant bit) of the result was set after the instruction. Note that this is not the same as if the sign flag *should* have been set (i.e., in an overflow condition).

To see the flags in action, we will look at the "byte" versions of these instructions so that we don't have to write long 64-bit values.

Let's imagine code for adding 0b01111111 (127) and 0b01111111 (127):

```
movb $0b01111111, %al
addb $0b01111111, %al
```

The result of this addition will be 0b11111110. If we were dealing with *signed* bytes, this would be a problem, because the addition causes an overflow and sets the sign bit when it shouldn't. However, we can check the overflow flag (OF) to see if this occurred. The jo instruction will jump if the overflow flag is set, and the jno will jump if it is not set. You can also check the signed flag similarly, with js and jns.

You can also use the cmp family of instructions for signed comparisons as well as unsigned comparisons. The cmp instruction is the same, but different jump instructions check different flags if you are treating the values as signed instead of unsigned values. For the instruction cmpq ARG1, ARG2, the following occurs:

jl: Jump if ARG2 is less than ARG1.

jle: Jump if ARG2 is less than or equal to ARG1.

jg: Jump if ARG2 is greater than ARG1.

jge: Jump if ARG2 is greater than or equal to ARG1.

While the unsigned jump evaluations (i.e., ja and jb and friends) are usually checking the carry flag (CF) and zero flag (ZF), the signed jump evaluations are also checking the sign flag (SF) and the overflow flag (OF).

8.4 Bigger Integers

Since 64 bits gives you a very large number of possible values, it is no longer often the case that programmers need larger values than fit in standard-sized registers. Nonetheless, understanding this will help understand the details of multiplication and division better.

If you needed bigger integers (i.e., more than 64 bits), it is fairly straightforward to do with multiple registers and/or multiple memory locations. Let us say that you want to work with 320-bit numbers (i.e., 5 quadwords big), and you wanted to add together two 320-bit signed numbers. The basic process for this would be the following:

1. Load the least significant 64 bits of each addend into registers.

2. Perform an addq instruction. This will perform an addition and set the carry flags.

3. Store the result.

4. For the remaining bytes

   (a). Load in the next least significant bytes of each value.

   (b). Add them together with the adcq instruction. This instruction will not only add the values together, it will take into account the carry flag (CF) from the previous addition.

   (c). Store the result.

5. After all the additions have occurred, check the overflow flag (OF) to see the result was bigger than 320 what can be kept in 320 bits.

Here, we introduced a new instruction, adcq (add with carry). As mentioned, this instruction not only adds the operands, it also adds the carry flag if it is set (and also sets the carry flags if appropriate). Note that the overflow flag only needs to be checked at the end. adc is setting it every time, but we only need to know the value at the very end.

So, as you can see, we can "chain together" multiple smaller values to make a larger value.

8.5 Division and Multiplication

In Chapter 4, we introduced the div and mul instructions. However, since we were just starting out, we didn't include a lot of detail. However, multiplication and division both have strange caveats that have to be taken into account.

With addition and subtraction, if a value goes beyond the space we provided, it will only be a single bit. Therefore, the processor can use the %eflags register to store the value of this bit using the carry flag (CF) and the overflow flag (OF). However, with multiplication, the size of the destination can *double*.

To see this, let's compare the addition of the decimal numbers 999 and 999 to their multiplication. Here is addition:

```
      9   9   9
+     9   9   9
_____
  1   9   9   8
```

Notice that it only extends a single digit beyond the original addends. This "extra" is small enough that can be stored in a single digit (which, in binary, is the carry flag in %eflags). Now look at multiplication:

```
          9   9   9
×         9   9   9
_____
  9   9   8   0   0   1
```

As you can see, multiplication has the ability to double the number of digits required!

Therefore, if we multiply two 64-bit numbers, how will the results be stored? What happens if the result is larger than 64 bits? To solve this problem, the CPU stores the result of multiplication in *two* registers! Previously, we mentioned that the result was in %rax. However, %rax is actually the least significant bits of the result. If the result overflows %rax, then the additional bits are stored in %rdx (which is one of the reasons it is known as the data register). When two registers are combined together this way, it is often written out as %rdx:%rax, though you would not write this as code (just as documentation/communication).

The div instruction is the opposite. The dividend (the number *being* divided) is stored in %rdx:%rax, and the divisor (the number it is divided by) is specified as an operand to the instruction. The result is then stored with the quotient (main result) being stored in %rax and the remainder being stored in %rdx. This is why we said in Chapter 4 to be sure that %rdx is zero before issuing a div instruction—it is actually included as part of the dividend!

Note that it is possible for the div instruction family to fail in multiple ways. If the starting value uses more than 64 bits, it is possible for the result to be more than 64 bits. Additionally, dividing by zero is illegal, so the divisor can't be zero. If either of these conditions are met, the instruction is considered illegal and the program will terminate.

Note also that the mul and div instruction families are unsigned instructions. The signed versions of these instructions are imul and idiv. For all multiplication instructions, the carry flag (CF) and overflow flag (OF) are set if the result overflows into the second register.

Additionally, the imul and idiv instruction families can operate with two operands as well, similar to how the add family operates. However, since only one register is specified for the destination, if the result overflows the destination, it is simply truncated to be the size of the destination register (but the flags are still set).

8.6 Looking at Individual Bits

Oftentimes you will want to test individual bits of a value. There are several reasons for this:

- You might want to know if a signed value is negative or not (i.e., if the most significant bit is set).

- You might want to know if a value is odd or not (for unsigned values, whether the least significant bit is set).

- You might be treating a value as a collection of on/off flags and want to know if a particular flag in that value is set.

While there are many bit operations available, we will look at two because of their utility: AND and OR. The AND operation compares two bits, and the result is 1 if both bits are 1 and 0 otherwise. The OR operation compares two bits, and the result is 1 if either bit is 1 (or both bits are 1).

To see this in action, let's consider the following instructions:

```
movb $0b01100010, %al
movb $0b11110100, $bl
andb %al, %bl
```

What this will do is line up the bits of %al with %bl and, for each bit, perform an AND function, and the result will be stored in the corresponding bit of %bl (the destination register):

```
      0   1   1   0   0   0   1   0
AND   1   1   1   1   0   1   0   0
      _____
      0   1   1   0   0   0   0   0
```

As you can see, only the positions where *both* %al and %bl contained a 1 did the bit get set in the resulting value.

Let's now look at an or operation between these two values:

```
     0   1   1   0   0   0   1   0
OR   1   1   1   1   0   1   0   0
     _____
     1   1   1   1   0   1   1   0
```

As you can see, if there was any place where either value was 1, then it was set in the final value.

The way that AND and OR are used in programming is often to check and to set individual bits. For instance, let's say we have a byte that represents the status of a transaction. Let's say that the least significant bit represented whether or not the transaction was completed (we'll ignore the meaning of the rest of them). It will be 1 if it is completed and 0 if it is not.

If we just wanted to pull out that one, single bit to examine, we could use the AND function. We would AND the value with a value that only had the bit set that we were interested in. That way, the result would *only* have the value of that bit in it. For instance, let's say the value of our status byte is 0b01001101. If we AND the value with 0b00000001, then the result will be 0b00000001 if the final bit is set, and 0b00000000 if it isn't.

A value that is used to specify which bits we are interested in is known as a **bitmask** (or just a mask), because it is silencing (zeroing out, masking) all the bits that we *aren't* interested in.

Interestingly, no matter which bit we are checking, we can always see if it is set using the zero flag (ZF) on the %eflags register. This is because if the bit isn't set, the result will always be zero. If the bit is set, then the result will be nonzero. So we can use the jz and jnz instructions to test this.

If we don't want to store the result of the andb instruction, we can use the testb instruction instead. This instruction will perform an AND operation and then discard the results, but keep the flags set. So, if I wanted to know if the least significant bit of %bl is set, I can do the following:

```
testb $0b0000001, %bl
jnz bitwasset
```

To set a flag to 1, you can use an OR operation. Let's say that we have a transaction status of 0b01001100, and we want to set the last bit to 1. To do this, we can do the following:

```
movb $0b01001100, %al
orb $0b00000001, %al
```

This will set the least significant bit of %al to 1.

To set a flag to 0, you can use an AND operation with all bits set to 1 *except* the one you want to set to zero. Let's say that %al has my status, but for some reason, I want to mark the transaction as incomplete (set the least significant flag to 0). This can be done with the instruction andb $0b11111110, %al. This will keep all flags to their original value, except for the least significant bit, which it will set to zero.

Other popular bit operations include

NOT: This operation has a single operand and simply flips the bit(s) (0 goes to 1 and 1 goes to 0). This is accomplished with the not family of instructions. notb %al will reverse all of the bits of %al.

XOR: This means **exclusive or**. This is similar to OR except that if *both* values are 1, the result is 0. This is accomplished with the xor family of instructions.

8.7 Numbers with Decimals

While it may seem appropriate to mention numbers with decimals here, the fact is that this is a whole separate topic and isn't really in scope for an introductory text. However, Appendix F provides an introduction. It is included in the appendix rather than the main text because it requires additional knowledge learned throughout the rest of the book (namely about the function of stacks). For now, just know that dealing with numbers with decimals is entirely different, and takes entirely different considerations, than dealing with ordinary integers.

Exercises

1. Write a program that adds two signed numbers. If the addition overflows, it should give back 1; otherwise, it should give back 0.

2. Write a program that uses a combination of masks and rotates to count the number of 1s in a register.

3. Write a program that will add two 320-bit values and store the result in memory. Since this is too large to output via the exit system call, you will need to use the debugger to verify that this works.

CHAPTER 9

More Instructions You Should Know

In this chapter, we will discuss instructions which are not used quite as often, but are still important to know in order to be able to write and read assembly language code well.

9.1 More Jump Instructions

The jump instruction we have seen so far (jmp) is pretty straightforward. You simply give it an address to jump to (usually as a label) and jmp goes there. However, there is more to it than that.

There are basically four types of jump instructions: short, near, far, and indirect. A **short jump** is a jump that is within 127 bytes of the current instruction. This allows the assembler to use less space for the instruction itself, encoding it in only 2 bytes. A **near jump** is a jump that is somewhere within the current address space. It is encoded as being *relative* to the instruction pointer, using 32 bits.[1] This is the "typical" jump that we think of. We don't have to worry about figuring out the relative address as the assembler will do that for us. In fact, we don't even have to worry about the difference between short and near jumps, as the assembler will decide whether to encode the jump as a short or near jump automatically.

A **far jump** isn't really used anymore. It used to be that memory on x86 processors was grouped into "segments," with each segment having its own set of addresses. However, Linux employs what is known as a **flat memory model**, which basically means that every address for a process is in the same segment, and each memory location the process has access to has a unique address for that process. Far jumps were used to jump

---

[1] This constrains jump targets to be within 2GB of the current instruction. That's not incredibly limiting, but important to recognize.

© Jonathan Bartlett 2021
J. Bartlett, *Learn to Program with Assembly*, https://doi.org/10.1007/978-1-4842-7437-8_9

to memory locations that were in different segments. Since everything you need is in the same segment, far jumps are unhelpful.

The indirect jumps are a little more interesting. Indirect jumps allow us to jump to an address that we won't know until runtime. Essentially, we will be storing the address we want to jump to in a memory location or a register. The indirect jump will then read that memory or register location and then jump to the 64-bit address specified.

Indirect jumps utilize the same jmp instruction, but they have an asterisk (*) before their operand to signify that it is indirect. For instance, jmp mytarget transfers control directly to the address mytarget, but jmp *mytarget will read the 64-bit address *stored* in mytarget and then jump to whatever location that specifies.

The need for indirect jumps may not be especially clear at this time, but we will make a lot of use of them in Chapter 18. For now, we will just show a demonstration of its usage:

```
target_pointer:
    .quad 0

mycode:
    movq $mytarget, target_pointer
    jmp *target_pointer

    # Code to jump over
    # ...

mytarget:
    # We're here!
```

Note that when we get to the call instruction in Chapter 11, all of this information will apply to the call instruction as well, except that there are no short calls.

9.2 Bit Manipulation

One of the advantages of assembly language is that since you are working at such a low level of code, accessing individual bits and bytes actually tends to be easier and more straightforward than in high-level languages. High-level languages actually try to hide the underlying representation from you (for good reason), but then that makes accessing that underlying representation harder.

9.3 Basic Logic Functions

A **logic function** is something that takes one or two bits individually and performs some standard operation on them. For example, the "and" function takes two bits and results in 1 if both the input bits are 1 and 0 if one input bit is 0 or both of the input bits are 0. So it only returns 1 if the first AND the second input bits are 1.

In assembly language, the instruction andq takes two quadwords and performs the "and" function on each bit of both quadwords. Like most instructions, it uses the second operand as the location to store the results.

Let's say that %rax contained the bits 0110100010101110000010101011111111110101 00101101010101010000011111 and %rbx contained the bits 0110111010100010000011111 01111001110101001011010101010101000011011. The instruction andq %rax, %rbx would result in each bit being "and"ed together and the result stored in %rbx. In the following, I have lined these values up and shown the result so you can more clearly see what is happening:

```
rax:    0110100010101110000010101011111111110101001011010101010000011111
rbx:    0110111010100010000011111011110011101010010110101010101000011011
----------------------------------------------------------------
result: 0110100010100010000010101011100111010100101101010101000011011
```

As you can see, it takes each pair of bits from %rax and %rbx individually and performs the "and" operation.

Other standard logic instructions are

> **orq**: This instruction performs an "or" operation, which results in a 1 if *either or both* operands has a 1.

> **norq**: A "nor" operation is the opposite of an "or" operation. Basically, whenever an "or" would return 1, the nor returns 0, and vice versa.

> **xorq**: An "exclusive or" operation is like the "or" operation, but returns 0 if both inputs are 1.

> **notq**: The "not" operation only takes one operand. It simply returns the opposite bit for each bit position. If the bit was a 1, it returns 0. If it was a 0, it returns 1.

All these instructions (except notq) set flags, with the zero flag (ZF) being the most important.

There are a lot of uses for these instructions, but some typical uses are listed as follows:

- The andq instruction is used for **masking** bits. That is, if there is a subset of bits we are interested in, we can use the andq instruction to set all other bits to zero. For instance, if I wanted to know the low-order three bits of register %rcx, I could do it with the instruction andq $0b111, %rcx.

- Many operations take an operand which has a set of "bit flags." That is, each individual bit within a single quadword has a meaning. You can combine individual flags using the orq instruction. That is, each flag that is set in either operand will be set in the destination operand.

- The most efficient way to load a register with the value of zero is to "exclusive or" it with itself. This is fast because the instruction can be encoded with a smaller number of bytes. So, to load zero into %rax efficiently, you can do xorq %rax, %rax. However, be aware that this does set flags.

Note that sometimes it is useful to actually have the assembler do "or" functions for you. Again, thinking about a bit flag operand, if you had symbolic names for each bit, you can specify the set of flags you are wanting in a more understandable way.

Let us say that we have the following definition of bits—the lowest-order bit means that a person knows how to program (0b1), the next lowest-order bit means that a person knows chemistry (0b10), and the next lowest-order bit means that a person knows physics (0b100). Let us say that we wanted to load a value into %rax that indicated that someone knows physics and programming but not chemistry. If we memorized the flags, we could simply do movq $0b101, %rax. However, this requires a lot of memorization, and someone reading the code for the first time isn't likely to understand its meaning. Instead, we could have a program like the following:

```
.equ KNOWS_PROGRAMMING, 0b1
.equ KNOWS_CHEMISTRY, 0b10
.equ KNOWS_PHYSICS, 0b100

movq $(KNOWS_PROGRAMMING | KNOWS_PHYSICS), %rax
```

The | symbol tells the assembler to perform an "or" operation *while assembling*. This is possible because KNOWS_PROGRAMMING and KNOWS_PHYSICS are constant values, so it can be computed at assembly time.

Note that we can then use andq to mask off individual bits and determine if the value has that bit set. If we want to know if %rax has the KNOWS_PHYSICS flag set, we can simply "and" against that flag, and the zero flag (ZF) will be set if the person does not know physics and unset if they do. Therefore, you could use jnz to do some special code if the person knows physics. The following is a snippet that shows how this works:

```
# %rax has the flags
andq KNOWS_PHYSICS, %rax
jnz do_something_special_because_they_know_physics
```

Scanning for Bits

Another set of instructions will take an operand and essentially "search" the operand for bits. The first instruction is lzcntq. This instruction takes a source parameter, which is the operand to scan, counts the number of "leading zeroes" (the number of high-order zeroes before hitting the first 1 bit) in the operand, and stores the result in the destination operand.

Let's say that %rbx contained the value 23 (which, in binary, is 10111 with 59 leading zeroes). If we performed the instruction lzcntq %rbx, %rcx, then the value 59 would be stored in %rcx.

The instruction bsfq ("bit scan forward") searches a value for the first nonzero bit that it finds (starting with the least significant bit as bit 0). It stored the index of the first nonzero bit in the destination operand. If no bits are set, the destination operand is undefined, and the zero flag (ZF) is set.

Let's say that %rdx contained the value 200 (which, in binary, is 11001000). If we performed the instruction bsfq %rdx, %rax, then the value 3 in %rax because "bit 3" is the first bit set (remember, we start counting at bit zero), and ZF will be zero.

There is another instruction, bsrq ("bit scan reverse"), which searches the opposite direction, starting at the most significant bit (bit 63).

Note that if you were searching for the first 0 rather than the first 1, you could use notq to flip all the bits of the operand and then use bsfq or bsrq to search.

The x86-64 instruction set has a whole lot more bit fiddling instructions, but these should handle a majority of the cases that you will need.

Always remember that bits are counted from least significant to most significant, starting with zero. If we are writing the binary form of a number, bit 0 is the rightmost bit.

9.4 Managing Status Flags

Occasionally, you may need to clear or set flags in the status register. The instruction set has several instructions that can clear or set flags. These instructions have no operands.

clc: Clears the carry flag (CF)

setc: Sets the carry flag (CF)

cld: Clears the direction flag (DF)

setd: Sets the direction flag (DF)

lahf: Loads the common flags from %eflags into %ah

sahf: Stores the common flags from %ah into %eflags

We will use the direction flag (DF) in the next section.

The instructions lahf and sahf utilize the following bit pattern for the flags:

0. carry flag (CF)

1. always 1

2. parity flag (PF)

3. always 0

4. auxiliary carry flag (AF)

5. always 0

6. zero flag (ZF)

7. sign flag (SF)

Bits 1, 3, and 5 are ignored in the sahf instruction.

9.5 Memory Block and String Operations

You may have wondered why the registers %rsi and %rdi are so named. %rsi is known as the **source index** register, and %rdi is known as the **destination index** register. The reason for these names is that there are several instructions which specifically target these two registers, which generally contain a "source address" for a location in memory and a "destination address," respectively. These instructions generally revolve around managing strings or blocks of memory.

Copying Blocks of Memory

The simplest instruction is movsq. This instruction looks in %rsi for an address, looks up the quadword value at the address specified there, and copies that quadword to the address specified in %rdi. After the data is moved, something else happens—%rsi and %rdi are then *incremented* to the next memory location (i.e., 8 bytes more since we are using quadwords). Alternatively, if the direction flag (DF) is set, then the memory locations are *decremented* instead.

That's a lot to pack into a single instruction! As you can see, this is ideal for copying blocks of memory. A single instruction moves a quadword of data from one block to another and increments both the source and destination address to the next quadword.

But that's not all! The movsq instruction can also be *prefix* with the rep modifier. This modifier will repeat the instruction multiple times, counting down using the %rcx register as a counter.

The following code will copy the first three of the five values from source to dest:

```
.section .data
source:
    .quad 9, 23, 55, 1, 3
dest:
    .quad 0, 0, 0, 0, 0

.section .text
_start:
    movq $source, %rsi
    movq $dest, %rdi
```

```
movq $3, %rcx
rep movsq

# Rest of program
```

As you can see, a lot is packed into the single instruction rep movsq. When copying large blocks of data, this can move data very fast.

Comparing Blocks of Memory

Sometimes you need to check if two blocks of memory are equivalent. For example, to see if two blocks of memory are equivalent, you would need to iterate through each value in the block to see if all the values are equal. Just like the movsq instruction moves blocks of memory, the cmpsq instruction compares blocks of memory.

By itself, the cmpsq instruction will load values from the addresses listed in %rsi and %rdi, compare them (similar to the cmp instruction), set the flags appropriately, and advance %rsi and %rdi based on the direction flag (DF). This instruction, too, can be prefixed by the rep prefix to use %rcx as a counter. However, this prefix by itself doesn't actually help much. If you think about its operation, it would only wind up setting the flags for the last value compared.

Instead, there are other versions of the rep prefix which perform additional functions. Here, the repe prefix will also only continue while the comparison is equal. That is, it will terminate the repetition as soon as two non-equal values are found. This way, you can use repe to find out if *any* value differs anywhere in the two memory blocks.

Interestingly, if you are using multiple quadwords to store really huge values, the result of this operation will also tell you which one is greater than or less than the other. This feature can also be used to compare two strings (the size of the shorter string would be stored in %rcx).

Scanning Blocks of Memory

Let's say that you were looking for a specific value in a block of memory. For this, the scasq instruction would work perfectly. This instruction uses %rdi and loads the value in the address specified by %rdi and compares it to the value in %rax. Then, based on the direction flag (DF), %rdi is moved to the next address.

Again, this can be prefixed with a variant of the rep prefix. Here, the repne prefix is helpful. This means to continue scanning as long as the comparison is *not* equal (i.e., as long as we haven't found the value). When the instruction terminates, you can use %rcx or %rdi to tell you where the value occurred.

Finding the Length of a String

Oftentimes, you will need to find the length of a string. We can use the scasb instruction to count the number of bytes in a string. To do this, we will start by loading %rcx with an extremely large value. The simplest way to do this is to set %rcx to all ones using the following code (think back to Chapter 8 to see why this would set %rcx to all ones):

```
movq $-1, %rcx
```

Now, let's say that we have some string data:

```
mystring:
    .ascii "This is my string\0"
```

Now, we want to count the characters. Therefore, in our code we can do the following:

```
movq $mystring, %rdi    # load the address of the string
movb $0, %al            # looking for a null value
repne scasb             # repeat until found
```

At this point, %rdi will be pointing to one byte beyond the null terminator of the string (remember, scasb always finishes by incrementing the address). Therefore, we need to subtract the starting address and then subtract one to get the correct value:

```
subq $mystring, %rdi
decq %rdi
```

Now, %rdi will contain the length of the string. We can then use this for %rcx for copying the string (using movsb) or comparing the string to another string (using cmpsb).

9.6 The No-Operation Instruction

Pretty much every assembly language has an instruction that does nothing, called the nop ("no operation") instruction. This instruction may seem unimportant, but it winds up being useful for a number of reasons, mostly revolving around providing "spacing" in code.

One reason for this is that sometimes code needs to be modified by other programs. Perhaps an instruction or two need to be inserted at a certain location. Providing several nop instructions can provide the space to do this. Then, if the instructions wind up being a slightly different length than expected, it doesn't cause problems, because the nop instructions left behind will simply do nothing.

Another reason for nop instructions is for code alignment, which will be discussed further in Chapter 13.

9.7 Instruction Families and Instruction Naming

I wanted to make a note about instructions, instruction families, and instruction names. In this book, with minor exception, we always append the size of the data being used to the instruction. That is, for a mov instruction, when utilizing 64 bits, we use the movq instruction. When using 8 bits (1 byte), we use the movb instruction.

However, when utilizing registers as operands, the assembler can usually figure out what you mean based on the size of register you are using. Therefore, instead of writing movq %rax, %rbx, you can simply write mov %rax, %rbx, and the assembler will understand that you are referring to the quadword version of the instruction.

For the purpose of this book, I prefer keeping the suffixes as it is more consistent and more explicit than what is happening. Additionally, if you see a suffix (such as q) on an instruction, it is usually safe to assume that there are b, w, and l versions of that instruction as well.

Additionally, different instructions have different limitations on what can be used as operands. Some operations disallow immediate-mode values, some operations disallow byte-size operations, all operations disallow using memory locations for both operands, etc. Being an introductory book, this book is not focused on providing the precise limitations of every instruction. In any case, the assembler should let you know if you do something invalid, either as an error or a warning.

Exercises

1. Write a program that returns bit 5 of a number.

2. Write a full program that calculates the length of a string using `scasb`.

3. Write a program that looks through an array of values for a specific value and then returns the index of that value.

4. Write a program using bit flags that takes three different values and finds the bits they all have in common. Return the number that has all those bits in common.

PART II

Operating System Basics

## CHAPTER 10

Making System Calls

So far, we have been learning the basics of assembly language itself—how to move, store, add, subtract, compare, branch, etc. Now that we have the basics under our belt, it is time to learn how to interface with the rest of the computer through your operating system.

Different processes on a computer have different levels of access within the CPU. Normal processes (such as the ones we have been writing) are known as user-mode tasks, because they are run by individual users to accomplish what they want. Other processes are kernel-mode tasks, because they are run by the operating system's kernel to accomplish system-level activities.

The kernel we are interacting with is the Linux kernel. While every program running under an x86-64 processor uses the same basic instructions no matter what the operating system, the interactions with the operating system may be different on different operating systems. Some progress in standardization have been made (such as the Windows Subsystem for Linux), but, for the purposes of this book, we will focus specifically on Linux.

10.1 The Kernel

So what does the kernel do? The kernel is doing several things for you:

- The kernel abstracts the hardware interface, so changes in hardware only require changes to the drivers, not to the application code.

- The kernel provides even higher-level abstractions of the world (on top of its abstractions of hardware), such as filesystems and networks, that the application code can utilize.

- The kernel provides a mechanism for processes to communicate with each other.

© Jonathan Bartlett 2021
J. Bartlett, *Learn to Program with Assembly*, https://doi.org/10.1007/978-1-4842-7437-8_10

- The kernel provides sharing mechanisms so that processes can all use system resources without causing injury to each other.

- The kernel provides permission enforcement, to prevent processes from doing things that they shouldn't be allowed to do (like erasing or hijacking the operating system).

- The kernel provides a restricted sandbox that your program plays in so that any bugs aren't likely to cause problems outside of the sandbox.

- The restricted sandbox that the kernel provides also makes it easier for programs to manage themselves, as they don't have to worry about other processes—they essentially act like they own the whole computer while they are running.

The way that your program and the kernel interact is essentially as follows. Your program operates as if it is the only thing running on the machine. When your program needs something outside of itself (access to a file, the network, more memory, a device, etc.), it makes a **system call**. A system call puts your program on hold and then switches control to the operating system kernel. The kernel then looks at what you requested; checks to make sure the request is valid, that your program has the access rights to what it is asking for, etc.; retrieves or performs the requested task; and then returns control back to your process.

10.2 Making a System Call

We already have some practice making the exit system call. However, let's add some more detail to this.

System calls are made using the syscall instruction. This call transfers control to the kernel. Now, the kernel needs to know why you are invoking it. It needs to know what you want.

System call numbers are values that refer to the request that you are making of the kernel. As we have seen, the value 60 (0x3c) refers to the exit system call. When the kernel is invoked with the syscall instruction, it reads the system call number from %rax.

The kernel, however, usually needs to know more information than just which system call to make. For the `exit` system call, all it needs to know is the exit status, which we place in `%rdi`. However, many system calls require much more information than just a single value. Each piece of information, or parameter, is stored in a separate register. The parameters, if needed, of a system call are placed in the following registers:

1. `%rdi`

2. `%rsi`

3. `%rdx`

4. `%r10`

5. `%r8`

6. `%r9`

The reason for this order is a bit esoteric, but, because of some special uses of these registers, it basically reduces the number of kernel instructions required to perform the system call. If a system call takes less than six parameters, it simply ignores the contents of that register.

System calls usually return (`exit` is an obvious exception to this). Even though the kernel code uses basically the same CPU instructions that you do, the kernel takes care not to clobber any of your registers you are using. There are, however, three exceptions to this. The `syscall` instruction itself clobbers registers `%rcx` (this stores where the next instruction will be when the kernel returns) and `%r11` (the current contents of `%eflags` get copied to `%r11`). Then, if the system call has a value to give back to the program, it will store that value in `%rax`.

Therefore, if you have anything important in these three registers, you should move them somewhere else before making the system call.

10.3 Getting the Unix Time

Unix systems measure time in "seconds since the epoch," where the "epoch" is midnight, January 1, 1970 (a somewhat arbitrarily chosen point in time). The system call number is 201 (`0xc9`). It takes one parameter, a pointer to the 64-bit value to store the time in. On success, `%rax` will have the value of the pointer (the same value you put in `%rdi`).

The following is code that will wait approximately 5 seconds. It gets the Unix time and then loops, continually asking for the current time until it receives a time at least 5 seconds after the time it found when the program first started:

wait5.s

```
.globl _start

.section .data
curtime:
    # The time will be stored here
    .quad 0

.section .text
_start:
    ### Initialize

    # Get the initial time
    movq $0xc9, %rax
    movq $curtime, %rdi
    syscall

    # Store it in %rdx
    movq curtime, %rdx

    # Add 5 seconds
    addq $5, %rdx

timeloop:
    # Check the time
    movq $0xc9, %rax
    movq $curtime, %rdi
    syscall

    # If I haven't reached the time specified in %rdx, do it again
    cmpq %rdx, curtime
    jb timeloop
```

timefinish:

```
    # Exit
    movq $0x3c, %rax
    movq $0, %rdi
    syscall
```

Note that we didn't have to load %rdi with $curtime in the loop because it was already in there. However, I left it in to be more obvious about what was happening. Also, this code doesn't check the return value of the result; it just assumes it is successful. That's a fairly safe bet with this particular system call. However, in general, it is good to check the return value of the system call.

Here, the only real error would be if we sent in an invalid address. This would result in %rax being set to an error value, which is usually indicated by a negative number.

10.4 Writing Output

The write system call writes data to a file. On Unix, however, the concept of a "file" is pretty wide. Pretty much everything on Unix systems tend to be files. On Linux, even your processes are files. If you do ls /proc, in addition to other system information, you will see a directory for each process you are running, and each directory will contain files that describe your running process.

When a file is opened, the open file is given a number by the operating system that you use to refer to that file. This number is known as the **file descriptor** and is usually a smallish value. When a process is started, there are typically three file descriptors available to you. File descriptor 0 refers to the "standard input" file, which is usually your keyboard input on the command line. File descriptor 1 refers to the "standard output" file, which is usually the text screen display on the command line. File descriptor 2 refers to the "standard error" file, which is meant for writing error messages, but, for simple programs, is also usually just hooked up to the text screen display on the command line. Note that the operating system allows rerouting of these file descriptors, so they can sometimes refer to other things as well, but these are their standard meanings.

Therefore, reading from file descriptor 0 reads from the keyboard, and writing to file descriptor 1 will write to the output. If you need to write an error message, it is best to write it to file descriptor 2.

The write system call number is 1 (0x01). The first parameter to the system call (stored in %rdi) is the file descriptor, the second parameter (stored in %rsi) is a pointer to the data to write out, and the third parameter (stored in %rdx) is the length of this data. If you want the data to display properly, it should be ASCII codes. Note that if it is null terminated, you should not send the null value. The kernel uses a count, not a termination character, to detect the end of the data.[1]

The following program writes a string and then exits:

simpleoutput.s

.globl _start

.section .data
mystring:
    .ascii "Hello there!\n"
mystring_end:
.equ mystring_length, mystring_end - mystring

.section .text
_start:
    ### Display the string

    # System call number
    movq $1, %rax
    # File descriptor
    movq $1, %rdi
    # Pointer to the data
    movq $mystring, %rsi
    # Length of the data
    movq $mystring_length, %rdx
    syscall

    ### Exit
    movq $0x3c, %rax
    movq $0, %rdi
    syscall

---

[1] The reason why the kernel uses a byte count instead of a null terminator is that many files are binary—full of noncharacter data. The null character is often a valid byte in this sort of output and therefore may need to be sent. By just giving a pointer and a byte count, the kernel can write any kind of data you need it to.

A few things to note on this program. First of all, we didn't end the string with a null terminator. This is because the system call uses string length instead of a sentinel character to determine the end of the string. Second, notice that the string ends with the character \n. This is a newline character. Without this, your next prompt would be on the same line as the output.

Also note that the three parameters (file descriptor, string start address, and string length) are loaded into %rdi, %rsi, and %rdx, respectively. This is the order specified in Section 10.2. All system calls will put their parameters in the order specified by Section 10.2. This is known as a **calling convention**. By "convention," that means that there is nothing physically in the computer which forces this order. However, some order *must* be chosen (because that's how the operating system knows what to do with those parameters). Therefore, by choosing a convention, this allows the program and the operating system to communicate.

You will find that, in programming, as in life, there are a lot of things which are done by convention—the rules themselves are not as important as having everyone follow the same set of rules. Indeed, we could imagine some other ordering for these parameters. While there is good reason for picking the ordering that was chosen (it minimizes the number of instructions that the kernel itself is executing), the kernel programmers could have chosen them differently. Ultimately, programming is about making choices, and following the choices of others, sometimes even if they are arbitrary. Everyone following the same conventions allows for more freedom in communication and operation.

10.5 Learning More System Calls

If you are curious about the system calls available, there is a good list of them available at https://chromium.googlesource.com/chromiumos/docs/+/master/constants/ syscalls.md. However, you can also find a list of them by running man 2 syscalls from the command line. You can find additional information for each system call by running man 2 NAME, where NAME is the name of the system call. Unfortunately, the information is about how to call them from C, not assembly language. However, the information in this chapter will help you map the information in the manual pages into assembly language code.

10.6 Going Beyond System Calls

While system calls are important, for the most part, you will not be using system calls directly. Instead, you will be using higher-level functions from the system library, which we will learn to access in Chapter 12. The goal of this chapter is to simply acquaint you with the system call mechanism, how it functions, and how it operates as the interface between your program and the operating system.

There are lots of reasons why calling system calls directly is usually not the right thing to do in a real program. For instance, when reading and writing to files (or standard output), the system library will handle a lot of strange or exceptional conditions for you, which you would have to do yourself if you wanted to make a robust program. If you exit the program using the system library (rather than the system call), it gives other libraries that you are using the chance to clean up after themselves before exiting. With the system call, you are telling the operating system to shut the program off *right now*.

That being said, having some familiarity with the system call mechanism is worthwhile, and, for very short programs with no outside dependencies (such as the ones we have written so far), there's nothing wrong with using system calls to do direct system interaction. If nothing else, you now know how the system library interacts with the operating system.

Exercises

1. Write a program that prints out two different strings one right after the other.

2. Write a program that prints out the same string ten times in a loop.

3. Write a program that takes a number stored in memory and determines if that number is odd or even. Rather than using the exit status to communicate this information, have the program choose between two different strings to write to standard output.

4. Write a program that loops ten times and alternates between printing two different strings each time.

CHAPTER 11

The Stack and Function Calls

The **stack** is an area of memory that is used to store values which will eventually be discarded.

11.1 Imagining the Stack

To understand what the stack is or why it is needed, imagine yourself doing a complicated task that involves a lot of paperwork. Imagine yourself doing taxes, and imagine doing it largely on paper, not the computer.

Now, while doing your taxes, you discover that you need to find out how much money you spent on tools for your job. This is a new (though related) task. You have to set down your old task in order to do it. You need the total to write down on your tax form, but you don't need the form itself to find out how much you spent.

So then you look through your bank statement to see what you spent money on. As you are going through your bank statement, you notice an anomalous charge. Now, you put down the bank statement and pick up the phone to call your banker about the charge. The banker needs your driver's license number, so you put the phone down to go find your license.

When you find the license, you write down the number, put the license away, and pick up the phone with your banker again. When you are done on the phone, you hang it up and set it aside, and you pick up where you left off reading through the bank statement. When you are done totalling the amount you spent on your tools, you set down the bank statement and pick up the tax forms again. You write the result into your tax form and continue on doing your taxes.

© Jonathan Bartlett 2021
J. Bartlett, *Learn to Program with Assembly*, https://doi.org/10.1007/978-1-4842-7437-8_11

Now, if you're like me, when you set down one task to do another, you probably just scattered the papers around. Computers, however, don't work like that. They need strict organization.

A more computer-oriented way to tackle this problem is to recognize that each "thing" you are doing (tax forms, looking through a bank statement, calling your banker, looking for your license) will have your attention. Additionally, when you are done, you are going to "go back" to what you were doing before. You might use the *result* of your inner task when you go back to the larger task, but on the whole, you can discard all of your intermediate results.

The way that we could organize such a system is by using a *stack* of papers. You might have all of your current papers laid out on your desk, but when you need to move into a task (such as looking through your bank statement), you take all of the papers that you are working on and put them onto the stack. Then you pull out your bank statement. When you call your broker, you put the bank statement on the stack and pull out your phone. When your broker needs your license number, you can put the phone on the stack while you go and do that.

As you complete each task, you can resume the previous task just by picking up whatever you last left on the top of the stack, because that is the last thing you were doing. You set the phone on the stack to go find your license, so when you are done, the phone is on the top of the stack. When you are done on the phone, the next thing on the top of the stack is your bank statement. When you are done reading the bank statement, the next thing on the top of the stack is your tax form.

So, having a stack gives you the ability to set down what you are currently doing, go do something else for which you need the results, and then come back and pick up where you left off.

11.2 The Computer Stack

This is what the stack on the computer does as well. The stack is an area of memory that is reserved for stacking temporary items. The operating system preallocates space for the stack and then puts the pointer to this memory in the **stack pointer**, %rsp. While pointers generally refer to the beginning of a memory region, at the beginning of a program %rsp points to the end of the memory region containing the stack.

You can then add things to your stack using the push family of instructions. When you push something onto the stack, it does two things:

1. It decrements %rsp to point to the next location on the stack.

2. It copies the value to the location specified by %rsp.

You can then get the values back using the pop family of instructions, which does the reverse.

As a simple example of using the stack, we will implement the factorial function. The factorial function takes a number and then multiplies it by all of the numbers between it and one. So, the factorial of 5 is 5 × 4 × 3 × 2 × 1, and the factorial of 3 is 3 × 2 × 1. What our program will do is to start at a given value and push each value we want to multiply by on the stack. Then, we will pop from the stack and multiply until we get the final answer. This is not the most elegant way to write a factorial function, but it will hopefully demonstrate in a simple way how the stack works. Also note that we will start by pushing a zero onto the stack as a sentinel value so we know where to stop.

factorialstack.s

```
.globl _start
.section .data

value:
.quad 5

.section .text
_start:
    # Push in the sentinel value
    pushq $0

    # Grab the value
    movq value, %rax

    # Push all the values from 1 to the current value to the stack
pushvalues:
    pushq %rax
    decq %rax
    jnz pushvalues

    # Prepare for multiplying
    movq $1, %rax
```

```
multiply:
    # Get the next value from the stack
    popq %rcx

    # If it is the sentinel, we are done
    cmpq $0, %rcx
    je complete

    # multiply by what we have accumulated so far
    mulq %rcx

    # Do it again
    jmp multiply
complete:
    movq %rax, %rdi
    movq $60, %rax
    syscall
```

11.3 The Importance of the Stack

The beauty of using the stack is that you can use it to separate out distinct parts of your program. Rather than having to memorize which variables are in use at which time, and making sure you don't actually clobber something (like a register), you can store register values (and other values) on the stack before jumping out to another part of the program. Then, when control comes back to where it was, the program can simply read its currently active values back from the stack.

This requires that any part of the program that uses the stack also cleans up after itself, being sure to pop all values that it pushed or take other equivalent measures to get the stack back to how it was before control was passed to this part of the program.

This is obviously not important in our simplistic programs so far, but as the complexity of your programs increase, the less you want to have to know about other parts of your program to modify the current part of your program. This is known as **loose coupling**—it means that we are going to try to make it so that when we work on one part of the program, we don't have to remember all of the details about how another part is implemented. This makes it simpler to make modifications (because you don't have to remember the registers being used elsewhere) and also makes it easier for people who aren't completely familiar with the code to make changes. Otherwise, they would have to have total knowledge of the complete program in order to know that they weren't causing problems in some way.

11.4 Reserving Space on the Stack

In addition to pushing and popping values on the stack, you can also manipulate the stack directly. Let's say that you want to reserve a space of 16 bytes on the stack. All you have to do in order to do that is simply subtract 16 from the stack pointer using `subq $16, %rsp`. You just have to remember to add it back when you are done with it with `addq $16, %rsp`. Remember, since the stack is, well, a stack, when cleaning up, everything has to be done in exactly the reverse order that it occurred when creating it.

So far, when we have wanted to use data in memory, we allocated specific storage in the `.data` section of the program. However, oftentimes you will want to just allocate a temporary amount of space that is just being used for the duration of a section of code. For this, reserving stack space works really well.

Another thing to keep in mind is that stack space, while big, is limited. On x86-64 systems, stack space by default is limited to 2 megabytes.

11.5 Functions

We've talked a bit about loose coupling. In computer programming, the first step to making your program loosely coupled is to divide the program into **functions**, also called **procedures** or **routines**.

Functions are the basic building block of larger computer programs. So far, our programs have been small enough that there was no reason to break them up into pieces. However, as program complexity grows, and as you need to pull in bits of code from other places, functions become more and more important.

Functions are defined as having

> **Name:** Obviously everything has a name. In a function, the name is also used as a label to the starting address of the function's code (the function **entry point**).

Input parameters: Functions have inputs, which are the things that the function uses to process. For example, a factorial function would take as an input parameter the value that you want the factorial to be taken of. Input parameters are also called **arguments**.

Return value: Functions have a return value, which is the value that is given back to the code that called the function. For example, on the factorial function, the return value is the final result of doing the factorial. In many languages, there is only one value that is allowed as the return value of the function. However, a function can simulate having multiple return values by passing in pointers as input parameters to memory where other results will be stored for output. Another option is for the return value to be a pointer to an area of memory containing multiple values.

Side effects: A side effect is something that is altered which is not specified in the input or output parameters. In general, programmers attempt to avoid side effects, but this is not always possible. For example, logging an error is a side effect—usually the log is not a parameter to a function, so sending data to the log file is a side effect.

The question, then, is how do we define functions so that they are loosely coupled, follow an understandable convention, and allow for these types of interactions?

11.6 Function Calling Conventions

Just as there is a convention for system calls, there is a predefined convention for function calls. This type of convention is known as an **application binary interface**, or **ABI**. The ABI that Linux uses is known as the "System V ABI," and here, we will describe the major features of the x86-64 version of the System V ABI.

Having this interface means that not only do we not need to define these conventions on every program, it also means that I can call functions written by other people, even in other programming languages, as long as they follow the conventions.

Preservation of Registers

The calling conventions require that the function being called should preserve the contents of the registers %rbp, %rbx, and %r12 through %r15. This means that if you want to use these registers, you have to save what is already there first to memory or the stack and restore them before you return. The remaining registers can be overwritten as needed. This also means that if you are calling a function, you should know that any register other than these may be overwritten during the function call.

Passing Input Parameters

Parameters come to the function primarily in registers. Parameters are identified by position, and the positions correspond to the registers as follows:

1. %rdi

2. %rsi

3. %rdx

4. %rcx

5. %r8

6. %r9

So, if there is only one parameter, it gets passed in %rdi. If there are two, the first parameter is passed into %rdi and the second is passed into %rsi.

If there are more than six parameters, all additional parameters get pushed onto the stack as quadwords (using pushq). The *last* parameter gets pushed onto the stack *first*.

So let's say you had a function called myfunc that should be given ten parameters and you wanted to pass the value 1 as parameter 1, the value 2 as parameter 2, and so forth; you would call the function like this:

```
movq $1, %rdi
movq $2, %rsi
movq $3, %rdx
movq $4, %rcx
movq $5, %r8
movq $6, %r9
pushq $10
```

```
pushq $9
pushq $8
pushq $7
call myfunc
```

Having such long parameter lists is pretty rare, but they do happen from time to time. The goal of the calling convention is to maximize the usage of registers to speed up the program.

Returning Output Parameters

Return values get returned in %rax. The ABI specification allows for using %rdx as well if there is a second return value, though I am not aware of where this has been used. Usually, if more return values are needed, either %rax will contain a pointer to a set of values, or the input parameters will include pointers to locations where those additional return values should be stored.

Saving Data on the Stack

This is a little more complex than the rest. As mentioned, temporary local values get saved in the stack. The section of the stack that belongs to a given function invocation is known as a **stack frame**. The stack frame consists of all of the local temporary storage needed for your function, as well as additional metadata that the system needs to make the function invocation. A visualization of the stack frame can be seen in Figure 11-1.

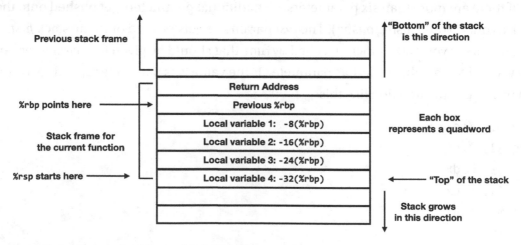

Figure 11-1. *Organization of a Stack Frame*

In this drawing, each box represents a quadword of data. The boxes are drawn so that the lower memory addresses are drawn toward the bottom. Note that since the stack grows "downward" in memory, when we talk about the "top" (conceptually) of the stack, it is actually lower in memory.

The actual value of the stack pointer is going to be changing as pushes and pops are made in your code. If you have local storage in the stack, it's tough to keep track of where that is relative to the stack pointer. Therefore, rather than actually refer to local values using the stack pointer, the ABI uses %rbp to store the value of the current stack frame. Therefore, all local values will be referenced as offsets to %rbp (which will be fixed for the duration of the function), and %rsp will be modified as needed during pushes, pops, and function calls.

When starting a function, you should first save the value of %rbp. This register is required to be preserved, as mentioned in a previous section. Therefore, the first thing that should be done is to push this value onto the stack. Immediately after pushing the value of %rbp onto the stack, %rsp should be copied to %rbp. This makes %rbp point to the previous version of itself.

Now, we need to make room for local variables. Subtract from %rsp (remember, the stack grows downward!) however much memory you need for local variables. You will refer to them as offsets from %rbp, but subtracting the value from %rsp is what reserves the space so that any function calls that the present function makes won't cause its local variables to be overwritten.

Nearly every function starts with these instructions to manipulate the stack, where NUMBYTES is the number of bytes of local storage space required:

```
# Save the pointer to the previous stack frame
pushq %rbp
# Copy the stack pointer to the base pointer for a fixed reference point
movq %rsp, %rbp
# Reserve however much memory on the stack I need
subq $NUMBYTES, %rsp
```

Then, at the end of the function, these steps should be reversed:

```
# Restore the stack pointer
movq %rbp, %rsp
# Restore the base pointer
popq %rbp
```

Now, creating a stack frame when entering a function and removing a stack frame when leaving a function are so common that instructions were added to do all these steps together: enter and leave.

The enter instruction simply takes a value that is the amount of additional memory you want on the stack and does all three steps for you. Therefore, the code for creating a stack frame in a function can be replaced with the following code:

```
enter $NUMBYTES, $0
```

Don't worry about the second operand in that instruction—just leave it at zero. That is used for a programming language feature called "closures" (also called "nested functions") which we don't worry about too much when writing assembly language directly. In truth, even for programming languages that use closures, they rarely are implemented using this feature of enter.

Likewise, the code for tearing down a stack frame can be replaced simply with the following:

```
leave
```

However, it is good to know the equivalent instructions so that you know what it is doing under the hood.

Note that some functions are sufficiently simple that they don't need to use enter and leave. If all of your computation can be done in registers, and you aren't overwriting any of the registers you are required to preserve, then there is no reason to use these instructions to create a stack frame.

I should note that the enter instruction is actually much *slower* than the equivalent set of instructions given before. However, we will continue to use the enter instruction for setting up a stack frame because (a) it is clearer, (b) it takes less space in the text, and (c) it allows you to visually see matching enter/leave instructions for setting up and tearing down stack frames, so you can more easily verify that you do either both or neither. The leave instruction is faster than the instructions it is replacing. Because of this, you will find a lot of compilers will set up a stack frame manually, but then use leave to tear it down.

Invoking and Returning with `call` and `ret`

Now, the big question is, how does the function you are calling know how to get back to you? If we issued a `jmp` instruction, the processor could start running the code, but then, when it was done, it would have no idea where to come back to.

The way this is solved is by pushing the address of the next instruction that you want to be executed when the function is completed onto the stack before jumping. This is known as the **return address**. This can be coded as follows:

```
    pushq $next_instruction_address
    jmp thefunction

next_instruction_address:
    # Next instruction here
```

However, this is so common that there is an instruction that does just this, the `call` instruction. Using call also gets rid of the need to put a label on the next instruction, because it just uses the next instruction that it would execute as the return address. Therefore, the preceding code can be replaced by

```
call thefunction
```

Likewise, popping the return address off of the stack and then jumping to it is accomplished with the `ret` instruction. This is done at the very end of a function with the following simple code:

```
ret
```

Aligning the Stack

According to the System V ABI, the stack is supposed to be **aligned** to a multiple of 16 bytes immediately before every function call. "Aligned to 16 bytes" means that the address of the stack pointer (`%rsp`) should be a multiple of 16. This is not always necessary, but some function calls will crash if this alignment is not properly heeded.

Since all function calls will involve storing the return address and the prior base pointer (for a total of 16 bytes), this means that when we request space using the `enter` function, we should always request a multiple of 16 bytes. This isn't strictly necessary if your function doesn't call other functions, but we will do it regardless so that we don't forget if we add in a function call later.

So, if you are going to allocate 8 bytes using enter $8, $0, to align it to 16 bytes, use enter $16, $0. Also, if you are calling a function that uses extra parameters that are passed on the stack, be sure to push extra bytes, words, or quadwords onto the stack before pushing the parameters to be sure that the final result is 16 byte aligned. Thankfully, most functions don't take that many parameters, so it is rarely a consideration.

More Complex Cases

There are more complicated cases than the ones we are considering here. The complete documentation for the x86-64 System V ABI is available online at https://gitlab.com/x86-psABIs/x86-64-ABI. If you want to send data that isn't an integer or a pointer or has more than six input parameters, you should probably check the ABI to see how it should be sent.

11.7 Writing a Simple Function

So, that's a lot to throw out at you. Let's put it together into a simple function. This function will take the first argument and raise it to the power of the second argument. We built a similar program in Chapter 5, but this time, we will write it as a function. Here is the code:

exponentfunc.s

```
.globl exponent
.type exponent, @function

.section .text
exponent:
    # %rdi has the base
    # %rsi has the exponent

    # Create the stack frame with one 8-byte local variable
    # which will be referred to using -8(%rbp).
    # This will store the current value of the exponent
    # as we iterate through it.
    # We are allocating 16 bytes so that we maintain
```

```
    # 16-byte alignment.
    enter $16, $0

    # Accumulated value in %rax
    movq $1, %rax

    # Store the exponent
    movq %rsi, -8(%rbp)
mainloop:
    mulq %rdi
    decq -8(%rbp)
    jnz mainloop
complete:
    # Result is already in %rax
    leave
    ret
```

Notice that we declared the name of the function to be .globl, but didn't worry about the other labels. Basically, the only labels that need to be available to other code are the function entry points.

We can then write a short program to call this function:

runexponent.s

```
.globl _start

.section .text
_start:
    # Call exponent with 3 and 2
    movq $3, %rdi
    movq $2, %rsi
    call exponent

    # result is now in %rax
    movq %rax, %rdi
    movq $60, %rax
    syscall
```

We can then build the program as follows:

```
as exponentfunc.s -o exponentfunc.o
as runexponent.s -o runexponent.o
ld exponentfunc.o runexponent.o -o runexponent
```

We can then run the program as usual.

11.8 Calling the Function from Another Language

Since we are following the ABI, this means that we can now call our function from another programming language, such as C.

The following is a section of C code that will call our function:

runexponent.c

```
int exponent(int, int);
int main() {
    return exponent(4, 2);
}
```

You can compile this together with the assembly language function using the following command:

```
gcc runexponent.c exponentfunc.s -o runexponent
```

This will compile together the C source code and the assembly language function into the program runexponent.

11.9 Writing Factorial as a Function

While there are a number of ways to write the factorial function, conceptually we think of the factorial function as being defined as

$$\text{factorial}(n) = n \times \text{factorial}(n-1)$$

with a special case of factorial(1) being 1.

In other words, we can define the factorial function in terms of the factorial function itself. This is a **recursive** function because it calls itself. It works because there is a **base case** where the value is actually directly computed.

Now that we have learned functions, we can actually structure our code like this as well. It may seem strange to have a function call itself, but stack frames allow the program to make sense of this concept. Every time the function calls itself, it will generate a new stack frame. Because on each invocation the function is always working with a different stack frame, the variables don't get confused.

The function is written as follows:

factorialfunc.s

```
.globl factorial
.section .text

factorial:
    # We will reserve space for 1 variable - the value we were called with
    # (aligned to 16 bytes)
    enter $16, $0

    # If the argument is 1, then return the result as 1.
    # Otherwise, continue on.
    cmpq $1, %rdi
    jne continue

    # Return 1
    movq $1, %rax
    leave
    ret

continue:
    # Save the argument into our stack storage
    movq %rdi, -8(%rbp)

    # Call factorial with %rdi decreased by one
    decq %rdi
    call factorial
```

```
# The result will be in %rax.  Multiply the result by our
# first argument we stored on the stack
mulq -8(%rbp)

# Result is in %rax, which is what is needed for the return value

leave
ret
```

We can then create a program to call this function:

runfactorial.s

.globl _start

.section .text
_start:
```
    # Call factorial with 4
    movq $4, %rdi
    call factorial

    # result is now in %rax
    movq %rax, %rdi
    movq $60, %rax
    syscall
```

You can then build these two together as follows:

```
as factorialfunc.s -o factorialfunc.o
as runfactorial.s -o runfactorial.o
ld factorialfunc.o runfactorial.o -o runfactorial
```

As you can see, functions allow you to structure your program in a way that is flexible and more understandable. Functions can be used to decompose a program into functionally related pieces where the interfaces between the functions are well specified. The ABI is a standardized convention which specifies the details on how these functions are handled which allows functions even in different languages to call each other.

11.10 Using .equ to Define Stack Frame Offsets

When there are just one or two variables, keeping track of their stack offsets is not too hard. However, as the number of local variables expands, it's harder and harder to remember which stack offset is used for which value. We can use .equ to give our stack offsets more clear names.

The following is the factorial function, with the only difference being that we defined a symbol, LOCAL_NUM, to refer to the stack offset that we are storing the number. We could have called this anything, but we prefixed the name with LOCAL_ just so we remember that this refers to a local variable offset. We also didn't define it as global because it only makes sense within the present function.

factorialfuncsym.s

```
.globl factorial
.section .text

# This is the offset into the stack frame (%rbp) that we store the
# number for which we are taking the factorial.
.equ LOCAL_NUM, -8

factorial:
    # We will reserve space for 1 variable - the value we were called with
    # (aligned to 16 bytes)
    enter $16, $0

    # If the argument is 1, then return the result as 1.
    # Otherwise, continue on.
    cmpq $1, %rdi
    jne continue

    # Return 1
    movq $1, %rax
    leave
    ret

continue:
    # Save the argument into our stack storage
    movq %rdi, LOCAL_NUM(%rbp)
```

```
# Call factorial with %rdi decreased by one
decq %rdi
call factorial

# The result will be in %rax.  Multiply the result by our
# first argument we stored on the stack
mulq LOCAL_NUM(%rbp)

# Result is in %rax, which is what is needed for the return value

leave
ret
```

Exercises

1. Look at the runexponent.c program. See if you can build a similar program to call your factorial function with.

2. Pick two programs from previous chapters and convert them to functions.

3. Create a function that, if given an even number, calls the factorial function with that value and, if given an odd number, raises that number to the third power using the exponent function. Then write a program that calls this function.

CHAPTER 12

Calling Functions from Libraries

In Chapter 11, we learned how to structure our code into functions so that other code can call these functions in a standardized way. However, your computer already comes preloaded with thousands of functions already built which you can call. In this chapter, we will look at how to call those functions, as well as some of the more helpful ones that are available.

The actual process of calling these functions you already know. If you know the name of a function, and you know its parameters, then you know the assembly language instructions to call it—move the parameters to the correct registers, save any registers that are not guaranteed to be preserved to the stack, and then call the function.

The questions, then, are, (a) how do we know what functions are available, (b) how do we learn what the parameters are, and (c) how do we include these functions in our program?

12.1 Linking with Static Libraries

There are two general types of libraries available on Linux—**static libraries** and **shared libraries**. Static libraries contain code that get directly added to your program. Whatever functions from the library that you use, those get physically copied into your final program. This chapter will deal with static libraries. We will consider shared libraries in Chapter 15.

Static libraries on Linux typically end with a .a extension, which stands for "archive." These are archives of functions that you can use yourself.

© Jonathan Bartlett 2021
J. Bartlett, *Learn to Program with Assembly*, https://doi.org/10.1007/978-1-4842-7437-8_12

12.2 Linking with Libraries

In this section, we are going to do a very short program to show how to use the standard library. The function we are going to use is the abs function, which takes one input parameter (a positive or negative integer) and yields the absolute value (the positive value) of that parameter. So, the absolute value of -5 is 5. It's a simple function, because the main thing is to just show how to call such functions and pull in the library.

What we are going to do is to load a negative number into %rdi and then call abs to convert it to a positive number. The code for the program is as follows:

abscall.s

```
.globl _start
.section .text
_start:
    # First parameter is -5
    movq $-5, %rdi
    # Call the function
    call abs

    # Result is in %rax, move to %rdi for the exit syscall
    movq %rax, %rdi
    movq $60, %rax
    syscall
```

Note that there is nothing special here. We are simply assuming the existence of the function called abs. We can assemble it just as we typically do with as abscall.s -o abscall.o. The assembler will assume that this is defined later. However, if we tried to link it just as we have done before, we will get an error saying, "undefined reference to 'abs.'" That is, the linker will notice that it can't find the symbol abs, so it has no idea where that call instruction should go.

This function is defined in the standard C library. Library files for static libraries are named libX.a, where X is considered the name of the library. For the standard C library, the file is just called libc.a. To tell the linker to link your file and include functions from the library, you would issue the following command:

```
ld abscall.o -static -lc -o abscall
```

The -static tells the linker that you want to physically incorporate the library functions into your program. The -lc tells the linker to *link* with the c library. It takes the c and expands it to libc.a, since we are looking for a static library (it would look for libc.so if we were linking to a shared library). Most libraries are named with more than one letter, but the standard C library is just c.

After this, the program abscall is ready to go just like any other program we have written.

12.3 Using the Standard C Library Entry point

Occasionally, some C functions require that certain setup functions have been run. Because of this, when linking with other libraries, it is common to *not* define _start in your program, but to instead define main. _start gets linked in from a separate library, which performs all necessary C library initialization.

The only change to your *code* is that the entry point is main, not _start. Here is the same absolute value function written to utilize the standard C library entry point:

absmain.s

```
.globl main
.section .text
main:
    # This is a function, but there are no local variables,
    # so we don't need to create a stack frame.

    # First parameter is -5
    movq $-5, %rdi
    # Call the function
    call abs

    # The result is already in %rax, so we just need to return

    # Since main is called from the standard C library,
    # we just need to return rather than call the exit system call.
    ret
```

This has two basic changes, both related to the fact that now main is being called from the C runtime library as a function.[1] First, we changed all mentions of _start to main. Second, we didn't have to call the exit system call. The C runtime library does that for us using the return value from main. Also, in this case, we didn't need to use enter and leave to create and tear down a stack frame, but we could have done so if we needed local variable storage.

Now, since we are using the C runtime library to supply the _start entry point for us, we have to link to additional code to provide that. However, the process to do this is sufficiently complex (and distribution specific) that we actually need the C compiler to assist us. GCC is the GNU Compiler Collection, which includes not only the C compiler but compilers for all sorts of languages, as well as tools to help you link and run them. GCC is also aware of assembly language and can be used to assemble and link assembly language files as well.

GCC can take care of assembling and linking all the needed components using the following single command:

```
gcc absmain.s -static -o absmain
```

When using gcc, it automatically links in the c library, but you can add additional libraries to link with using the same -l syntax and the name of the additional library you want to link in. The -static flag is similar to the one that we used to link with, specifying that we want to physically incorporate code from static libraries. Note that doing this adds about 500 kilobytes to the final code size. Even so, it is best practice to build your programs in this way when using the C library because you don't know which functions require the initialization code that this method brings in.

12.4 Working with Files

The C library has lots of functions that make working with input/output much easier. You may have noticed, for instance, that so far we have not done any code which actually prints out a number. That's because converting a number into its string representation using ASCII digits is somewhat of an annoyingly hard problem. It's not terribly hard (you should try it yourself sometimes); it's just tedious.

---

[1] The "C runtime library" is a different beast than the "standard C library" though they function together as a unit. As we will see in the following, we can use the compiler to handle bundling all of these components together, as the details get tricky.

However, the C library gives us all sorts of functions which allow us to read and write all sorts of data, both from the standard input and output and from files. The C library handles a lot of the complexity of Linux system calls for us, and we only need to concern ourselves with the actual reading and writing of data.

Now, the C library needs some additional data to handle this complexity, so it maintains a data structure (called the FILE) which maintains this data. The nice thing is that you don't have to know anything about this data. Opening a file will return an **opaque pointer** to you which represents the file, and then you pass that back to other functions you need to work with the file. An opaque pointer simply means that you don't have to worry about the specific data that the pointer points to. You just have to keep track of it and use it to refer to the file you are dealing with. The specific data that the pointer points to is managed entirely by the C library.

The functions we are interested in right now are the functions to open, write, and close files.

The function which opens a file is called fopen. This function takes two parameters. The first one is the pointer to a string which contains the filename, which will be relative to whatever the current working directory is. The second one is the pointer to a string which contains the "mode" that the file should be open in. Some of the options for the mode are "r" for reading, "w" for writing, "a" for appending (like writing, but starts at the end of the file if it already exists), and "r+" for both reading and writing. Both of these strings are null terminated.

The open results in the opaque FILE pointer we talked about earlier. You simply store that pointer and send it back in for other C library calls. If the open fails for any reason (you don't have permission and so on), then the call returns the literal value zero in %rax instead of the pointer. When a program has a zero in place of a pointer, that is called a **null pointer** because it is *supposed* to be a pointer to something, but instead points to nothing. Many functions return null pointers instead of real pointers when failures occur.

To write to the file, you use the fprintf function. The first parameter to fprintf is the FILE pointer. The second parameter is the "format string" which tells the function the outline of what to print. However, the format string can contain variables which get substituted and printed into the string. These variables are then passed, in order, after the format string. So, let's say that you wanted to write the age of a person to a file, which says, "The age of Sally is 53." You can do that using a format string that says, "The age of %s is %d.". What the %s does in the string is tell the fprintf function that the next parameter will be a pointer to a null-terminated string, and it should substitute that string in for %s. What the %d does in the string is tell the fprintf function that the next parameter will be an integer, and it will display that integer *as a decimal*, replacing the %d.

One important note is that, on functions that take a varying number of arguments (called **variadic functions**), you should set %rax to zero if you are not passing any floating-point values (see Appendix F for more information on this). Since fprintf can take a variable number of arguments (based on the number of substitutions specified in the format string), and we haven't even learned how to do floating-point values yet, %rax should be set to zero before calling this function.

When you are done with the file, you call the fclose function to close the file. Closing files is important because it makes sure that all of the data that was pending to be written in the file is fully written out to disk. If you forget to close the file, it is possible that some of the data won't be written before your program finishes, and the data will be lost. When you call fclose, you simply send in the FILE pointer you received before. fclose will return a zero if everything was successful and a nonzero value if it encountered any problems while closing the file.

The following code will open a file called myout.txt, write two formatted strings to the file, and then close the file:

filewrite.s

```
.globl main

.section .data
filename:
    .ascii "myfile.txt\0"
openmode:
    .ascii "w\0"

formatstring1:
    .ascii "The age of %s is %d.\n\0"
sallyname:
    .ascii "Sally\0"
sallyage:
    .quad 53

formatstring2:
    .ascii "%d and %d are %s's favorite numbers.\n\0"
joshname:
```

```
    .ascii "Josh\0"
joshfavoritefirst:
    .quad 7
joshfavoritesecond:
    .quad 13

.section .text
main:
    # Create a stack frame with one local variable
    # for the file pointer (aligned to 16 bytes)
    enter $16, $0

    # Open the file for writing
    movq $filename, %rdi
    movq $openmode, %rsi
    call fopen

    # Save the file pointer in the local variable
    movq %rax, -8(%rbp)

    # Write the first string
    movq -8(%rbp), %rdi
    movq $formatstring1, %rsi
    movq $sallyname, %rdx
    movq sallyage, %rcx
    movq $0, %rax
    call fprintf

    # Write the second string
    movq -8(%rbp), %rdi
    movq $formatstring2, %rsi
    movq joshfavoritefirst, %rdx
    movq joshfavoritesecond, %rcx
    movq $joshname, %r8
    movq $0, %rax
    call fprintf

    # Close the file
```

```
    movq -8(%rbp), %rdi
    call fclose

    # Return
    movq $0, %rax
    leave
    ret
```

Since we are using the standard C library, we are going to build this using the following command:

```
gcc filewrite.s -static -o filewrite
```

You can then run it by doing `./filewrite`. After running it, there should be a new file in your current directory called `myout.txt` which contains the output.

12.5 Using **stdout** and **stdin**

As mentioned in Chapter 10, the operating system has three open file descriptors for you at the beginning of your application—standard input, standard output, and standard error. In the C library, the library automatically creates FILE pointers for each of these for you, called `stdin`, `stdout`, and `stderr`.

These do not need to be opened or closed—that is done for you. You can use them just like you would any other file when calling file-related functions such as `fprintf`.

The following is the same program we just did, but with the output directed to stdout:

stdoutwrite.s

.globl main

.section .data
formatstring1:
    .ascii "The age of %s is %d.\n\0"
sallyname:
    .ascii "Sally\0"
sallyage:
    .quad 53

formatstring2:
    .ascii "%d and %d are %s's favorite numbers.\n\0"
joshname:
    .ascii "Josh\0"
joshfavoritefirst:
    .quad 7
joshfavoritesecond:
    .quad 13

.section .text
main:

```
    # No local variables - no stack frame needed

    # Write the first string
    movq stdout, %rdi
    movq $formatstring1, %rsi
    movq $sallyname, %rdx
    movq sallyage, %rcx
    movq $0, %rax
    call fprintf

    # Write the second string
    movq stdout, %rdi
    movq $formatstring2, %rsi
    movq joshfavoritefirst, %rdx
    movq joshfavoritesecond, %rcx
    movq $joshname, %r8
    movq $0, %rax
    call fprintf

    # Return
    movq $0, %rax
    ret
```

Note that, perhaps surprisingly, the load instruction is movq stdout, %rdi instead of movq $stdout, %rdi. The reason is that stdout is actually a pointer to the memory location where the FILE pointer lives, not the file pointer itself.

12.6 Reading Data from a File

Data can be read from a file using fscanf. fscanf takes very similar parameters as fprintf—a file handle, a format string, and a sequence of variables based on the variables in the format string. The difference, however, is that since you are reading the values, for fscanf, the integers are passed as pointers rather than values. You are telling fscanf where to put the values it scans.

The following is a program that uses our exponent function we made earlier. It prompts the user for two numbers separated by spaces and then computes the exponent of the first raised to the second:

exponentscanf.s

```
.globl main

.section .data
promptformat:
    .ascii "Enter two numbers separated by spaces, then press return.\n\0"

scanformat:
    .ascii "%d %d\0"

resultformat:
    .ascii "The result is %d.\n\0"

.section .text
.equ LOCAL_NUMBER, -8
.equ LOCAL_EXPONENT, -16
main:
    # Allocate space for two local variables
    enter $16, $0

    # Show the prompt to stdout
    movq stdout, %rdi
    movq $promptformat, %rsi
    movq $0, %rax
    call fprintf

    # Request the data
    movq stdin, %rdi
```

```
movq $scanformat, %rsi
leaq LOCAL_NUMBER(%rbp), %rdx
leaq LOCAL_EXPONENT(%rbp), %rcx
movq $0, %rax
call fscanf

movq LOCAL_NUMBER(%rbp), %rdi
movq LOCAL_EXPONENT(%rbp), %rsi
call exponent

movq stdout, %rdi
movq $resultformat, %rsi
movq %rax, %rdx
movq $0, %rax
call fprintf

leave
ret
```

This program calls the exponent function that you wrote in the file exponentfunc.s in Chapter 11. To build these programs together, issue the following command:

```
gcc -static exponentscanf.s exponentfunc.s -o exponentscanf
```

When run, this has a full input/output mechanism. This is how most programs in real life are written—the core "logic" of the program is written separately from the user interface, and the user interface sends the core logic the data it needs to process. Obviously, most real-world programs are much more advanced than this, but the principle remains the same.

12.7 Finding the Functions You Want

The standard C library is equipped with a huge variety of functions. Additionally, there are other libraries that have even more functions available. There are libraries and functions for networking, drawing, user interfaces, mathematics, typography, and more.

Unfortunately, there is not a universal location you can go to in order to find functions you need. You have to be generally familiar with the libraries and what they do and then read the documentation to figure out what the individual functions are called, what parameters they take, what results they return, and any side effects they have.

Most general-purpose functions are found in the C library that is available in Linux, known as the GNU C Library, or glibc. This is a superset of the standard C library and is automatically included in any program built on Linux using GCC.

The documentation for this library is a bit unwieldy simply because there are so many functions available. However, you can find the documentation online at www. gnu.org/software/libc/documentation.html. If you know a function name and want to find out more about it, you can usually find this out by typing man 3 NAME on the command line, where NAME is the name of the function of interest.

Functions are usually specified using the conventions of the C programming language. We won't get into the details of C here, but you can get the basics by looking at the declaration of the fopen function as follows:

$$\underset{\text{Return Value Type}}{\underline{\text{FILE *}}} \quad \overset{\text{Function Name}}{\underline{\text{fopen}}} \quad (\underset{\text{First Parameter}}{\underline{\text{const char *filename}}}, \underset{\text{Second Parameter}}{\underline{\text{const char *opentype}}})$$

Anything that has a * after it means that it is a *pointer* to that type of value. So this takes two pointers to character sequences (i.e., ASCII values) and returns a pointer to a FILE data structure.

The abs declaration is as follows:

```
int abs(int number)
```

Here, int refers to an integer (a 32-bit integer on a 64-bit Linux operating system). So this function takes an integer as its first (and only) parameter (in %rdi) and returns an integer (which will be in %rax).

While the number of types in C is fairly extensive, most of the common ones are as follows. The sizes vary depending on the platform, and the ones listed are for 64-bit Linux operating systems.

char: An 8-bit signed integer (called a char because this is the same type used to store individual ASCII character values)

short: A 16-bit signed integer

int: A 32-bit signed integer

long: A 64-bit signed integer

long long: A 64-bit signed integer (this is a separate type because on 32-bit platforms, it is also 64 bits)

These can also be prefixed with the word unsigned to indicate that they are always positive, and so the sign bit can be used to make the field take more potential values.

As mentioned, if a type ends with a *, that means it is a *pointer* to that type of data. Note that because the x86-64 platform is a little endian platform (see Chapter 7), this means that you can use pointers to larger sizes in places where smaller sizes are requested. So, if I have a pointer to a 64-bit value, I can send that pointer to something looking to store a 32-bit value, provided the other 32 bits are zeroed out beforehand.

Also note that, as far as calling conventions go, all of these can be essentially treated as 64-bit values.

Stickier issues occur when dealing with record types, called structs. These represent groups of values stored together in memory. These aren't difficult conceptually, but there are just a lot of rules about how these are stored in memory, which we can't effectively cover in this book.

Exercises

1. Now that you know how to perform input and output, convert two of your previous programs from having hard-coded inputs to having a prompt for the user and reading stdin for the value and then writing the result back out to stdout.

2. Now convert those programs to open two files, one for reading and one for writing. It should read the values from one file and write the results to the other.

3. Modify one of the programs that prompt the user for input so that, after displaying the answer, it goes back and starts the process all over. Note that pressing Ctrl+C will terminate the program if you need to.

4. Modify the previous program so that the user is prompted after each iteration and asked if they want to keep going. Have them enter the number 1 to keep going, so you can scan for a number.

5. The code to scan a single character is %c, which takes a pointer to a single byte (though you can also send it a pointer to a larger value than this if it is easier). Modify the program to ask the user to type Y to keep going.

CHAPTER 13

Common and Useful Assembler Directives

The GNU Assembler has a whole plethora of directives, and this book only has the space for a few of them. Nonetheless, only a small handful are widely used. We have covered a number of them—`.section`, `.quad`, `.ascii`, `.equ`, etc. Here, we will look at several that are helpful, useful, or you are likely to see when looking at other code.

13.1 Reserving Space for Data

So far, we have used the `.quad` directive extensively and a little bit with the `.byte` directive. Along those lines there are two other directives for other value sizes. A 16-bit value is defined with a `.short` directive or the equivalent `.value` directive. A 32-bit value is defined with the `.int` directive or the `.long` directive. These value directives can be quite confusing because they don't quite match other size annotations, either in x86 assembly language or in the C language.[1] If you want to be very specific, the directives `.2byte`, `.4byte`, and `.8byte` take up exactly as much space as they indicate.

Now, sometimes we need even more data than individual values. Perhaps we need a large buffer to store data from a file. Perhaps we need a large array of values. If we aren't too picky about what belongs in those data locations on startup, we can use the `.skip` directive to simply reserve space.

`.skip` takes one or two arguments. The first argument is the number of bytes to reserve. The second (optional) argument is the value to put in these reserved locations. If not specified, the value will be zero.

---

[1] Even more confusing are the additional directives `.hword` and `.word`. Even though `.hword` is supposed to mean "half-word," it is actually the same size as `.word` (16 bits). Because of this confusion, I recommend not using either one.

© Jonathan Bartlett 2021
J. Bartlett, *Learn to Program with Assembly*, https://doi.org/10.1007/978-1-4842-7437-8_13

The `.skip` directive has two synonyms. `.space` and `.zero` both do the exact same thing, though, for obvious reasons, it would be weird to use the second argument with `.zero`.

So, if you wanted to reserve a 1,000-byte space, you could do so like the following:

```
mydata:
    .zero 1000
```

Here, `mydata` refers to the starting address of the 1,000 bytes, which are all initialized to zero.

Another data-oriented operation is `.string`. This is identical to `.ascii`, but it automatically appends the null byte to the end so you don't have to write it. For this book, I prefer using `.ascii` since it is more clear exactly what is being stored. The `.asciz` directive is a synonym for `.string`.

13.2 Code and Data Alignment

Data alignment deals with what address that a value starts in memory. More specifically, whether that address is a multiple of some number.

You might find it odd that it matters whether an address is a multiple of a particular number. However, the physical organization of memory, data buses, and the CPU architecture mean that locating values at some multiples is faster than others. In the case of some advanced instructions, loading from an address that is not a multiple of the right number will actually fail and trigger a fault or exception.

In most computers, the speed issues are based on the word size of the computer. Since we are dealing with an 8-byte (64-bit) word, then it is optimal for memory fetches to be aligned to the nearest multiple of 8. Being out of alignment can slow down memory accesses. Some vector instructions use 16-byte (128-bit) words and *require* 16-byte alignment. This is why we always reserve space on the stack in multiples of 16 bytes (see Chapter 11). Even some functions that you may not expect to use vector instructions do so and will fault if the stack is not properly aligned.

Because of these issues, the assembler offers directives to force the alignment of the next address. There are several alignment functions available on the GNU Assembler:

.**balign**: This directive aligns the next address to the given multiple. If I give the directive .balign 8, then the next memory address used will be a multiple of 8. By default, the spacing will be zero if you are in a data section or filled with the nop instruction if you are in a code section. You can also specify, via another parameter, what value to use in the skipped space.

.**p2align**: This directive is very similar to .balign except that instead of giving the number of bytes to find a multiple of, you are actually requesting the number of bits used for alignment. In other words, to align to 8 bytes, I would issue the command .p2align 3, because $2^3 = 8$.

.**align**: This is not recommended to be used. For some configurations, it works like .p2align, and for others, it works like .balign. Therefore, it is best to use the specific one that you really want rather than this confusing directive. However, it normally acts like .balign.

Note that these alignment instructions, when done in .text sections, will pad with nop instructions rather than zero. This can be done to speed up code due to physical constraints of the processor. Essentially, heavily used sections of code and jmp targets both sometimes benefit from being aligned. nop instructions fill in the gap.[2]

13.3 Other Sections and Section Directives

Before we start talking about other sections, I wanted to point out that because the .data and .text sections are so frequently used, the assembler actually has specific directives for those. If you issue .data by itself as a directive, it is equivalent to issuing .section .data. Likewise with .text.

---

[2] Also note that x86 actually has several different nop instructions of different sizes. The GNU Assembler will choose the proper instruction (or set of instructions) that will best fill the gap.

However, these are not the only sections available. Other sections include

> **.rodata**: The .rodata section contains data that cannot be
> modified. This is loaded into memory when the application is
> loaded and is marked as read-only. Attempts to write to this
> memory will result in the program aborting.
>
> **.bss**: The .bss section contains uninitialized data. That is, rather
> than specifying values, you merely specify the size of data to be
> contained. This saves space in the executable, especially if there is
> a large amount of data here. The operating system initializes the
> .bss section to all zeroes. You can reserve data in the .bss section
> using the .zero or .skip directives.

These are not the only sections, but the other ones are somewhat internal to the
system and aren't especially useful to modify or mess with.

The following code will reserve 1,000 bytes in the .bss section and then also have a
read-only value:

```
.section .bss
mydata:
    .zero 1000

.section .rodata
myreadonlydata:
    .quad 7
```

Since it is in the .bss section, the data starting at mydata does not have to be stored
in the executable. Since it is in the .rodata section, the quadword at myreadonlydata
cannot be written to, only read.

13.4 Local and Global Values

You can reserve data in the .bss section and give the address a name in one directive
using the .lcomm directive. The .lcomm directive takes two parameters—the name of the
symbol for the address and the amount of space required. .lcomm myvar, 8 reserves a
quadword (8 bytes) in the .bss section and sets myvar to be the address of the start of
this memory. Symbols defined using .lcomm are *local* by default—they are not visible
outside of the current file unless otherwise marked with .globl.

The .comm directive is like the .lcomm directive, but the linker will merge any symbol with an identical name to point to the same location. It means that the symbol, though it may be defined in more than one file, is *common* to all of them.

We have already seen the use of .globl to mark a defined symbol as being "global," that is, relevant outside of the file it is defined in. If you want to, you can spell it all the way out with .global.

The GNU Assembler treats all undefined values as *external*, meaning that it is just going to assume that the linker will have another file that defines and exports them with a .globl directive. If you would like to be more specific about the symbols that you are assuming to be external, there is a .external directive available, but it does nothing on the GNU Assembler. It simply allows you to document which symbols you intend to use from other sources.

13.5 Including Other Code

When you break your code up into multiple files, oftentimes you will need to share various snippets/directives, especially .equ definitions. The .include directive will include the given file (put in quotation marks) into your source code. Note that the included file should *not* contain any code or data that are marked as .globl, as that will cause problems when files are linked, because then multiple assembly sources would be including the same externally facing definitions. Usually, included files don't contain any code or data at all.

Sometimes, you want to include a binary file within your code. Let's say that you wanted an image to be embedded within your object file. The .incbin directly will include a file verbatim into the resulting object file. The following code includes the file myimage.png at the address specified by the symbol myimage:

```
.section .data
myimage:
    .incbin "myimage.png"
```

13.6 Annotating Code

Another set of directives helps you annotate your code, both for debugging and other purposes. The most important annotation is the .type directive. For symbols marked with .globl, the .type directive lets the linker know what kind of symbol it is—whether function (specifying @function) or data (specifying @object).

The following code marks myvar as the address of data and myfunc as the address of a function:

```
.globl myvar, myfunc
.type myvar, @object
.type myfunc, @function

.section .data
myvar:
    .quad 0

.section .text
myfunc:
    # Do things
    ret
```

Within functions, a set of directives known as CFI (control flow integrity) directives tell debuggers about where you are within a function. These are rather complicated, but if you see directives starting with .cfi_, they are essentially information items passed to debuggers and other tools to describe the intended flow of the program. This can be used by debuggers to give you more information about the state of your program at any given point or by security tools to verify that nothing fishy is going on. However, their complexity is too much of a nuisance to trouble with for programmers. They are inserted by compilers for adding context to assist debuggers and profilers. I wanted to point them out because if you look at assembly language code generated by GCC, you will find a lot of these in the code.

Exercises

Go through some of the code written for previous chapters and make use of these new directives:

1. Convert `.ascii` directives to `.string`.

2. Add `.type` annotations to symbols marked as `.globl`.

3. Replace `.quad` directives with `.8byte`.

4. Replace `.quad` directives where the initial value isn't used with a `.skip` directive or an `.lcomm` directive. Also, move the data into the `.bss` section.

5. Look for values which are not modified and move them to the `.rodata` section.

CHAPTER 14

Dynamic Memory Allocation

So far, we have not gone into detail about what the memory layout of a Linux process looks like, primarily because we hadn't covered enough material to make sense of it. In this chapter, we will look at how Linux processes work with memory and how to make your process request more memory from the operating system.

14.1 Virtual Memory

In reality, all memory addresses that your process uses are a lie. In order to protect programs from other programs that may have bugs or go rogue, modern operating systems use a **virtual memory** system so that each program appears to be alone in memory. What happens is that memory is arranged into physical blocks called **pages**. When a process runs, the operating system gives your program a certain number of memory pages and marks what address they will live at for your process. When we have a pointer to memory, that pointer is actually to the virtual address. We have no access to the physical address of that memory, just the virtual address. The virtual memory addresses that we have access to are known as our process's **address space**.

Figure 14-1 gives a conceptual view of what this looks like. Each process "thinks" that it has access to a flat, unified, complete memory space. However, that is the *virtual* memory address space. The kernel actually takes those memory addresses and maps them onto physical RAM or to disk space (i.e., swap space).

The operating system can then use this to its advantage. As noted, a running program doesn't even have to have all of its memory in physical RAM. The operating system can opt to move some of a process's memory into **swap space**—a region of the hard drive designated to store such memory. The operating system then marks those pages as nonexistent. Then, when your process tries to access those pages, it triggers an

173

© Jonathan Bartlett 2021
J. Bartlett, *Learn to Program with Assembly*, https://doi.org/10.1007/978-1-4842-7437-8_14

error in the operating system. The operating system determines that you were trying to access memory that was on disk.

The operating system then temporarily suspends your program while it moves that memory from disk into physical RAM. Once it is loaded in RAM, that memory page is remapped into your process's address space, and the program is restarted at the instruction that caused the error. This time, however, since the page is physically in RAM, the instruction will succeed. All of this happens without your process having to know anything about what is going on.

14.2 Memory Layout of a Linux Process

The amount of space that is possible to cover with 64 bits is huge. However, in reality, the address space on x86-64 Linux is actually limited to 47 bits. That's still enough to address 128 terabytes of data! Of course, your computer doesn't have 128 terabytes of data. So how does the process decide how much memory to give you?

By default, Linux only gives your process the minimal amount needed for your code, your data, the stack, and some extra room for operating system-related items. Any additional memory that you need must be requested to be mapped in to your process. We will cover this requesting process later in this chapter.

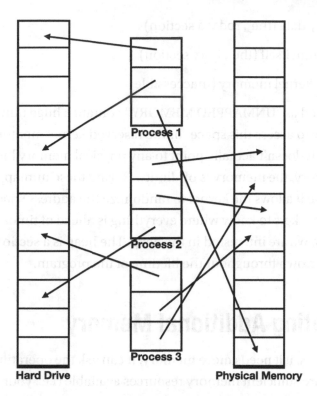

Figure 14-1. *Conceptualizing How Process Virtual Memory Maps to Physical Memory*

The way that Linux lays out the process is roughly as follows (from higher addresses to lower addresses):

- UNMAPPED MEMORY and kernel shared memory (inaccessible)

- The stack (see Chapter 11 and Appendix G)

- UNMAPPED MEMORY

- Dynamically loaded libraries (see Chapter 15)

- UNMAPPED MEMORY

- The heap

- UNMAPPED MEMORY

- Uninitialized data area (the .bss section)

- Global program data (the .data section)

- Read-only data (the `.rodata` section)

- The program itself (the `.text` section)

- Reserved kernel memory (inaccessible)

The areas marked as "UNMAPPED MEMORY" contain a huge number of memory addresses. If you try to access this space (or the reserved kernel memory), your program will crash, because it doesn't actually point to any physical memory location, or, in the case of kernel memory, the memory is off-limits. Having these unmapped areas is a safety issue, because it allows the kernel to randomize the address space a little bit and make it harder for hackers to know where everything is ahead of time.

For this chapter, we are interested in the heap. The heap is a section of memory that can be continually grown throughout the lifetime of the program.

14.3 Allocating Additional Memory

As your program runs, if it needs more memory, it can ask the operating system for more, and if there are sufficient memory resources available (i.e., your system is not out of RAM and swap space), the operating system will add additional valid addresses to your address space. The **program break** is the point at which memory addresses are no longer valid. The program break can be moved, however, by requesting more memory from the operating system.

Managing this memory can be a bit of a chore. Memory management is a huge area of interest for computer programmers and computer language designers because it can get very complicated, and it is hard to devise a system that is both easy for programmers to use and fast for language and library designers to implement.

In the C library, memory management is handled by two core functions—`malloc` and `free`. The `malloc` function (i.e., "memory allocate") asks the C library for memory. If there is free memory available in your process, `malloc` will return it. Otherwise, it will ask the operating system for more memory, and the operating system will move the program break to allow for you to have a larger address space to work with, assuming that there is in fact more memory available.

When you are done using the memory, you use the `free` function to return the memory. This doesn't actually give back the memory to the operating system, but rather marks the memory as free so that a future `malloc` will be able to use it.

malloc takes one parameter, the amount of memory you need, and returns the address of the memory that it allocated for you. free takes one parameter, the address of the memory that you requested, and doesn't return anything at all. When calling these functions, it is important to obey the following rules:

1. Always free any memory you allocated with malloc.

2. Never use a pointer after you have called free on it.

3. Never call free on a pointer that wasn't allocated with malloc.

4. Never call free more than once on a pointer.

If you fail to free a pointer allocated by malloc, that results in a **memory leak**, because you have memory that you are requesting but never disposing of when you are done.[1] If you use a pointer after it is freed, then you may wind up accessing an invalid memory region or, worse, overwriting data that gets allocated at a later time.

The following is a short program that allocates 500 bytes of memory and then uses that as a **buffer** (temporary, usually fixed-length storage location) to read in data from stdin and then writes the data back out to stdout. Note that we could have allocated this data on the stack as well. The goal here is simply to show the action of malloc and free.

mallocdemo.s

.globl main

.section .data
scanformat:
    .ascii "%499s\0"

outformat:
    .ascii "%s\n\0"

.section .text
.equ LOCAL_BUFFER, -8
main:
    # Allocate one local variable (aligned to 16 bytes)
    enter $16, $0

---

[1] Note that all memory gets disposed of when your program exits. Occasionally, there is reason to malloc without freeing if you plan on keeping the memory until the end of the program, but that is pretty rare.

```
# Get the memory and store it in our local variable
movq $500, %rdi
call malloc
movq %rax, LOCAL_BUFFER(%rbp)

movq $5, (%rax)

# Read the data from stdin
movq stdin, %rdi
movq $scanformat, %rsi
movq LOCAL_BUFFER(%rbp), %rdx
movq $0, %rax
call fscanf

# Write the data to stdout
movq stdout, %rdi
movq $outformat, %rsi
movq LOCAL_BUFFER(%rbp), %rdx
movq $0, %rax
call fprintf

# Free the buffer
movq LOCAL_BUFFER(%rbp), %rdi
call free

# Return
movq $0, %rax
leave
ret
```

As is usual with apps that use the C library, you can build and run this with the following command:

```
gcc -static mallocdemo.s -o mallocdemo
```

The format string for fscanf probably needs a little explanation. The %s format specifier tells fscanf to read a string up until it finds whitespace (a space or a return). However, you only send it a memory address where to store that string. This means that fscanf, just on this information, won't know how much space it is allowed to use.

The number between the % and the s is the maximum number of characters that can be read into our buffer. It's set to be 499 instead of 500 because fscanf will also include a null character, so we need to make sure our buffer has space for the null after all of the characters are in.

If you don't specify a number, then, if the user types more characters than you have allocated, the fscanf function can't know that. It will just keep adding characters to the buffer, *even if it goes beyond the end of the buffer*. This is known as a **buffer overflow**. If the buffer was allocated on the stack instead of the heap, this would be known as a **stack overflow**. These sorts of issues cause problems because it means that a function is overwriting memory not allocated for its use. In the best situations, this causes a fault. A worse situation is where it corrupts data and you don't even notice until a long time later. An even worse situation is if someone else discovers the problem before you do and exploits it as a security breach. As an example, on a stack overflow, if the attacker writes data beyond memory boundaries, they could potentially modify a return address and cause your program to execute their code.

14.4 Writing Your Own `malloc` Implementation

Most programmers use malloc all day long, but never stop to think how it is implemented. Here, I will show you a simple naive implementation of malloc and free. We will call them allocate and deallocate. Real implementations of malloc are much more complex, but this implementation should at least give you some insight into the kinds of considerations that go into these functions.

We mentioned the program break earlier. As we need more memory, we will ask the operating system to move the program break using the brk system call (call number 12). This system call tells the operating system where we want the new program break to be. If we send in a null pointer (0), it will tell us where the program break currently is.

The way we will keep track of our memory is that when we allocate memory, we will actually allocate two additional quadwords of memory than was asked for—one quadword for the size of the memory block and one quadword for whether or not the block is currently in use. We will actually return a pointer to the memory that is immediately after these two quadwords.

As each request for memory is asked, we will walk through our list of allocated memory looking for existing freed space that is sufficiently big to fill our needs. If it finds an open space, it returns it. If there are no open spaces, it asks the system to move the system break to allocate more space.

allocate.s

.globl allocate, deallocate

.section .data
memory_start:
    .quad 0
memory_end:
    .quad 0

.section .text
.equ HEADER_SIZE, 16
.equ HDR_IN_USE_OFFSET, 0
.equ HDR_SIZE_OFFSET, 8

.equ BRK_SYSCALL, 12

```
# Register usage:
#  - %rdx - size requested
#  - %rsi - pointer to current memory being examined
#  - %rcx - copy of memory_end
```
allocate_init:
```
    # Find the program break.
    movq $0, %rdi
    movq $BRK_SYSCALL, %rax
    syscall

    # The current break will be both the start and end of our memory
    movq %rax, memory_start
    movq %rax, memory_end
    jmp allocate_continue
```
allocate_move_break:
```
    # Old break is saved in %r8 to return to user
    movq %rcx, %r8
```

```
# Calculate where we want the new break to be
# (old break + size)
movq %rcx, %rdi
addq %rdx, %rdi
# Save this value
movq %rdi, memory_end

# Tell Linux where the new break is
movq $BRK_SYSCALL, %rax
syscall

# Address is in %r8 - mark size and availability
movq $1, HDR_IN_USE_OFFSET(%r8)
movq %rdx, HDR_SIZE_OFFSET(%r8)

# Actual return value is beyond our header
addq $HEADER_SIZE, %r8
movq %r8, %rax
ret
```

allocate:
```
# Save the amount requested into %rdx
movq %rdi, %rdx
# Actual amount needed is actually larger
addq $HEADER_SIZE, %rdx

# If we haven't initialized, do so
cmpq $0, memory_start
je allocate_init
```

allocate_continue:
```
movq memory_start, %rsi
movq memory_end, %rcx
```

allocate_loop:
```
# If we have reached the end of memory
# we have to allocate new memory by
# moving the break.
cmpq %rsi, %rcx
```

181

```
    je allocate_move_break

    # is the next block available?
    cmpq $0, HDR_IN_USE_OFFSET(%rsi)
    jne try_next_block

    # is the next block big enough?
    cmpq %rdx, HDR_SIZE_OFFSET(%rsi)
    jb try_next_block

    # This block is great!
    # Mark it as unavailable
    movq $1, HDR_IN_USE_OFFSET(%rsi)
    # Move beyond the header
    addq $HEADER_SIZE, %rsi
    # Return the value
    movq %rsi, %rax
    ret

try_next_block:
    # This block didn't work, move to the next one
    addq HDR_SIZE_OFFSET(%rsi), %rsi
    jmp allocate_loop

deallocate:
    # Free is simple - just mark the block as available
    movq $0, HDR_IN_USE_OFFSET - HEADER_SIZE(%rdi)
    ret
```

A slightly better implementation would align addresses to 16-byte boundaries, as those are preferred on the x86-64 architecture. However, getting this set up and calculated correctly would probably make the code a lot harder to follow.

The following is a short demonstration program to see this allocator in action. Basically, you can see that it will allocate several addresses, free one of them, and then only reuse that space if there is a small enough allocation requested to fit in it. It then ends by doing an fscanf and fprintf to show the usage of the allocated memory in action. Even if you are not familiar with the C language, you should be able to follow the code reasonably well.

usealloc.c

```
#include<stdio.h>

void *allocate(int);
void deallocate(void *);

int main() {
    char *a1 = allocate(500);
    char *a2 = allocate(1000);
    char *a3 = allocate(100);

    fprintf(stdout, "Allocations: %d, %d, %d\n", a1, a2, a3);
    deallocate(a1);

    char *a4 = allocate(1000);
    char *a5 = allocate(250);
    char *a6 = allocate(250);
    fprintf(stdout, "Allocations: %d, %d, %d, %d, %d, %d\n", a1, a2, a3,
    a4, a5, a6);

    fscanf(stdin, "%s", a5);
    fprintf(stdout, "%s", a5);
}
```

To build the code with the allocator, just do

```
gcc -static allocate.s usealloc.c -o usealloc
```

You can then run the program using ./usealloc.

Note, however, that using this allocator can be problematic if integrating with other code because the system malloc and free are probably also using the brk system call. As mentioned, this is primarily for demonstration purposes anyway.

14.5 The mmap System Call

In addition to setting the program break, you can also request larger blocks from the operating system. This is done using the mmap system call (system call number 9). In order that mmap and brk don't compete with each other, mmap usually allocates from much higher up in the address space. Unlike brk, which asks for specific memory locations, the addresses given by mmap are determined by the Linux kernel itself. Linux allows you to request an address, but Linux can override your decision. Also unlike brk, mmap is limited to allocating in page-size increments, which is 4096 bytes on Linux x86-64. You can request other sizes, but the allocation itself will be rounded up to the nearest page size.

We aren't going to go into detail about mmap in this book, but the call is extremely flexible. Not only can you ask it for memory, you can ask it to treat a file as if it were just memory! That is, given an open file, the operating system will simply cause a region of memory to act as if it were your file itself. Loading from the memory reads the file and writing to the memory writes to the file.

The mmap system call takes the following parameters:

1. **Requested target address**: Leave this as a null pointer to let Linux choose the address for you. Linux can override this address.

2. **Length of allocation in bytes**: It is best to make this a multiple of 4096 since Linux allocates in page-size increments anyway.

3. **Protection flags**: These allow you to specify whether this memory is read-only (0x01) or read-write (0x03). Other advanced options are available as well.

4. **General flags**: There are a *lot* of flags available. For most purposes, you should set the MAP_PRIVATE flag (0x02). If your allocation is not based on a file, you should set the MAP_ANONYMOUS flag (0x20), which tells Linux to ignore the file descriptor and just allocate more memory. Combining these two flags gives you 0x22.

5. **File descriptor**: If you are mapping a file into memory, this should be the file descriptor (received from a previous file open system call). If you are just requesting memory not tied to a file, you should have the MAP_ANONYMOUS flag set in the "general flags" and set this to -1.

6. **Offset**: If you are mapping a file into memory, you can use this to tell Linux where in the file to start. Otherwise, set this to zero.

The return value (in %rax) is the memory address allocated if successful or –1 if not.

To request a memory block that is two pages long would require a request like the following:

```
movq $9, %rax        # mmap syscall number
movq $0, %rdi        # Linux chooses the destination
movq $8192, %rsi     # Two pages of memory
movq $0x03, %rdx     # Memory should be read-write
movq $0x22, %r10     # Requesting private memory not tied to a file
movq $-1, %r8        # No file descriptor attached
movq $0, %r9         # No offset requested
syscall
# Result in %rax
```

To return allocated memory to the operating system, use the munmap system call (call number 11). It takes two parameters—the memory address to unmap (%rdi) and the size (%rsi).

The mmap system call is very flexible, but adds a significant amount of complication. It's sufficiently important that I wanted to bring it to your attention, but sufficiently complicated that using it effectively is outside the scope of this book.

If we were to imagine an allocator similar to the one earlier based on mmap, it would need to request whole pages at a time. Therefore, you would need to have two levels of allocation—block allocation and then individual memory allocations. Then, when a program requests memory, it would need to walk both the blocks and the individual allocations within that block to find the memory.

Exercises

1. Create a program that uses your allocate function that allows a user to type in how many bytes they want to allocate, allocates that amount of memory, displays the address that was allocated, then fills the space with the letter a terminated with a null, and then prints out that string.

2. Create a program similar to the previous one, but which does so in a loop. Be sure to free the allocations when you are done with them. Notice how the allocations are reused if the allocation is small enough, but are allocated new if the allocation is too large to fit in a previous allocation.

3. Modify the `allocate` function to make sure all allocations occur on 16-byte boundaries.

4. If you are really adventurous, try rewriting the `allocate` function to use `mmap` instead of `brk`.

CHAPTER 15

Dynamic Linking

So far, all of our code that we have written has been statically linked. This means that all of the code is physically contained within the final executable. The linker literally brings all of the code together, figures out which object file has which functions and memory locations defined in them, and builds a single executable which can be loaded and run on Linux. If you make calls to the standard C library (or other libraries), those functions are themselves physically copied into your program.

An alternative approach is known as **dynamic linking**. With dynamic linking, libraries stay as separate files, and they are merely *referenced* by your code. They are only brought together when (or sometimes after) your program is run. This is more flexible because if code lives in libraries, the libraries can be upgraded separately from the applications. Therefore, if there is a security problem in a library, the only thing that has to be changed is the library itself. This also saves disk space because the individual functions are not copied into each application program, but only exist in one place in the filesystem. These libraries are called **shared libraries**.

On Linux system, shared libraries are also known as **shared objects** and have the extension .so. On Windows systems, they are known as **dynamic link libraries** and have the extension .dll, and on Macs, they are called **dynamic libraries** and have the extension .dylib (although the .so extension is used as well). These terms are all basically interchangeable, and which one is used depends largely on preference.

In this chapter, we are going to discuss how to build and use shared libraries on Linux.

© Jonathan Bartlett 2021
J. Bartlett, *Learn to Program with Assembly*, https://doi.org/10.1007/978-1-4842-7437-8_15

15.1 Linking to a Shared Library

Let's write a short program that merely calls `fprintf`:

link_example.s

```
.globl main

.section .data
output:
    .ascii "hello\n\0"

.section .text

main:
    enter $0, $0

    movq stdout, %rdi
    movq $output, %rsi
    call fprintf

    movq $0, %rax

    leave
    ret
```

Typically, we have compiled this into a static executable using a command like this:

```
gcc -static link_example.s -o link_example
```

This statically links the program into `link_example`, so you can run it with `./link_example`. If you look at the size of the file using `ls -l link_example`, it is fairly large—almost a megabyte on my system. Part of this is debugging information. You can strip off excess debugging information using the `strip` command. If you type in `strip link_example`, it will reduce the file size by about a third. However, this is still pretty large.

To see that this is a statically linked file, we can trace the dynamic loading of files using the `ldd` command. `ldd` tells us all of the shared libraries. We can run `ldd link_example`, and it will say, "not a dynamic executable." In other words, we compiled it with everything statically linked.

Note that even as a static executable, the file still has a format, known as ELF (Executable and Linking Format). This format is used by the Linux kernel to load the file into the right location in memory and start it. The `objdump` command can be used to inspect ELF executables, even if they are statically linked. Running `objdump -x link_example` will show you all of the metadata contained in the ELF format. On an unstripped executable, there's actually quite a bit of information. But, for a statically linked, stripped executable, it is primarily a list of program sections, where they will be loaded into memory, and any additional details on how the section will be loaded into memory.

To link to the C library dynamically, all we have to do is replace `-static` with `-rdynamic` in the command line:[1]

```
gcc -rdynamic link_example.s -o link_example
```

This new `link_example` program runs identically to the previous program, but it now loads its libraries dynamically when it in invoked. The executable size has dropped from a megabyte to about 16 kilobytes! That's because the `fprintf` function brought in a *lot* of dependencies in the C library, which, when statically linked, added up to a lot code compiled in to the final executable. Now that we are dynamically linking, all of that stays in the C library!

You can see the list of dependencies by running `ldd link_example`. This will list out the libraries and where they are loaded into memory (which may vary each time you call it). On my computer, the output looks like this:

```
linux-vdso.so.1 (0x00007fffd373a000)
libc.so.6 => /lib/x86_64-linux-gnu/libc.so.6 (0x00007fedf3205000)
/lib64/ld-linux-x86-64.so.2 (0x00007fedf33d4000)
```

Let's start at the end of the list. That last entry is the **loader**.[2] The loader is a program that reads your program file and loads it into memory as well as any relevant libraries. The loader is usually named with some form of `ld.so`.[3] This is the library that actually does the loading itself. In fact, it is itself an executable. You can even run `/lib64/ld-linux-x86-64.so.2`, and

---

[1] Actually, on most systems, simply dropping `-static` will default to `-rdynamic`, but for beginners, I think being explicit is more helpful.

[2] Note that the loader is sometimes referred to as a linker as well, since it links together the executable and libraries at runtime. To avoid confusion, it will always be referred to as the loader here.

[3] The name of the file indicates that it is the loader for Linux x86-64 binaries, version 2. Linux actually supports multiple loaders.

it will give you a help screen. When you run your dynamic executable, it actually starts by loading up this program and sending it your program name as a parameter. The command /lib64/ld-linux-x86-64.so.2 ./link_example will produce equivalent results as running the program directly.

The next entry is libc.so.6. This is the C library, version 6. libc.so.6 is known as the **soname** (shared object name) and is the official name of the library. The arrow after the library soname indicates *where* on the system the library can be found. This allows the executable to know *what* library to link to and the dynamic link loader to know *where* to find it.

Finally, the linux-vdso.so.1 library is a special library, called the **vDSO** library, provided by the Linux kernel itself. This library allows fast execution of certain kernel functions, such as time functions, which don't require any particular privilege level to access. Calling these functions allows you to get public system information without actually invoking a system call. Calling the functions from this library directly is not recommended unless you are building a C library yourself.

If we had linked against other libraries, they would also be listed here.

You can use objdump to see what the loader sees. If you run objdump -R link_ example, it will show you what relocations the loader will make for your program. Some of them are internal to how GCC works, but you should also see relocations for stdout and fprintf. These records tell the loader which symbols it is going to have to look up.

15.2 How the Loader Works

When your code compiles, it has a list of symbols that it couldn't find within the main code itself. The compiler/linker then examines the list of libraries you asked it to compile with.[4] It makes sure that all of the symbols that it couldn't find within your code are found in one of the shared libraries. It then records all of the shared libraries that you requested that it link with into the executable. It doesn't record the loader or the vDSO library, as those are provided/invoked by the kernel itself.

Each function symbol that is found is added to both the **Procedure Linkage Table**, or **PLT**, and the **Global Offset Table**, or **GOT**. The PLT contains an indirect jump instruction to the location specified in the GOT. Interestingly, the GOT doesn't start out

---

[4] The C library is implicitly assumed to be in the list of libraries to link with—it doesn't need to be explicitly requested.

with the location of the function. Rather, it contains a bit of "glue code" which tells the loader to look up the symbol and replace the symbol in the GOT with the *actual* value of the function (this is known as **lazy loading**).

This indirection allows the executable to be loaded quickly (without having to wait for relocations that may never be used), but speeds itself up by replacing the indirect lookups with the actual values as the program continues to run.[5]

So, for instance, the instruction `call fprintf` will cause the loader to do the following:

1. Create an entry for `fprintf` in the GOT, initially set to be the search function for this symbol.

2. Create an entry for `fprintf` in the PLT, set to be an indirect jump to function listed in the GOT. This symbol is named `fprintf@plt`.

3. Modifies the `call fprintf` to `call fprintf@plt`. This way, the code is unmodified, and only the GOT will be modified at runtime.

4. When the call to `fprintf@plt` is invoked the first time, the loader fixes up the value in the GOT to point to the real `fprintf` function.

5. On subsequent calls to `fprintf@plt`, the indirect jump to the GOT entry will point to the `fprintf` function itself.

For data fields (such as `stdout`), these are recorded into the GOT immediately when the loader loads the program. However, our code can use them directly (without going through the GOT) because, even though `stdout` is defined by the external library, the definition of `stdout` is actually localized into the main program. It will live where the linker for the executable tells it to live. This is known as a **copy relocation**.

---

[5] You can actually force the loader to do this ahead of time. If you set the environment variable LD_BIND_NOW to a non-empty string, it will resolve all of the functions in the PLT before the program even starts.

15.3 Building a Basic Shared Library

In this section, we'll learn how to build a basic shared library. This library will have an extremely simple function in it, squareme, which squares its first parameter. The code is as follows:

squareme.s

```
.globl squareme

.section .text
squareme:
    movq %rdi, %rax
    imulq %rdi
    ret
```

We will also write a program which uses squareme:

run_squareme.s

```
.global main

.section .data
value:
    .quad 6
output:
    .ascii "The square of %d is %d\n\0"

.section .text
main:
    enter $0, $0

    movq value, %rdi
    call squareme

    movq stdout, %rdi
    movq $output, %rsi
    movq value, %rdx
```

```
movq %rax, %rcx
call fprintf
leave
ret
```

We can build these together statically relatively easily by just compiling them together as usual:

```
gcc -static squareme.s run_squareme.s -o run_squareme
```

However, let's say that we wanted a math library of reusable math functions. Let's call this library libmymath.so. To do this, we can build squareme into a library using the following command:

```
gcc -shared squareme.s -o libmymath.so
```

We can then compile the main application to reference the library:

```
gcc run_squareme.s -lmymath -L . -o run_squareme
```

This will build run_squareme against our shared library. The -lmymath argument says to link against the libmymath.so library (it automatically adds the lib prefix and .so suffix), and the -L . argument says to add the current directory to the list of directories to look in for libraries.

However, if you try to run this command right now, it will give an error. Running ./run_squareme will give the error error while loading shared libraries: libmymath.so: cannot open shared object file: No such file or directory. This is because while we told GCC where to find the library, the loader has no idea where it is. Therefore, we have to tell the loader where else it should look for libraries as well. We can do that with the LD_LIBRARY_PATH environment variable. If you run export LD_LIBRARY_PATH=. and then run the command, it will work.

Libraries are usually permanently installed by copying them to /usr/lib and then running ldconfig as root (this latter part is not always necessary). This is one of the default locations the loader looks for libraries.

15.4 Position-Independent Code

The problem with shared libraries is that the loader can actually map them anywhere in memory. In fact, one of the security precautions that Linux distributions usually take is to randomize address spaces, so that libraries can be loaded anywhere in the address space. The location that a library is loaded into memory is known as the **base address**.

However, this means that libraries have to be specially written so that moving them around in memory does not cause them to break. This type of code is known as **position-independent code**, or **PIC**.

There are three main areas where code needs to be modified in order to be position independent:

1. References to external functions

2. References to the `.data` section of the library

3. References to externally defined data (such as `stdout`)

The references to external functions are handled relatively automatically by the linker and loader using the same PLT/GOT mechanism described before. If you look at PIC assembly language generated by other tools (see Chapter 16), they will normally have the `call fprintf@plt` encoded directly in the assembly language, rather than having the linker take care of that. Either way works perfectly fine, though explicitly referencing the PLT can help you remember that the function call is going through a level of indirection.

Referencing the `.data` Section

References to addresses in the `.data` section of the library are handled through an addressing mode known as **PC-relative addressing**. This addressing mode records addresses of data *as an offset of the current instruction pointer*.

The following function illustrates how this is done:[6]

multbyten.s

`.globl` multbyten

`.section .data`

---

[6] The code loads the value 10 from the `.data` section instead of using immediate mode in order to illustrate the concept.

```
ten:
    .quad 10

.section .text
multbyten:
    movq ten(%rip), %rax
    imulq %rdi
    ret
```

The line `movq ten(%rip), %rax` utilizes PC-relative addressing. This says that we need the address `ten`, but to encode it as a relative offset of the instruction pointer at this location. Therefore, no matter where in memory the library (and its data) gets loaded, it will still know where `ten` is, because it is a fixed offset from that location in the code.[7]

PC-relative addressing was introduced in the x86-64 instruction set architecture. Before that, a much more complicated scheme was required in order to access data section variables.

Referencing Externally Defined Data

To reference externally defined data such as `stdout`, we will have to do two-step lookups using the GOT. However, to do this, we actually need to use a special symbol, `GOTPCREL`.

Let's say, for instance, we want to load `stdout` into `%rdi`. Previously, we could do this with just `movq stdout, %rdi`. However, we don't actually know *where* `stdout` will wind up living (remember, it's actually defined elsewhere). Therefore, we have to look up the address of `stdout` in the GOT and then use that address to load the actual value.

To do this, we need to execute two instructions:

```
movq stdout@GOTPCREL(%rip), %rdi
movq (%rdi), %rdi
```

The first instruction finds the location of the variable in the Global Offset Table using PC-relative addressing and then loads that into `%rdi`. The special symbol `GOTPCREL` is a

---

[7] Note that PC-relative addressing actually violates the address calculation method described in Chapter 6, but it is easy to remember that if `%rip` is the base register, then the value will simply be the offset from the current location in code to that value. Also note that PC-relative addressing does not support the index or the scale. If those are needed, you will need to use the `leaq` instruction to get the address and then use other instructions to manipulate the address how it is needed.

PC-relative location of the GOT. The second instruction then uses that location to look up the value of stdout itself.

The following is the code for a simple function, printstuff, that uses this idea:

printstuff.s

.globl printstuff

.section .data
mytext:
    .ascii "hello there\n\0"

.section .text
printstuff:
    enter $0, $0

    movq stdout@*GOTPCREL(%rip)*, *%rdi*
    movq *(%rdi)*, *%rdi*
    leaq *mytext(%rip)*, *%rsi*
    call fprintf@*plt*

    leave
    ret

This code loads stdout into %rdi using the GOT. Then, it loads the address of the string into %rsi using PC-relative addressing. Finally, it calls fprintf using the PLT. Also remember that enter and leave are required when calling other functions in order to make sure that the stack is properly maintained.

15.5 Calling from C

We can now compile all three of these into a single shared library. Issue the following command to add all three functions to libmymath.so:

```
gcc -shared printstuff.s multbyten.s squareme.s -o libmymath.so
```

Because we follow the ABI conventions, we can call this either from an assembly language program or from a C program. The following is a simple program that uses these functions:

use_mymath.c

```
#include<stdio.h>

long squareme(long);
long multbyten(long);
void printstuff();

int main() {
    long number = 4;
    fprintf(stdout, "The square of %d is %d\n", number, squareme(number));
    fprintf(stdout, "Ten times %d is %d\n", number, multbyten(number));
    printstuff();
}
```

To build, we just do

```
gcc -rdynamic use_mymath.c -lmymath -L . -o use_mymath
```

Then we can run it with ./use_mymath (assuming LD_LIBRARY_PATH is still set).

15.6 Skipping the PLT

When calling functions, you can actually skip the PLT and call the entry in the GOT directly. This will force the loader to load the value immediately before the program starts rather than lazy loading it like it does when called through the PLT.

To do this, simply replace function calls with PC-relative indirect calls to the entry in the GOT. For instance, to call fprintf, rather than issuing call fprintf or call fprintf@plt, you can use the following instruction:

```
call *fprintf@GOTPCREL(%rip)
```

Doing this improves execution speed, but with some cost of startup speed on large programs.

15.7 Position-Independent Executables

Not only can libraries be position independent, so can your main program! You can write your main program as if it were a shared library and then compile it to be a **position-independent executable** (or **PIE**). The advantage of this is that it makes it harder for exploits to misuse your code because the executable itself may not be loaded into the normal location.

The following code is just like the previous code for link_example.s, except written in a position-independent manner:

link_example_pie.s

```
.globl main

.section .data
output:
    .ascii "hello\n\0"

.section .text
main:
    enter $0, $0

    movq stdout@GOTPCREL(%rip), %rdi
    movq (%rdi), %rdi
    leaq output(%rip), %rsi
    call fprintf

    movq $0, %rax

    leave
    ret
```

Then, to build this as a PIE, you can run the following:

```
gcc -pie link_example_pie.s -o link_example_pie
```

The result isn't significantly different than before, but if you run it under GDB (GNU debugger) (see Appendix C), you will notice that the addresses changes every time it is run.

15.8 Force-Feeding Functions to the Executables

Another benefit of shared libraries and dynamic loading of libraries is the ability to force-feed functions into a program. In a program, any function which is in a shared library can be overridden by the user.

The loader supports an environment variable called LD_PRELOAD, which preloads a library's symbols into an executable *before* it loads in the shared libraries requested by the executable. Therefore, if a symbol was already defined by the library specified by LD_PRELOAD, then that symbol is preferred to symbols loaded later. You can use this feature to override library functions with your own, even if the code is already compiled, and you don't have access to the source code!

This is oftentimes used to provide better versions of various system functions such as malloc, such as providing a more optimized version, or even providing a garbage-collecting version of it. This is harder than it seems, as many functions have a lot of unknown interactions with global variables, other functions, and various other side effects, so just replacing functions willy-nilly will often just lead to crashes.

As a simple example, though, the following code can be used as a drop-in replacement for fprintf in simple cases. Instead of doing what you wanted fprintf to do, it will instead print, "Haha! I intercepted you!" using the write system call.

fprintf_override.s

```
.globl fprintf

.section .data
mytext:
    .ascii "Haha! I intercepted you!\n"
mytextend:

.section .text
fprintf:
    movq $1, %rax
    movq $1, %rdi
    leaq mytext(%rip), %rsi
    movq $(mytextend - mytext), %rdx
    syscall
    ret
```

To compile this, do `gcc -shared fprintf_override.s -o liboverride.so`. Then, to force this to preload on commands, enter `export LD_PRELOAD=./liboverride.so`. Now, any command that you run which called `fprintf` will now call your function instead!

To try it out, use the following commands:

```
export LD_PRELOAD=./liboverride.so
./use_mymath
```

To unset `LD_PRELOAD`, you can either set it to an empty string or run `unset LD_PRELOAD`. I would advise doing this before accidentally running other commands and having them error out because `fprintf` isn't working!

15.9 Loading Libraries Manually

In addition to the loader loading libraries when your application starts, you can also load them manually as well. The `dlopen` and `dlsym` functions allow you to open a shared library and get symbol references from them. This is often used for adding plugins to code.

The `dlopen` function specifies the filename of a shared library to open, as well as a parameter of flags for opening the library. It returns a pointer to the handle for the shared library, which you can use to look up symbols with `dlsym`. The `dlsym` function searches the shared library for the specified symbol and, if found, returns its value (usually a pointer).

The following code will load the `libmymath.so` library manually, find the pointer to the `printstuff` function from the library, and then call it:

manual_load.s

```
.globl main

.section .data
filename:
    .ascii "libmymath.so\0"
functionname:
    .ascii "printstuff\0"
```

```
.section .text
main:
    enter $0, $0

    movq $filename, %rdi
    movq $1, %rsi   # the flag for lazy-loading
    call dlopen

    movq %rax, %rdi
    movq $functionname, %rsi
    call dlsym

    call *%rax

    leave
    ret
```

To get access to these functions, we will need to link with the libdl.so library. Therefore, we will need to build with the following command:

```
gcc -rdynamic manual_load.s -ldl -o manual_load
```

Now, running ./manual_load will load the library manually and call the function from it!

Exercises

1. Take two programs from earlier in this book and rewrite them as PIE executables.

2. Add the factorial function built earlier to the libmymath.so library.

3. Write a program that uses both the C library to read a number and the libmymath.so library to find the factorial of the number. Be sure to set the environment variables so the loader can find the library before you run it.

4. Look at the various shared libraries on your system. Search the Internet to find out what some of them do.

PART III

Programming Language Topics

CHAPTER 16

Basic Language Features Represented in Assembly Language

The goal of this part of the book is to demonstrate how features from higher-level programming languages map onto assembly language. Whether assembly language is your first programming language or your hundredth, its primary usage for the average programmer is to give them insight into what's really happening under the hood of whatever language they are programming in.

However, there are a large number of programming languages out there. We aren't going to pick any particular programming language, but will generally look at languages that come from the C family of languages. We will look at various programming language options (such as memory management and object orientation) and how those can be translated into the lowest levels in assembly language.

If you have used any C-like language (Java, C++, Swift, Go, etc.), the pseudo-code here should look familiar. The point, however, is that my goal is not for you to know all the particulars of a specific language implementation, but more to better imagine how these things *can* work so that if you're interested in a language, you can read their documentation and have a better starting point for what they are talking about.

If assembly language is your first language, I would suggest that you gain some familiarity with other programming languages before proceeding on to this part of the book.

This chapter mostly covers things that should be fairly obvious from previous chapters in the book, but we also try to expand the ideas further. The one genuinely new concept is the discussion of tail-call elimination at the end of the chapter.

© Jonathan Bartlett 2021
J. Bartlett, *Learn to Program with Assembly*, https://doi.org/10.1007/978-1-4842-7437-8_16

16.1 Global Variables

Global variables are usually just implemented as labeled parts of the `.data` section. We have run into code like this over and over again:

```
my_variable:
    .quad 29
```

This is essentially equivalent to having a global variable `my_variable` set to the value `29`.

However, many programming languages allow you to also have global variables which are uninitialized at the beginning of the program. These are usually placed in a different section of your assembly language program. The `.bss` section is like the data section, except that you don't specify any values, just the amount of space needed. This allows you to *reserve* space for the running program, without actually taking up that space on disk if there isn't a starting value.

A global variable using the `.bss` section looks like this:

```
.section .bss
my_variable:
    .skip 8
```

The `.skip` directive tells the assembler to advance the current address it is thinking about (8 bytes in this case).

Another important directive related to global variables is the `.balign` directive. This directive makes sure that the next address is aligned to the specific byte boundary. This is important because proper alignment can make the processor faster (see Appendix I), and a very few highly specialized instructions require certain alignments. The directive `.balign 8` will align the next address to an 8-byte boundary, while the `.balign 16` will align the next address to a 16-byte boundary.

16.2 Local Variables

Local variables can be implemented either simply as registers or as reserved memory on the current stack frame (see Chapter 11). The `enter` instruction is used to set up all of the local variables used for a function no matter where in the function they are declared. Most programming languages allow you to declare a variable anywhere you want in the function, but, under the hood, they all get wrapped up into the same enter instruction at the beginning of the function.

Additionally, it is not uncommon for programming languages to reuse registers, stack variables, and the like if a previous variable stops being used. This is bad practice if you are hand-coding assembly language, because it makes the code much harder to read.

16.3 Conditional Statements

Conditional statements are fairly easy to imagine how to put into assembly language. Imagine the following code:

```
if(a > b) {
    // DoSomething
} else {
    // DoAlternate
}
// CodeContinues
```

This can be implemented by adding two labels to the code. The first label is to the success branch (i.e., DoSomething). The second label should be on CodeContinues. In assembly language, assuming %rax contains a and %rbx contains b, this looks like

```
    cmpq \rbx, \rax
    jg DoSomething

    # DoAlternate here

    jmp CodeContinues

DoSomething:
    # DoSomething here

CodeContinues:
    # Continue on here
```

As you can see, the branch DoSomething naturally flows onto CodeContinues, but DoAlternate has to jump there to avoid also executing DoSomething.

16.4 Loops

Loops are not much different than conditional branching. They simply contain an additional jump at the end of the loop back to the beginning.

Let's look at the following basic while loop:

```
a = 0
// LoopStart
while(a < b) {
    // DoSomething

    a++
}
// CodeContinues
```

This loop has a comparison, but, actually, it is the *reverse* of the comparison that we are interested in. If the comparison succeeds, then we just continue to DoSomething. However, if the comparison fails, that's when we jump out to CodeContinues. So we will need to reverse our comparison here. Then, at the end of the loop, we will need to jump back to LoopStart.

Assuming a is in %rax and b is in %rbx, here is the assembly language code:

```
    movq $0, %rax        # Initialize the loop

LoopStart:
    cmpq %rbx, %rax
    jge CodeContinues    # Opposite of original while comparison

    # DoSomething

    incq %rax
    jmp LoopStart        # Go back to the beginning of the loop

CodeContinues:
    # Continue on here
```

You can write any loop (such as a for loop) in terms of a while loop, so the preceding translation works for pretty much any loop you might run into.

16.5 Function Calls and Default Values

Function calls are fairly straightforward, as we already discussed them at length in Chapter 11. Additional information when dealing with passing floating-point values is available in Appendix F.

However, many programming languages also allow default values to be specified for various parameters. This can be accomplished in a variety of ways:

- It can be done at compile time, where the functions always include all parameters, but if a parameter is left out, the compiler adds in a default value to the function.

- An additional parameter can be passed that has bits set on or off for which parameters were included in the call and which need defaults. Then, the function itself can check to see which values were sent to it in the call.

- The function can be separately implemented for each combination of default values (see next section).

- The same function can have different entry points depending on which values are defaulted in.

We will show here how to do the last one of these. Let us say we have the following function definition:

```
int myfunc(int param1, int param2 = 3, int param3 = 5)
```

We can code this in assembly language by having multiple targets: myfunc will be the main entry point, myfunc_default_param3 will set up the third parameter for us, and myfunc_default_param2_param3 will set up both of them. Remember that the first parameter is stored in %rdi, the second parameter in %rsi, and the third parameter in %rdx.

```
myfunc_default_param2_param3:
    movq $3, %rsi
myfunc_default_param3:
    movq $5, %rdx
myfunc:
    # Main function here
```

As you can see, the different endpoints are basically monkey patching the parameters to include the various default values.

16.6 Overloaded Functions

Some languages, such as C++, also implement what are called **overloaded functions**. This is where a single function name can be implemented in different ways by different parameters.

That is, we can have two functions, both called myfunc. Which one is chosen depends on the types (and number) of the parameters. One version might take an integer, and another version might take a floating-point variable.

This is usually done by **name mangling**. This means that the language will modify the name of the function internally to include the types of arguments. Then, function calls will choose which one to call and change the name of the function (again, internally) to specify which one they want to call.

There are a lot of C++ name-mangling rules, so we won't get into them all. However, for simple functions, the following rules will get you pretty far:

1. All mangled names begin with _Z.

2. Next is the number of characters in the function name (6 for myfunc).

3. Next is the function name itself (myfunc).

4. Last is a letter for each argument type. l for a 32-bit integer, x for a 64-bit integer, c for a character, d for a double, etc.

5. The return value is not included in the function name.

So, the function long myfunc(long long a, long b) would be named _Z6myfuncxl.

16.7 Exception Handling

Exception handling can be implemented in a number of ways, and we will simply show one that is conceptually simple to follow.

The problem with exceptions is that they can transfer control way outside of the scope of the immediate function or calling function. For instance, consider the following code:

```
void myfunc() {
    try {
        myfunc2();
        // DoMoreStuff
    } catch {
        // HandleException
    }

    // ContinueMyFunc
}
void myfunc2() {
    myfunc3();
}
void myfunc3() {
    throw_exception my_exception_code;
}
```

Here, `throw_exception` will transfer control not only back out to the calling function, func2, but all the way out to myfunc. Additionally, this is not even the return address for myfunc (which would go to DoMoreStuff), but to the exception handler in HandleException.

Additionally, each stack frame must be given the chance to "unwind." That is, many times there are actions which must be taken for a function to clean up after itself, such as closing files, deallocating memory, etc. So, control has to be transferred far outside the current scope, but we also need to perform cleanup operations along the way.

A simple way to take care of this is to simply have the address of the exception handler be pushed onto the stack before making the function call. Every function will implement some type of exception handling, even if it doesn't explicitly handle exceptions. If a function doesn't catch exceptions and no cleanup is needed, it will simply transfer control to the next cleanup on the list. If a function doesn't catch exceptions but needs cleanup, it can do so before transferring to the next exception handler. Finally, if a function does catch the exception, then they can both clean up and do exception handling and not propagate the exception further.

The following is an implementation of this idea:

exception.s

```
.equ my_exception_code, 7 # Just picking a value at random
myfunc:
    enter $0, $0

    push $0  # Needed to keep the stack aligned
    push $myfunc_exceptionhandler
    call myfunc2

    # DoMoreStuff

myfunc_ContinueMyFunc:
    # Do more stuff here

    leave
    ret

myfunc_exceptionhandler:
    # HandleException - do any exception-handling code here

    # Go back to the code
    jmp myfunc_ContinueMyFunc

myfunc2:
    enter $0, $0

    pushq $0 # keep the stack aligned
    pushq $myfunc2_exceptionhandler

    call myfunc3

    leave
    ret
```

```
myfunc2_exceptionhandler:
    # Nothing to do except go to the next handler
    leave              # restore %rsp/%rbp
    addq $8, %rsp   # Get rid of return address
    jmp *(%rsp)     # jump to exception handler

myfunc3:
    enter $0, $0

    # Throw
    movq $my_exception_code, %rax  # store exception code
    leave                          # restore %rsp/%rbp
    addq $8, %rsp                  # Get rid of return address
    jmp *(%rsp)                    # Jump to exception handler

    # What would have happened if we didn't throw the exception
    leave
    ret
```

We are pushing zero onto the stack because the stack is supposed to maintain a 16-byte alignment. Then we are pushing the exception handler information for the function. A "throw," then, consists of setting %rax to the exception information (here it is just a number) and then performing an alternate series of steps to return to the function, so that we return via the exception handler, not to the return address. The exception handler can either handle the exception and continue processing (as happens with myfunc), or it can propagate the error on up the chain (as happens with myfunc2). No exception handler was shown for myfunc3 both for brevity's sake and because it is unneeded.

Note that this also makes it straightforward to implement finally clauses that do finalization without actually catching the exception. In myfunc2, any finalization could have been done before propagating the exception on to the next function in the call stack.

16.8 Tail-Call Elimination

One interesting optimization that can be done in certain cases is known as **tail-call elimination**. Many programming languages encourage (or even force!) programmers to write programs recursively. This is usually fine, except that sometimes the recursion happens so many times that the program runs out of stack space!

To mitigate against overusage of stack space, programming languages often implement tail-call elimination. The idea behind this is that if the last thing that a function does is return the value of another function call (it doesn't need to process that value or anything—just return it), then at the point of the call, the stack frame is actually not needed. The current stack frame can be discarded with a leave instruction, and then, rather than issuing a call instruction, a jmp instruction can be issued instead. This means that a return (ret) from the called function will not return control back to the present function, but to the preceding function! Since we were just going to keep the return value in %rax anyway, there was nothing else the present function needs to do, so there is no reason to return to the present function.

This not only eliminates waste in stack space usage, it also saves the processor a lot of time returning from the huge stack of recursive functions. If each tail call is just a jmp instead of a call, then the stack is not building up, and the return of the last call is just single return instruction.

Let's consider a tail-call version of the factorial function. In this version, the current accumulated value of factorial is sent along with the current value. In pseudo-code, the function would look like this:

```
int factorial(int value) {
    return factorial_recursive(value, 1);
}

int factorial_recursive(int number, int value_so_far) {
    if(number == 1) {
        return value_so_far;
    }
    int curval = number * value_so_far;
    return factorial(number - 1, curval);
}
```

This is a recursive implementation, but it doesn't have to build up stack frames if the compiler implements tail-call elimination. The following is the assembly language that could be used to implement the preceding function using tail-call elimination. Notice that all tail recursive calls are implemented with a `jmp` rather than a `call`.

factorialtail.s

```
.globl factorial
.section .text
factorial:
    # No stack frame needed, just get ready to call factorial_internal

    # %rdi already has number,
    # value_so_far gets set to 1
    movq $1, %rsi

    # We can eliminate this as a tail call as well!
    jmp factorial_internal

factorial_internal:
    # No stack frame needed
    # %rdi has number
    # %rsi has value_so_far

    cmpq $1, %rdi
    je factorial_internal_completion

    # multiply number and value_so_far
    movq %rsi, %rax
    mulq %rdi

    # Next value
    decq %rdi         # number
    movq %rax, %rsi   # value_so_far

    # Tail call elimination
    jmp factorial_internal
```

```
factorial_internal_completion:
  # This is the base case - return value_so_far
  movq %rsi, %rax
  ret
```

Remember, this *only* works if (a) the *very last thing* the function does is make a function call and (b) it returns exactly the value it received from this function call.

Interestingly, the technique doesn't actually require that the call is a recursive call, though that is where it is most useful. As long as the call is at the end of the function, tail-call elimination can be applied.

Recursive programs are often thought of as easier to reason about than looping programs, because it is easier to write programs where all variables are only assigned once, and therefore you can easily see where the value comes from since there is only one line of code where the value is assigned. Historically, this technique was not viewed favorably because it was deemed inefficient due to having the overhead of function calls everywhere. However, when tail-call elimination is used, the resulting assembly language is nearly as efficient as if a simple loop were employed.

16.9 Reading Assembly Language Output from GCC

Many programming languages themselves support output to assembly language directly. The GNU Compiler Collection (GCC) will do this for you using the -S switch. If you want to see what assembly language the compiler generates for the file foo.c, you can run gcc -S foo.c, and it will generate a file called foo.s containing the assembly listing.

This is useful for a variety of reasons. First, it's helpful when learning assembly language to learn what compilers are actually generating. This helps both learning assembly language and how the target language is implemented. Additionally, if you want to use assembly language to optimize something, it is sometimes easier to have the compiler have the first turn. Humans are good at inventing rules; computers are good at applying them. Therefore, if there are known rules for optimization, the compiler probably knows them and will apply them. Then, for non-rule-based optimizations, you can implement them yourself.

The following is a simple program written in C:

example_compile.c

```c
#include <stdio.h>

long squareme(long x) {
    return x * x;
}

long myval;
int main() {
    fprintf(stdout, "Enter a number: \n");
    fscanf(stdin, "%d", &myval);
    fprintf(stdout, "The square of %d is %d", myval, squareme(myval));
}
```

If it is compiled with gcc -S example_compile.c, it generates the following output on GCC 10.3.0 (some extraneous lines removed for readability):

example_compile.s

```asm
    .text
    .globl      squareme
    .type       squareme, @function
squareme:
.LFB0:
    .cfi_startproc
    pushq       %rbp
    .cfi_def_cfa_offset 16
    .cfi_offset 6, -16
    movq        %rsp, %rbp
      .cfi_def_cfa_register 6
    movq        %rdi, -8(%rbp)
    movq        -8(%rbp), %rax
    imulq       %rax, %rax
    popq        %rbp
    .cfi_def_cfa 7, 8
    ret
```

217

```
        .cfi_endproc
.LFE0:
    .size       squareme, .-squareme
    .globl      myval
    .bss
    .align 8
    .type       myval, @object
    .size       myval, 8
myval:
    .zero       8
    .section       .rodata
.LC0:
    .string      "Enter a number: \n"
.LC1:
    .string      "%d"
.LC2:
    .string      "The square of %d is %d"
    .text
    .globl      main
    .type       main, @function
main:
.LFB1:
    .cfi_startproc
    pushq       %rbp
    .cfi_def_cfa_offset 16
    .cfi_offset 6, -16
    movq        %rsp, %rbp
    .cfi_def_cfa_register 6
    movq        stdout(%rip), %rax
    movq        %rax, %rcx
    movl        $17, %edx
    movl        $1, %esi
    movl        $.LC0, %edi
    call        fwrite
    movq        stdin(%rip), %rax
```

```
movl        $myval, %edx
movl        $.LC1, %esi
movq        %rax, %rdi
movl        $0, %eax
call        __isoc99_fscanf
movq        myval(%rip), %rax
movq        %rax, %rdi
call        squareme
movq        %rax, %rcx
movq        myval(%rip), %rdx
movq        stdout(%rip), %rax
movl        $.LC2, %esi
movq        %rax, %rdi
movl        $0, %eax
call        fprintf
movl        $0, %eax
popq        %rbp
.cfi_def_cfa 7, 8
ret
.cfi_endproc
```

Some differences from our expectations appear here:

1. Unsurprisingly, all of the data storage names were computer generated. Generally, the compiler introduces local values with the .L prefix.

2. The compiler adds a lot of additional annotations to make sure that the assembler exactly matches what the compiler writers want.

3. The specific assembler directives used are a little different than the ones we generally use when writing code ourselves. For example, it uses .text rather than .section .text as we typically do.

4. The compiler often uses explicit pushing of values rather than the enter instruction. The reason for this is that in many processors, it is actually faster to execute multiple instructions than for the processor to execute the enter family of instructions.

5. The code generally prefers to use 32-bit addresses rather than
    64-bit. This is why it is loading string addresses into 32-bit
    registers rather than their 64-bit equivalents.

6. The compiler can **inline** functions in certain circumstances.
    Note that the first `fprintf` actually gets converted into an `fwrite`
    function. This is because the compiler figured out that it could do
    this without causing issues and would avoid an extra function call.

In any case, it should be sufficiently close to what you have learned so far that you
can follow the details closely.

Exercises

1. Write a short program in C which contains both a for loop and a
    function call.

2. Take the program you just wrote, and now write an assembly
    language version of it.

3. Compile the program with `gcc -S` to see how GCC translates your
    program into assembly language. How did that differ from your
    version?

4. Compile the program with `gcc -S` with different optimization
    levels/options turned on (optimization levels are specified by
    `-OLEVEL` where `LEVEL` is a number zero or greater). How does this
    affect the output?

5. Write a C++ program. Try to predict the name mangling of your
    functions. Use `gcc -S` to see if you are correct.

6. Write a program in another language GCC supports. Can you
    more or less predict the output?

CHAPTER 17

Tracking Memory Allocations

Nearly every programming language has some features to track memory allocations. Some, like the C programming language, are primitive. In Chapter 14, we learned how to implement basic procedures for allocating and deallocating memory for a program and managing the amount of memory we requested from the kernel.

However, even with having functions to allocate and deallocate memory, there are still a lot of issues that programmers have when tracking memory. Trying to figure out when a piece of memory *can* be deallocated is tricky. If a program has lots of subsystems, and memory gets passed around, it is tough to tell when we are done with it. Simply providing functions to allocate and deallocate memory is literally the least we can do.

In this chapter, we will look at more advanced facilities of memory management.

17.1 Memory Pools

One way to keep track of memory is with memory pools. To understand the benefit of memory pools, think about a web service. Web services get a request, process a request, and then, basically, forget about the request. They don't have to keep any of the request-specific data around while they wait for the next request. There is some data that they need to keep the server running, but none of the data that they worked with during the request really matters anymore.

In this type of environment, **memory pools** work really well. Memory pools are like multiple areas of memory from which you can request allocations and deallocations. Imagine segmenting out your memory so that not only do you request an amount of memory you want, you also request which memory pool you want it allocated from.

Why is this helpful?

221

© Jonathan Bartlett 2021
J. Bartlett, *Learn to Program with Assembly*, https://doi.org/10.1007/978-1-4842-7437-8_17

Go back to our web request example. During a request, you are going to allocate memory—maybe lots of it. Rather than having to manage all these pointers to be sure you free them all at the right time, what if you could just say, "Hey computer—free everything that I allocated for this request!" Memory pools allow you to do this.

Basically, you would create a memory pool and designate it as being for requests. Then, as requests come in, allocations would occur from that specific memory pool. Finally, when the request is finished being handled, all of the memory in that pool would be flushed at once.

The following is a modification to the allocator from Chapter 14 that allows a user to specify a pool number to allocate from and also provides a `deallocate_pool` function to deallocate all allocations from a particular pool.[1] Basically, it has an additional field on each allocation which is the pool number that the allocation belongs to. Then, when deallocating a pool, the deallocator simply walks the list of memory allocations and deallocates each one that belongs to the pool.[2]

mempool.s

.globl allocate, deallocate, deallocate_pool

.section .data
memory_start:
    .quad 0
memory_end:
    .quad 0

.section .text
.equ HEADER_SIZE, 32 *# Only need 24, but this is a 16-byte aligned value*
.equ HDR_IN_USE_OFFSET, 0
.equ HDR_SIZE_OFFSET, 8
.equ HDR_POOL_OFFSET, 16

.equ BRK_SYSCALL, 12

---

[1] Note that this code performs best when memory pool 0 is not used. This is because the pool number is reset to zero when deallocations occur, so that `deallocate_pool` will skip them.

[2] While this uses a separate field for the memory pool, if you wanted, you could probably tweak the code so that HDR_IN_USE_OFFSET and HDR_POOL_OFFSET shared a quadword—that is, if it is zero, then it's unallocated; if it is nonzero, it references the memory pool it belongs to.

```
# Register usage:
#  - %r10 - memory pool #
#  - %rdx - size requested
#  - %rsi - pointer to current memory being examined
#  - %rcx - copy of memory_end
```

allocate_init:
```
    # Find the program break.
    movq $0, %rdi
    movq $BRK_SYSCALL, %rax
    syscall

    # The current break will be both the start and end of our memory
    movq %rax, memory_start
    movq %rax, memory_end
    jmp allocate_continue
```

allocate_move_break:
```
    # Old break is saved in %r8 to return to user
    movq %rcx, %r8

    # Calculate where we want the new break to be
    # (old break + size)
    movq %rcx, %rdi
    addq %rdx, %rdi
    # Save this value
    movq %rdi, memory_end

    # Tell Linux where the new break is
    movq $BRK_SYSCALL, %rax
    syscall

    # Address is in %r8 - mark size, availability, and pool
    movq $1, HDR_IN_USE_OFFSET(%r8)
    movq %rdx, HDR_SIZE_OFFSET(%r8)
    movq %r10, HDR_POOL_OFFSET(%r8)

    # Actual return value is beyond our header
    addq $HEADER_SIZE, %r8
```

```
    movq %r8, %rax
    ret

    # This version of allocate has
    # two parameters - pool # and size
allocate:
    # Save the pool number int r10
    movq %rdi, %r10
    # Save the amount requested into %rdx
    movq %rsi, %rdx
    # Actual amount needed is actually larger
    addq $HEADER_SIZE, %rdx

    # If we haven't initialized, do so
    cmpq $0, memory_start
    je allocate_init

allocate_continue:
    movq memory_start, %rsi
    movq memory_end, %rcx

allocate_loop:
    # If we have reached the end of memory
    # we have to allocate new memory by
    # moving the break.
    cmpq %rsi, %rcx
    je allocate_move_break

    # is the next block available?
    cmpq $0, HDR_IN_USE_OFFSET(%rsi)
    jne try_next_block

    # is the next block big enough?
    cmpq %rdx, HDR_SIZE_OFFSET(%rsi)
    jb try_next_block

    # This block is great!
    # Mark it as unavailable
    movq $1, HDR_IN_USE_OFFSET(%rsi)
```

```
    # Set the pool #
    movq %r10, HDR_POOL_OFFSET(%rsi)
    # Move beyond the header
    addq $HEADER_SIZE, %rsi
    # Return the value
    movq %rsi, %rax
    ret
```

try_next_block:
```
    # This block didn't work, move to the next one
    addq HDR_SIZE_OFFSET(%rsi), %rsi
    jmp allocate_loop
```

deallocate:
```
    # Free is simple - just mark the block as available
    movq $0, HDR_IN_USE_OFFSET - HEADER_SIZE(%rdi)
    movq $0, HDR_POOL_OFFSET - HEADER_SIZE(%rdi)
    ret
```

deallocate_pool:
```
    # %rdi has the pool number
    # Walk the allocations and deallocate
    # anything with the pool number
    movq memory_start, %rsi
    movq memory_end, %rcx
```

deallocate_pool_loop:
```
    cmpq %rsi, %rcx
    je deallocate_loop_complete

    cmpq %rdi, HDR_POOL_OFFSET(%rsi)
    je deallocate_from_pool
    addq HDR_SIZE_OFFSET(%rsi), %rsi
    jmp deallocate_pool_loop
```

deallocate_from_pool:
```
    movq $0, HDR_POOL_OFFSET(%rsi)
    movq $0, HDR_IN_USE_OFFSET(%rsi)
```

```
    addq HDR_SIZE_OFFSET(%rsi), %rsi
    jmp deallocate_pool_loop
```

deallocate_loop_complete:
```
    ret
```

You can call this allocator like this:

```
int main() {
    // Get 400 bytes from pool 1
    char *a1 = allocate(1, 400);
    // Get 32 bytes from pool 2
    char *a2 = allocate(2, 32)
    // Get 80 bytes from  pool 2
    char *ae = allocate(2, 80);

    // Release all of pool 2
    deallocate_pool(2);
}
```

If more thought was given on how these pools were structured, the flushing event, rather than having to iterate through all allocations, could essentially happen instantaneously.

Memory pools are fairly rare phenomena in computer programming, but I thought they were worth a mention because they have very interesting properties. The Apache Portable Runtime uses memory pools for exactly the purpose outlined here—web request processing. However, they can be helpfully applied anytime you have many allocations which are aligned with a particular part of the life cycle of a program.

17.2 Reference Counting

Memory pools are nice, but the problem with them is that their usage is tied to fairly specific application styles and life cycles. Another, more general way to semiautomate memory management is with **reference counting**. In reference counting, instead of the programmer keeping track of whether or not they need to free memory, there is a counter (called the **reference count** or **refcount**) stored on the memory saying how many parts of the program are *using* the memory. When a part of the program starts to use a piece of memory, or if the pointer to that memory gets stored somewhere, the program adds 1 to the counter. When that part of the program is done with that piece of memory (or the pointer goes away or points elsewhere), it subtracts 1 from the counter. When that counter drops to zero, the memory gets deallocated.

This adds a bit of overhead, as you will have to continually be calling the function to add/subtract from the counter and check for zero. Nonetheless, this simplifies the process greatly.

However, there are two big problems with reference counting:

1. If there are circular reference (i.e., the memory refers to other memory, which has a pointer back to the memory itself), then the reference count gets stuck and can't go to zero. This can't really be managed by the system and has to be fixed by the user being smart about when they add to the reference count and when they don't. In programming languages that support reference counting, there is usually an option for a pointer to be a *weak reference* (i.e., does not contribute to the reference count). However, this creates other problems, such as the fact that something that is being pointed to could in fact disappear.

2. There are several edge cases when dealing with reference counting and knowing who is responsible for what is very important. For example, when an object is returned from a function, what should its reference count be? If it were zero, it should already be deallocated. If it is one, then who is responsible for deallocating it? What if the result is ignored by the programmer?

The programming languages most famous for reference counting are Objective-C and Swift. Interestingly, because of the intricacies of how they operate, they both have different answers to the second question. In Objective-C, originally, programmers had to maintain reference counts themselves, using the functions `retain` (increase the reference count) and `release` (decrease the reference count and deallocate if needed). This meant that it was not unusual for a programmer to ignore a return value from a function. To prevent programmers from having to explicitly release return values from functions, a function known as `autorelease` was established which meant, essentially, "`release` this at a later time." Then, if programmers wanted to ignore a value, they could, and it would be cleaned up later. They only had to interact with it if they wanted to keep in (in which case they would issue a `retain` on it).

Swift, however, does the opposite. Since the compiler is in charge of retaining and releasing, it simplifies things by having returned values always have a reference count of 1, and the calling function is responsible for releasing it if they don't want the value.

The following code is a modification of the allocator in Chapter 14. Instead of just having a flag telling whether the memory is in use, this is now a counter which tells how many times the memory has been retained. The value starts at 1 when the memory is allocated with `allocate`. The `retain` function will add one to the reference count. The `deallocate` function has been removed in favor of `release`, which decrements the reference count and checks to see if it is ready to deallocate.

Since we are not autoreleasing, we are following the semantics of Swift, where returned values are assumed to have a reference count, and the calling functions have to release them when they are no longer being used.

Interestingly, we actually can use the *exact same* `allocate`/`deallocate` code from Chapter 14. What we will do is transform the "in use" quadword from a flag to a count, which means that `allocate` already sets that to what we want it to be. All we need are two short functions for adjusting the reference count. Additionally, because "deallocating" simply means marking the "in use" quadword as a zero, there is nothing additional we need to do because that is the same thing that happens when the reference count goes to zero!

The following code gives two short functions that add reference counting to our memory management system:

refcount.s

```
.globl retain, release

.section .text
.equ REFCOUNT_OFFSET, -16

retain:
    incq REFCOUNT_OFFSET(%rdi)
    ret

release:
    decq REFCOUNT_OFFSET(%rdi)
    ret
```

The following code will exercise the reference count functionality:

```
int main() {
    char *a = allocate(500);
    retain(a);
    retain(a);
    release(a);
    char *b = allocate(300); // New allocation
    retain(a);
    release(a);
    release(a);
    char *c = allocate(300); // New allocation
    release(a); // Object is deallocated here
    char *d = allocate(300); // Re-uses space from a
}
```

Note that when writing in assembly language, this can be done even faster. While it causes more tight coupling, if the programmer knows the way the reference counting system works, the programmer can avoid the function call altogether and simply increment/decrement the reference count in a single instruction, no matter where it is! No more trying to shuffle things into %rdi and taking care to save your registers. You can literally do this by incrementing the correct offset (-16 in our case) of your pointer.

17.3 Garbage Collection

The ultimate in automatic memory management is **garbage collection**. In garbage collection, the programmer ultimately doesn't have to care at all about memory management. They can simply allocate and store. The rest is taken care of by the system.

The system goes through memory periodically and checks to see if there is anything that is unreferenced. Anything unreferenced then gets automatically freed.

Garbage collection even avoids the problem of circular references. The garbage collector starts with a set of "base memory regions" and works out from there. Anything unreachable from those base memory regions is assumed to be garbage. So, even if two things point to each other, it doesn't matter because if there isn't a reference to one of them reachable from the starting set of memory regions, then they aren't reachable by code.

This sounds like a complicated process, and, in fact, it can be, but there are also easier ways to do it if you allow for some assumptions.

The assumptions for our garbage collector are as follows:

- We will assume that every pointer is stored on an 8-byte boundary.

- We will assume that when the garbage collector is called, there are no pointers in registers that aren't also stored somewhere as well.

- We will establish the .data and .bss sections, as well as the stack, as being our "base memory" regions.

The garbage collection process will look like this:

1. We will walk through all allocations and mark them *all* as free.

2. We will then walk these memory regions looking for anything that "looks like" a pointer (i.e., the value could be pointing somewhere on the heap).

3. For any pointer-like value that we find, we will push it onto the stack.

4. We will then go through the stack, and for each pointer-like object, we will

    (a). Walk through the allocations to see if it is a real pointer.

    (b). If it is a real pointer, we will check to see if it is marked as in use.

    (c). If it is already marked as in use, we will skip it and go on to the next value in the stack.

    (d). Otherwise, we will mark it as in use and go through each quadword in this region looking for pointer-like values and adding them to the stack.

5. Once we are all the way through the stack of values, our job is done.

This is a "conservative" garbage collector, because it is treating anything that could be a pointer as if it were a real pointer. If we were in charge of a programming language, we could make the garbage collector only care about real pointers. In our case, we are just looking for values that *could* be pointers into the heap.

Because this chapter is already running long, and this code is longer than most, the code is available in Appendix J. It's more complicated than other code in this book, but it is probably less complicated than you might have expected garbage collection to be!

To use the garbage collector, just `gc_allocate` freely, and then periodically call `gc_scan` (no parameters needed) to actually perform the garbage collection.

17.4 Adding Finalizers

When using automatic memory management, sometimes you would like to be notified when memory gets reclaimed. Perhaps you want to know when something is no longer used. Perhaps the memory is a file structure or something that contains a file descriptor that needs to be closed or some other important piece of information that has to be dealt with before the data structure goes away.

This requires a **finalizer**. A finalizer is basically a function that is run right before memory is deallocated. All of these schemes can have finalizers added to them, though the complexity of doing so varies with the approach.

We won't implement them here, because it actually takes quite a rewrite to add them. Essentially, however, you can add a finalizer by

1. Reserving a spot in the memory header to store a finalizer function

2. Having a function call to set the finalizer

3. Executing the finalizer when the object is destroyed

This is not incredibly hard to do with the reference counting. We just need to add more fields to the memory header. For the garbage collection, however, we would need to add more states so that we knew which memory allocations switched from allocated to deallocated.

Exercises

1. Think more about the memory pool allocator. Rather than using an integer to identify the pool, create functions to allocate and deallocate entire pools, giving a user a pointer to the pool upon creation from which to allocate their data.

2. Think about the memory pool allocator. How might you modify this so that memory pools are flushed without having to iterate through every allocation? Note that it will require restructuring the code and data quite a bit.

3. Take one of the allocators from this chapter and add a finalizer system to it.

CHAPTER 18

Object-Oriented Programming

This chapter takes a look at object-oriented programming from an assembly language perspective. Object-oriented programming is most useful when you are a programmer writing libraries for other programmers to use. Since we have programmers building things for programmers, in this chapter, the term "library programmer" will be used to refer to the programmer who is creating the data structures, functions, and objects, and the term "application programmer" will be used to refer to the programmer who is using those things. Oftentimes, the library programmer and the application programmer are the same person, but nonetheless, the roles are distinct.

In the programming we have done so far, we have emphasized the importance of all parts of your program knowing and understanding the layout of data on your computer. Since computer memory consists entirely of numbers, we have to know what the numbers mean in order to use them. However, this makes programming a lot less flexible.

What if there was a way to program where the application programmer didn't have to pay as close of attention to the specific layout of each data structure, but could operate on the data in a way that was more focused on functionality?

Object-oriented programming is a style of programming and programming languages which allow you to treat data structures by their *functionality* rather than by their data layout.

Object-oriented programming is typically defined by three key ideas: **encapsulation**, **polymorphism**, and **inheritance**.

© Jonathan Bartlett 2021
J. Bartlett, *Learn to Program with Assembly*, https://doi.org/10.1007/978-1-4842-7437-8_18

18.1 Encapsulation

Essentially, the library programmer defines functions, called **methods**, around the data structure to control how the data structure is manipulated and accessed. Application programmers, rather than accessing the data structure directly, use the methods instead. This allows a level of indirection and encapsulation which shields the application programmer from having to know too much about the internals of the data structure.

We've dealt with encapsulation before without mentioning it. The FILE structure from Chapter 12 exhibits features of encapsulation. The fopen function returned a pointer to the FILE structure, but we never actually knew what was in it. We only knew the functions that took it as a parameter. These functions essentially act as gateways to the structure, ensuring that we only utilize the FILE structure in legitimate ways. We call the function and the library manages any actual changes required to the data.

This allows a level of safety for the application programmer using the function as well as a means of compatibility for future changes. Since the application programmer's usage of FILE is entirely through functions, the library programmer can modify the implementation easily without causing problems for the application programmer. The type of record (the data layout plus the methods defined around it) is known as the **class** of the object. An instance of the data structure itself is known as the **object**.

An object's **life cycle** usually includes three types of functions: **constructors**, **methods**, and **destructors**. A constructor is what build your object. It allocates data, sets initial values, and hands back to the program a pointer to the underlying record. The fopen function is essentially a constructor. It allocates data for the FILE structure, sets it up, and hands back a pointer to it.

Methods do all of the "main" tasks of the object. Most of the functionality of the object is defined in various methods. We normally write methods such that the first parameter is a pointer to the object that the method is written for. fprintf is a good example of a method. The first parameter is a pointer to the FILE structure. The function encapsulates and abstracts the operation of the FILE structure. You don't need to know any of the underlying system calls to use the method or even what the data inside the FILE pointer looks like. The application programmer simply gives fprintf the pointer, and fprintf knows the right way to deal with it.

Finally, a destructor takes care of getting rid of your object. For some objects, this just deallocates the memory. For other objects, this is more involved. The destructor for the FILE structure is the fclose function. It not only deallocates the memory, it also tells the operating system that we are done with the file and closes it out.

The following is how we might imagine these functions being used together (this is not a real programming language, just an example of what one might look like):

```
function main() {
    File *myfile = File.fopen("myfilename.txt", "w"); // Constructor
    myfile.fprintf("Hello there!\n");                 // Methods
    myfile.fprintf("Hello again!\n");
}
```

A few things to note. First of all, the constructor is usually defined on the class itself. Since there isn't an object available yet, constructors are often defined as `class_name.constructor_name`. However, they always yield a pointer to a data structure of the right type for the class.

Second, note that the destructor wasn't explicitly called. This is true of many object-oriented programming languages. The destructor is called *implicitly* when the object is garbage collected or goes out of scope.

Finally, notice how the syntax is `object_variable.method_name`. Under the covers, this is just a function call where the object is merely the first parameter (though, as we will see shortly, there is a bit more to it than that). It is written this way (among other reasons) to emphasize that the `fprintf` method is defined *on* the `myfile` object. In other words, `fprintf` has a special relationship with (and special access to) the `FILE` data structure.

18.2 Polymorphism

Encapsulation helps us think about and structure our code more clearly. However, it is just as much a style as it is a technology. Essentially, it says, "The library programmer knows the data structures, the application programmer should just use the functions that the library programmer defines and not worry too much how it is implemented."

Polymorphism, however, does the real magic of object-oriented programming. Polymorphism means that when I'm writing functions or methods, I don't even have to be worried too much about the specific types of objects that are passed in as parameters. What I care about is the *behaviors they support* more than their specific types.

Let's look at an example to see what I mean. This is a fictitious programming language, so don't imagine that this will actually build a working program anywhere.

```
interface Animal {
    function speak();
    function eat();
}

class Dog implements Animal {
    method speak() {
        stdout.fprintf("Ruff, ruff\n");
    }

    method eat() {
        stdout.fprintf("I love dog biscuits\n");
    }

    method fetch() {
        stdout.fprintf("I love to play fetch\n");
    }
}

class Cat implements Animal {
    method speak() {
        stdout.fprintf("Meow\n");
    }

    method eat() {
        stdout.fprintf("Yum, yum fish\n");
    }

    method playWithString() {
        stdout.fprintf("Ball of string, Yay!\n")
    }
}

function doThings(Animal *a) {
    a.speak();
    a.eat();
    a.speak();
    a.speak();
}
```

```
function main() {
    c = Cat.new();
    d = Dog.new();

    doThings(c);
    doThings(d);
}
```

In this example, we define two classes—a Cat class and a Dog class. These classes both *implement* the Animal **interface**. In object-oriented terms, an interface is a set of methods which may be supported by one or more classes.

What this means is that I can define functions which don't care what specific data structure they receive. They only care what *interfaces* those data structures support. In the example, the doThings function took any object that supports the Animal interface. The program calls it with a Dog object one time and a Cat object another time. In each case, the code will do the appropriate functions for that object!

What this allows for is the ability of programmers to build highly extensible programs. By defining standard interfaces, they can write code which allows them to extend by adding additional classes that implement those interfaces. The main application code does not need to be changed, because the application code merely works with the interfaces. Adding new types of objects typically requires relatively little programming changes at the edges.

So how is this implemented?

Polymorphism is usually implemented by simply having a record for each interface that each class implements. This record, known as a **vtable**, is simply a list of pointers to each function in the interface that the class implements.

Then, when passing an object to a function that operates on an interface, both the pointer to the object and a pointer to the vtable are passed. Since the interface is known ahead of time, the offsets into the vtable are also known, and the function simply looks up the function it wants to call on the vtable. This combination of two pointers—an object pointer and a vtable pointer—is often referred to as a **fat pointer**.

The following is our cat/dog example in assembly language. There's quite a bit of code for such a simple example, but hopefully, you can see how flexible this makes your code, especially if all the complexity is being handled in a programming language by the compiler rather than trying to do it by hand.

First, let's look at how the objects themselves are defined. Each one will allocate memory, because, in theory, these would have data behind them. Ours don't, but that's okay. Also, for brevity, the unused cat- and dog-specific functions (fetch and playWithString) were removed.

Here is the code for the Cat class:

vtable_cat.s

```
## Cat Class
.globl cat_new, cat_eat, cat_speak, cat_destroy
.section .data
speak_text:
    .ascii "Meow\n\0"
eat_text:
    .ascii "Yum, yum fish\n\0"
play_text:
    .ascii "Ball of string, Yay!\n\0"

.section .text

.equ CAT_SIZE, 64

cat_new:
    enter $0, $0
    movq $CAT_SIZE, %rdi
    call malloc
    leave
    ret

cat_speak:
    enter $0, $0
    movq stdout, %rdi
    movq $speak_text, %rsi
    call fprintf
    leave
    ret
```

```
cat_eat:
    enter $0, $0
    movq stdout, %rdi
    movq $eat_text, %rsi
    call fprintf
    leave
    ret

cat_destroy:
    enter $0, $0
    # %rdi already has the address
    call free
    leave
    ret
```

Notice that the functions are fairly straightforward. All of them (except the constructor) simply take a pointer to the object as its first parameter. In the current implementation, since the method knows the complete type information of the object, we don't need vtable information. We will see the shortcomings of this in the section on inheritance. However, this is the method used in languages such as Go which support polymorphism but not inheritance.

The code for the Dog class is very similar:

vtable_dog.s

```
## Dog Class
.globl dog_new, dog_eat, dog_speak, dog_destroy
.section .data
speak_text:
    .ascii "Ruff, ruff\n\0"
eat_text:
    .ascii "I love dog biscuits\n\0"

.section .text

.equ DOG_SIZE, 32

dog_new:
    enter $0, $0
    movq $DOG_SIZE, %rdi
```

```
    call malloc
    leave
    ret
```

dog_speak:

```
    enter $0, $0
    movq stdout, %rdi
    movq $speak_text, %rsi
    call fprintf
    leave
    ret
```

dog_eat:

```
    enter $0, $0
    movq stdout, %rdi
    movq $eat_text, %rsi
    call fprintf
    leave
    ret
```

dog_destroy:

```
    enter $0, $0
    # %rdi already has the address
    call free
    leave
    ret
```

Next, we will define the interface, which is essentially just defining how the interface vtable looks with each set of methods. Note that the vtable is literally just a list of functions which tell how the Animal interface is defined for that object. One vtable is needed for each class for each interface it implements.

vtable_animal.s

```
.globl VTABLE_ANIMAL_SPEAK_OFFSET, VTABLE_ANIMAL_EAT_OFFSET
.globl dog_vtable_animal
.globl cat_vtable_animal

.equ VTABLE_ANIMAL_SPEAK_OFFSET, 0
```

```
.equ VTABLE_ANIMAL_EAT_OFFSET, 8

dog_vtable_animal:
    .quad dog_speak
    .quad dog_eat

cat_vtable_animal:
    .quad cat_speak
    .quad cat_eat
```

Next, we will look at the doThings function which uses the vtables. Notice how the first parameter to doThings is the object and the second parameter is the vtable. This tells the function both *where* the object exists in memory (the pointer to the object) and *how* it is utilized (the pointer to the vtable). Then, all the function calls are made as *indirect* function calls, made as offsets into the vtable.

Here is the code:

vtable_dothings.s

```
.globl doThings
.section .text

doThings:
    .equ LCL_ANIMAL_OBJ_OFFSET, -8
    .equ LCL_ANIMAL_VTABLE_OFFSET, -16
    enter $16, $0
    movq %rdi, LCL_ANIMAL_OBJ_OFFSET(%rbp)
    movq %rsi, LCL_ANIMAL_VTABLE_OFFSET(%rbp)

    # %rdi already contains the object
    call *VTABLE_ANIMAL_SPEAK_OFFSET(%rsi)

    movq LCL_ANIMAL_OBJ_OFFSET(%rbp), %rdi
    movq LCL_ANIMAL_VTABLE_OFFSET(%rbp), %rsi
    call *VTABLE_ANIMAL_EAT_OFFSET(%rsi)

    movq LCL_ANIMAL_OBJ_OFFSET(%rbp), %rdi
    movq LCL_ANIMAL_VTABLE_OFFSET(%rbp), %rsi
    call *VTABLE_ANIMAL_SPEAK_OFFSET(%rsi)

    movq LCL_ANIMAL_OBJ_OFFSET(%rbp), %rdi
```

```
    movq LCL_ANIMAL_VTABLE_OFFSET(%rbp), %rsi
    call *VTABLE_ANIMAL_SPEAK_OFFSET(%rsi)

    leave
    ret
```

As you can see, the vtable is stored in %rsi. If we want to call the eat function, we use the symbol VTABLE_ANIMAL_EAT_OFFSET to know where that function lives. Therefore, VTABLE_ANIMAL_EAT_OFFSET(%rsi) contains the address of the function that will be executed. We use the * with the call instruction to let the CPU know that VTABLE_ANIMAL_EAT_OFFSET(%rsi) is not where it should jump to, but rather the memory location that holds the address where the jump should go.

Finally, we have our main function, which constructs the objects, calls doThings (passing in both the object and the correct vtable), and then destroys the objects:

vtable_main.s

```
.globl main
.section .text

main:
    .equ LCL_CAT, -8
    .equ LCL_DOG, -16

    enter $16, $0

    # Construct a cat
    call cat_new
    movq %rax, LCL_CAT(%rbp)

    # Construct a dog
    call dog_new
    movq %rax, LCL_DOG(%rbp)

    movq LCL_CAT(%rbp), %rdi          # Object
    movq $cat_vtable_animal, %rsi     # VTable
    call doThings

    movq LCL_DOG(%rbp), %rdi          # Object
    movq $dog_vtable_animal, %rsi     # VTable
    call doThings
```

```
# Destructors
movq LCL_CAT(%rbp), %rdi
call cat_destroy

movq LCL_DOG(%rbp), %rdi
call dog_destroy

leave
ret
```

To build these together, just do the following (all on one line):

```
gcc -static -o vtable vtable_main.s
    vtable_dothings.s vtable_animal.s
    vtable_dog.s vtable_cat.s
```

Then, to run it, just do ./vtable.

18.3 Inheritance

Let us say that we had a cat that made a different noise than "meow." In object-oriented programming, this is usually handled through inheritance. Inheritance allows you to define new classes that are essentially identical to the original class, but may add or replace existing methods and can add data fields.

This has many implications in how the object system works. For a simple case, let us look at a class called ScreechyCat, which, rather than saying, "Meow," says, "Screech!" Inheritance allows us to *only* code the methods that changed from the Cat class. The methods that are the same don't need to be reimplemented. The class that provides methods is known as the **superclass** (or **base class**), and the class that inherits methods is known as the **subclass** (or **derived class**).

Here is the code:

vtable_screechy.s

```
## ScreechyCat Class
.globl screechy_cat_new, screechy_cat_speak, screechy_cat_destroy
```

```
.section .data
speak_text:
    .ascii "Screech!\n\0"

.section .text
.equ SCREECHY_CAT_SIZE, 128

screechy_cat_new:
    enter $0, $0
    movq $SCREECHY_CAT_SIZE, %rdi
    call malloc
    leave
    ret

screechy_cat_speak:
    enter $0, $0
    movq stdout, %rdi
    movq $speak_text, %rsi
    call fprintf
    leave
    ret

screechy_cat_destroy:
    enter $0, $0
    call free
    leave
    ret
```

Two things to note:

1. We allocated *more* memory than the Cat class. We can allocate
    the same amount or more, but not less, because the individual
    methods that are inherited from Cat think they know what the
    layout of the data is. Therefore, while more fields can be added
    (which the original methods would then ignore because they
    aren't aware of them), the layout of the base class cannot be
    changed.

2. We didn't implement an eat method for ScreechyCat because it is inheriting that method. We could make this more clear by adding in a constant, such as .equ screechy_cat_eat, cat_eat. This would make it easier to remember, but isn't strictly required.

Next, for the vtable, the vtable for Animal for the ScreechyCat class looks like this:

vtable_screechy_animal.s

screechy_cat_vtable_animal:
   .quad screechy_cat_speak
   .quad cat_eat

Notice that since the eat method is the same for both classes, the cat_eat address is placed directly into the vtable. Object-oriented programming means that the functions that aren't overridden are copied directly into the vtable.

Now, the problem with our implementation mechanism is that if a method is called *from* a base class to an overridden method in the *same class*, there is not enough data to find the overridden method. Instead, the base class (non-overridden) method would be called.

In order to support that sort of behavior, a vtable is created for each class containing all of its methods, and this is sent with every call to methods in the class. Then, *all* calls (including calls to other functions within the same class) are called through the vtable.

This requires a significant rewrite of our system and so isn't shown here.

18.4 Runtime Type Information

Oftentimes, programs need additional information about the objects that they are working with. The program may need to know what specific class it belongs to, what interfaces it supports, or other details. This is known as **runtime type information**, and this is a common facility provided by most object-oriented languages.

The way that runtime type information is implemented is often by adding either a pointer to this data as the first field of an object (so that it is easily findable even if you don't know the type of object) or by having a function that retrieves this information be the first entry in every vtable record.

This runtime type data for a particular class is often known as a class's **metaclass**. Sometimes metaclasses are just structs with some functions defined on them, and other times they are implemented as full-blown classes themselves, themselves having a metaclass and vtables.

18.5 Duck Typing

There is another way of implementing object-oriented programming which allows for "duck typing." Duck typing comes from the old saying, "if it walks like a duck and talks like a duck, it's a duck." In other words, rather than having types and interfaces, you are allowed to attempt to call any method name on any object at all.

In this mechanism, instead of knowing exactly where the entry for the function of interest is, your code merely has an identifier for the function. That is, each function name resolves to a specific number. The object stores *all* of its method pointers as identifier/pointer pairs. Then, instead of doing a lookup on a vtable for the function, the code walks the list of functions, looking for a matching identifier. When it finds a matching identifier, *that* is the function it calls.

This requires more code for every function call, because each call requires a search through the list of functions. In some languages, this occurs in multiple stages—one for each level of superclass. Essentially, the present class is searched for implementations. Then, if not found, the superclass is then searched, then that class's superclass, and so forth.

In some languages, if no method is found, an opportunity is given to the class to *create* one at runtime. This allows for things such as autocreating database access methods based on the fields present in the database.

18.6 General Considerations

In all, object-oriented programming allows programmers to implement software in a highly dynamic way, separating out *functionality* from *implementation*. This tends to be tedious when hand-coded in assembly language. However, when produced from a programming language, this leads to flexible programs which are easy to write, read, and understand.

Therefore, assembly language programmers are much less likely to write in an object-oriented fashion. However, building an object-oriented programming language requires extensive knowledge of assembly language, even if the compiler is what ultimately generates it.

Exercises

1. Create a `Triangle` and `Rectangle` class, each of which hold the base and height of the object. Then create a method called `findArea` which calculates the area of each. Create a `Shape` interface which has this method, and encode a vtable for it.

2. Reimplement the `Cat` and `Dog` classes using duck typing. This will require assigning a unique number to represent each method name. Create a function called `call_method` which takes the object and the method number and looks up the function for the object and calls it. This will require having the first field of the object be a pointer to this method lookup table.

## CHAPTER 19

Conclusion and Acknowledgments

My goal for this book was to demystify what happens in computer programming. I think many people—even professional computer programmers—sometimes forget what is really happening under the hood. If you know assembly language, however, you can see how what you are doing in a high-level language is getting mapped onto the core constructs of assembly language. When a programming language implements a new feature, you can better understand both the feature itself and its possible limitations, because you can better imagine how it was implemented.

This is what assembly language programming has done for me, and I hope it does the same for you.

In my day job, I switch around between a lot of different languages. On a regular basis, I will program in Go, Ruby, Kotlin, Swift, Python, and JavaScript. These are all very different languages. However, knowing assembly language helps me understand their similarities and differences in a more visceral way.

Before I go, I want to say thanks to a lot of people who helped bring this book to fruition. First, I would like to thank my dad, who initially taught me to program when I was very young. He bought the family a TI-99/4A computer and taught me the basics of programming. To get a sense of how old this is, the computer did not have either a hard drive or a floppy drive, but actually made sounds that were captured by a cassette tape recorder to save and load files and programs (not kidding!). Second, I would like to thank my wife, who has always encouraged and supported me and didn't seem to mind too much when I was writing instead of doing something more productive around the house.

I would also like to thank everyone who reviewed this book ahead of time, especially Paul Cohen and Brent Shambaugh for their thorough reviews. I also want to thank Nathan Bartlett, Tavo Soto, Jonathan Ruggles, Steven Dodson, Lawrence Kincheloe,

© Jonathan Bartlett 2021
J. Bartlett, *Learn to Program with Assembly*, https://doi.org/10.1007/978-1-4842-7437-8_19

Alex Ayon, and David Bartlett for reading early versions of this manuscript and providing valuable comments. I want to thank Eric Holloway for making several helpful suggestions which contributed to this book. Finally, I want to thank Bill Parker and Randall Hyde, whose early books on Apple II assembly language (*Intermediate Apple* and *How to Program the Apple II Using 6502 Assembly Language*) first got me started programming in assembly language as a teenager.

PART IV

Appendixes

APPENDIX A

Getting Set Up with Docker

Docker is a tool that allows you to run numerous **containers** on your system at the same time. A container is similar to a virtual machine running inside your computer, but without most of the overhead of a full virtual machine. Docker also allows you to quickly and easily download third-party machine images and run them locally on your computer. Even on a Mac or Windows computer, you can run Linux images from Docker. The only requirement is that since Docker is not a true virtual machine, your computer must have an x86-64 processor. If you are running 64-bit Windows or any version of MacOS that's at least as recent as Catalina (10.15), you have the hardware you need to run the code in this book under Docker. You can also do this under Linux as well, though it is hardly necessary as Linux should already have all the tools you need.

A full discussion of Docker is outside the scope of this appendix, but there are plenty of resources available for learning about it. Here, we will only include the bare minimum to get you up and running.

Docker containers are essentially command line only. If you are not familiar with the command line, please refer to Appendix B.

You can edit files inside a Docker container, but you are essentially limited to using command line tools (again, see Appendix B). Additionally, the Docker container stops as soon as you exit the container. Finding the old, running container and restarting it is possible, but the details of that are outside the scope of this appendix. Therefore, what we are going to focus on is running a Docker container, but having the data files live on your host computer on a directory that is shared with the container. This way, all of the changes will be on your main computer, will be available to you on any container, and you can edit them from your host computer with your favorite editor. Changes will be immediately available within the Docker container for you.

© Jonathan Bartlett 2021
J. Bartlett, *Learn to Program with Assembly*, https://doi.org/10.1007/978-1-4842-7437-8_20

I have built a Docker image specifically for this book to make it really easy to get started. Assuming that Docker is installed and running successfully on your computer, to get the image up and running, just do the following steps:

1. Choose a directory on your hard drive to store your code.

2. Go into the command line on your own machine (this will be known as the "host" machine).

3. On the command line, go to the directory you chose in step 1.

4. If you are on a Mac or Linux computer, run the following command (all on one line):

    ```
    docker run -it --rm
    --mount "type=bind,src=`pwd`,target=/my-code"
    johnnyb61820/linux-assembly
    ```

Be sure that pwd is wrapped in backticks (`` ` ``), not single quotes, as this tells the computer to run the command pwd and put the result in place. If you are on a Windows computer using the traditional command prompt, instead of `` `pwd` ``, you will want to put %cd% (*without* backticks). It will look like this:

```
docker run -it --rm
--mount "type=bind,src=%cd%,target=/my-code"
johnnyb61820/linux-assembly
```

If you are using Windows PowerShell, you need to replace icode `` `pwd` `` with $pwd (again, without backticks). It will look like this:

```
docker run -it --rm
--mount "type=bind,src=$pwd,target=/my-code"
johnnyb61820/linux-assembly
```

If you don't know if you are on the traditional command prompt or PowerShell, then you should assume you are using the traditional command prompt.

The first time you run this, it will download the given image if needed (this can take a while, depending on your connection speed). After the download is finished, it will give you an interactive Linux terminal in a new container that is outfitted with all of the tools you need. In the container, the directory will be called /my-code, but this will actually have the directory from your host computer mounted in. Any changes either on the container or on the host will be immediately reflected on the other side, because you are sharing the directory between them.

The parts of this command line are fairly straightforward. `docker run` tells Docker to run a new container. The `-it` flag will allow the Docker instance to act as a console. The `--rm` flag tells Docker that when you exit the container to delete it.[1] The `--mount` flag and its arguments tell Docker to mount a directory from the host machine on the new container. We are using a *bind mount* which makes a directory from the host machine available to the container. The source on the host machine is simply the current working directory (which is what `` `pwd` `` discovers or, on Windows, what %cd% means). It is set to mount the directory onto the /my-code directory on the host machine, which is the directory that the container is set to start you in. This means that, after starting the container, you will be in the /my-code directory, but it will have all the same files as the directory you were in on your host computer. Essentially, it will be like nothing happened except that now you are on a Linux machine with the Linux developer toolchain available to you. The final argument, `johnnyb61820/linux-assembly`, is the image you want to run. If this is your first time running the command, Docker will download the image for you and then run it. From that moment on, you will have the image on your computer, and Docker will not need to download it again.

To verify that you are running inside the container, run `as --version`. This should print information about the tool (the GNU assembler), including the system it was built to target. It should include some text about the target being `x86_64-linux-gnu`. If it says that the command isn't found or that the target is `x86_64-apple-darwin`, then you are not inside the container.

---

[1] This sounds more destructive than it really is. Remember, all of your files are actually stored on the host machine, so this simply keeps stopped containers from building up on your system. Of course, it isn't really harmful to leave stopped containers around as they utilize practically zero resources. Each container *shares* its base image files, so running new containers doesn't take up any significant disk space (just a few kilobytes for overhead), and if they are stopped, then they don't take up any memory or processing power.

APPENDIX B

The Command Line

The **command line** is one of the most useful tools for a programmer in the long run, but it is one that is tucked and hidden away from ordinary users. With the command line, instead of pointing and clicking to tell the computer what to do, you type commands that the computer reads and then runs. For the most part, each command is actually its own tiny (or not so tiny) program that does just one job for you. It is like a mini programming language that executes as you type each line.

B.1 Why Use the Command Line

It may sound a little scary, but there was a time not so long ago when *everyone* accessed their computer through the command line. Everybody from salespeople to secretaries to managers to programmers. In the days before Mac and Windows, the command line was how everybody worked with their computers.

Today, almost no one even knows what the command line is. Operating system developers have buried it far in the dusty corners of the computer. Nonetheless, for a computer programmer, having a basic comfort level with the command line is essential. You can think of the command line as an unfiltered dialog between you and the computer. Pretty much all of the graphical tools associated with modern computers are there to filter your dialog with your computer. The menus and buttons are there to *limit* what you can do. For ordinary users, this limitation is great. It prevents the user from doing the wrong thing. But, for the programmer, the effect is reversed. Ultimately, the entire reason to program computers in the first place is because you want the computer to do something that the original creators of the computer didn't expect. And, to do that, such limitations get in your way rather than help you forward.

Additionally, in a web-oriented world, the command line gives you the most straightforward access to remote computers. While we won't cover remotely logging into computers here, I can tell you that knowing the command line is essential for administering and debugging computers remotely.

257

© Jonathan Bartlett 2021
J. Bartlett, *Learn to Program with Assembly*, https://doi.org/10.1007/978-1-4842-7437-8_21

For this book, there is another, more practical reason to use the command line. Programs that run on the command line are much easier to *write* than graphical programs. When writing graphical programs, you have to setup menus, position icons, etc. Command line programs don't need any of that. In fact, your first program will only be three instructions long—hardly enough to get a windowed application even up and running.

In any case, this book assumes at least a passing familiarity with the command line. If you have never used the command line before, this appendix is meant to help get you started. There are, unfortunately, some differences between the command line on all of the platforms—Mac, Windows, and Linux—though thankfully the differences between Mac and Linux are hardly noticeable.

B.2 Starting the Command Line

As mentioned, the command line is pretty well buried on most computers. Here is how to start it one each platform:

> **Mac**: On a Mac, open up your Finder (usually it's the smiley-face guy at the bottom-left of your Dock), then go into "Applications", then go into "Utilities." In that folder, you will find a program called "Terminal." Opening that program will bring up the command line. I recommend dragging the Terminal application to your Dock so that you can easily access it later.

> **Windows**: On Windows, you can find the command line by opening the "Run box" by holding down the Windows key and pressing R. This will bring up a dialog asking you what you want to run. Just type in cmd and then click "OK." This will bring up the command line.

> **Linux**: On Linux, it varies by distribution. However, since Linux is usually geared toward more advanced users, the command line is usually somewhere in the standard menus. Look for menu items saying, "Command Prompt," "Terminal," "Shell," etc.

When the command line starts up, it is usually a black background with white text. You generally can't use your mouse at all within the command line. Think back to the early days of computers before there was a mouse attached, and you only had a single black screen and no graphics—only text. The command line is a window into that world.

Try pressing the return key. Notice that it goes to the next line. The text to the left of your cursor is known as the **command prompt**. The actual text is highly dependent on your operating system, but it usually gives you status information such as your username and the name of the computer. It also usually tells you what directory you are in.

Now, the specific instructions that are available at the command line depends on both your operating system (which has the commands as programs) and the **shell**, which is what reads your commands and interprets them to the operating system (and implements some of the commands directly). Thankfully, for what we will be doing, the different shells behave similarly.

It's not incredibly important, but common shells include:

> **Bash** This is the most common shell on Linux, and is also the default shell on older Macs. Bash stands for "Bourne Again Shell," which is a joke based on the fact that it is a revision of the older "Bourne Shell," originally developed by Stephen Bourne. If you're not a fan of bad puns, it's possible that the world of programming may not be your cup of tea.

> **Z Shell** Starting with Catalina, Macs usually default to the Z Shell, or zsh. It is similar to Bash, but newer, more customizable, and is more consistent than Bash.

> **Windows Command Shell** This is the shell that is run by default on Windows when you run the cmd command mentioned above.

> **Windows Powershell** For more advanced users, Windows also offers Powershell, which is similar to the Windows Command Shell, but is more integrated into the operating system. Windows Command Shell is somewhat of a holdover from the DOS days.[1] It's preferred for this book because it is more widely available and easier to get access to than Powershell, but professional Windows programmers tend to use Powershell instead.

---

[1] DOS stands for "Disk Operating System" and was the command line operating system that PCs ran before Windows became available.

As a note, be aware that most people use the terms "command line," "command prompt," "terminal," and "shell" pretty interchangeably.

B.3 Navigating Your Computer Using the Command Line

When the command line comes up, you are "in" a directory on your computer. This is known as the **current directory** or **working directory**. This is likely your **home directory**, which, on most computers, is the directory above all of the typical directories you think of on your computer—your desktop (which is itself a directory), the "Photos" directory, the "Documents" directory, etc. Your home directory contains these.

However, your home directory itself is embedded within the filesystem of the computer as a whole. To see exactly where you are on the computer, you will need to print the working directory. On most shells, you can do this by typing pwd and pressing enter (you tell the computer you are finished typing your command by pressing enter). However, on the Windows Command Shell, you type in echo %cd% instead.

To see the files in the current directory, just type in dir.[2] This will print out a list of all of the files in your current directory.

On Mac and Linux, all of your hard drives are contained within the same filesystem. However, on Windows, the different drives get assigned a letter. The standard hard drive is usually the C: drive (drive letters are followed by a colon). To change the drive that you are on in Windows, just type the name of the drive followed by a colon and then press enter. For instance, to change to the E: drive, just type E:.

Then, for all shells, to change the directory, you would use the cd (change directory) command. For new users, it is best to only change one directory at a time. For instance, to go into your "Desktop" directory, you would do cd Desktop. Note that, since the command line uses spaces to separate parts of the command, if the directory you want to go in to contains a space, you will need to group the name together by enclosing the name of the directory in double-quotes. For instance, if the directory you want to go into is named "My Directory" then, to go into it, you would type cd "My Directory".

If you want to go "up" (to the directory that is above your current directory), you can do cd .. . The .. directory is a special directory which always refers to the directory

---

[2] On some Linux systems, dir is not available, and you will need to type in ls instead.

that contains the current directory. Similarly, the . directory always refers to the current directory.

Another important note is that, on Windows, directories are separated by backslashes (\) and, on the other operating systems, directories are separated by ordinary forward slashes (/).

To create a new directory inside the current one, use the mkdir command. To create a directory called "MyStuff" you would issue the command mkdir MyStuff. Again, if you want it to contain spaces, you need to enclose it in double-quotes.

You should practice navigating through the directories on your computer to get used to it.

If you want to view a file, you can do that on the command line as well. However, most files will just look like gibberish because they are not written to be displayed on the command line (they aren't pure text, even if they contain text). If the file is called myfile.txt, then, on Linux and Mac, you would do this by typing cat myfile.txt, and on Windows you would do this by typing type myfile.txt.

B.4 Running Programs

You have already been running programs on the command line. The dir command is actually a separate program that lists out the directories for you.[3] Shells contain a variable called the **path** which tells them the standard places where they should look for programs. For example, on my computer, the dir command is actually in the /bin directory. Since /bin is in my path, the shell finds this command when I run it.

However, if a command you want to run isn't in your path, you have to specify exactly where the program exists. That's why, in this book, when you run your own programs, you are always going to start them with a ./ before the name of the program. For instance, to run the first program in the book, you will run ./myexit (no spaces).

---

[3] Commands which change the state of the shell itself are usually implemented by the shell instead of as a separate program. For instance, the cd command isn't a separate program, because it is changing where your current shell is running. However, dir takes your current directory, and then just prints out what is there and returns to the shell, so it is implemented as a separate program.

This tells the computer that you want it to run the command in the . directory (i.e., the current directory) named myexit.[4]

Every command exits with a **status code**, which is a number between 0 and 255 which represents the status that the program exited with. For most programs, the status code will just be 0, which means the program exited without problems. However, we will use the status code quite a bit in the first part of the book to send back results of the program before we get into proper input and output.

To see the exit status of the last command you ran, type the command echo $?. This only works on Linux, but you won't need an equivalent command on Windows.

B.5 The Environment

One other thing to note is that we will occasionally refer to the **environment** or to **environment variables**. The environment is a set of values that is passed into a program without being explicitly set on the command line. Essentially, you carry your environment with you on the command line, and any command you execute inherits your current environment variables. On the whole, the environment is ignorable—you don't have to worry about it in most cases. However, for the cases where environment variables need to be set, read on.

To set an environment variable, you do export VARNAME=VALUE. This will set the environment variable VARNAME to be equal to VALUE. This will be automatically set in any program you run going forward until you log out. To unset the variable, do unset VARNAME. For the most part, unless the program is looking for a specific environment variable, it will be ignored by the program. However, some environment variables do important things.

Just remember that if you log out, all of your environment variables will be reset to their defaults, so if you want to have them you will have to enter them in again. Also, if you accidentally set an environment variable that causes problems, just logging out and logging back in will fix the problem. This issue is especially pertinent for Chapter 15.

---

[4] Note that, on Windows, this would actually be .myexit, but, you will be running all of these things on Docker, which gives you a Linux machine inside your Windows machine. Therefore, when you actually run the command, you will run it as ./myexit, because, even though you got there *through* the Windows Command Shell, you are actually running Linux at that point.

B.6 Editing Files

Even people who use the command line regularly tend to edit files using graphical (non-command line) programs. Additionally, editing a file in the command line depends highly on what command line editors are installed. However, if you are using the Docker image mentioned in Appendix A, I installed several common command line editors for you.

To edit a file, just type the name of the editor followed by the name of the file to edit. For instance, to use the `nano` editor to edit a file named `myfile.txt`, just run `nano myfile.txt`. The file doesn't have to exist before running the command. When you save the file from the editor, it will create it if it doesn't already exist.

Editors included with the Docker image include `nano`, `mle`, `tilde`, `jed`, `mg`, `emacs`, and `vi`. We are going to focus on `nano` because it is the easiest for basic editing. Others are better for more advanced usage (I've written most of my books using `vi`), but they are harder to learn the basics.[5]

`nanoa` is nice because it gives you the list of common commands at the bottom of the screen for reference. The ^ character means to hold down the Ctrl key while pressing the other key. With `nano` you can just type like normal. You can use your arrow keys to move around (remember, the mouse doesn't work at the command line!) and then type in control-o to save and control-x to exit.

B.7 Other Modifications to Your Computer

Another thing you should consider doing to your computer is to tell it to display file extensions. The *extension* is the three- or four-letter code that is tacked on to filenames on your computer (after a period) to tell the computer (and you) what format the file is and/or what application should open the file. Word documents, for instance, have an extension of `.doc` or `.docx`, Excel files have an extension of `.xls` or `.xlsx`, and pure text files that aren't used for programming have an extension of `.txt`. This extension is

---

[5] In fact, even saving and quitting the programs can be difficult in many editors. If you want to try something other than nano be sure to research how to use the them *before* starting them, though you can always just close the window if you get stuck.

actually a part of the name of the file, but many operating systems hide these to make it easier on the user.[6]

As a computer program, you *need* to see all of the intricacies of what is going on in your computer, so it is best to enable seeing file extensions. Every version of every operating system puts this in a different place, so I can only give you a broad description of how to find it. If you open up your file browser (Finder on the Mac, Explorer on Windows), you can usually find the option somewhere in the preferences menu, possibly under some sort of "advanced" section of the menus.

---

[6] In my opinion, this actually makes it harder for the user for a lot of reasons. Many operating system writers these days prefer *lying* to users (i.e., not telling them the full name of the file) instead of *explaining* things to users. This is one of the many things that makes users more disconnected from the technology they rely on, and keeps them in ignorance rather than help them gain understanding about what their computer does. The long-term effect is that a lot of things are happening that the user doesn't understand because relevant information was hidden from them. This is supposed to be a *simplification*, but I've generally found that there is a difference between *simplifying* the truth and *distorting* the truth, and, unfortunately, modern frontend developers tend towards the latter.

APPENDIX C

Debugging with GDB

The primary intention of this book is to teach you how the computer works under the hood. As such, I don't spend a lot of time focusing on debugging. Nevertheless, the standard GNU debugger (GDB) has support for assembly language programming if things go awry and you are having trouble figuring it out.

One of the nice things about knowing assembly language is that you can use GDB to debug any compiled program, even those without debugging information. Since they all compile to the same machine code, they will all work successfully with GDB, even if there is no debugging code included.

C.1 Starting GDB

To start GDB, simply type in `gdb` on the command line. This will give you a prompt that looks like this:

```
(gdb) _
```

At the prompt, type

```
file FILENAME
```

where `FILENAME` is the path to the program you want to run. This will load the program into the debugger.

You can run the program by just typing in `run`, but, since you haven't told it where to stop, this will simply run the program to completion, which is probably not what you are wanting to do if you plan on debugging your program.

So, before running the program, you need to tell the debugger where to stop. This is known as a **breakpoint**. To add a breakpoint to the entry point of the program (i.e., `_start`), you just issue the following command:

```
break *_start
```

© Jonathan Bartlett 2021
J. Bartlett, *Learn to Program with Assembly*, https://doi.org/10.1007/978-1-4842-7437-8_22

The * just means that _start refers to an address in memory. In this particular case, if you left it out, GDB would know what you mean, but I recommend you keep it there because, in other cases, GDB might not know what you mean.

Now, you can run the program using the run command:

```
run
```

This will immediately stop, letting you know that the debugging hit the breakpoint that you added.

C.2 Stepping Through Code

So, now you are actively debugging your program, what can you do?

Remember that, to the computer, you code is actually machine code—lots of bytes strung together into machine-readable instructions. Therefore, what you will want to do is to have the debugger **disassemble** the machine code for you. Since the process of converting assembly language to machine code is known as assembling, the process of converting machine code back to assembly language is known as disassembling. However, remember that any fanciness that you put in your code (comments, local labels, etc.) are thrown away during the assembly process. Therefore, the resulting assembly code will be very simplistic.

To see the disassembly of the present function, simply issue the following command:

```
disassemble
```

The following is the disassembled code from the myexit.s file from Chapter 3:

```
(gdb) disassemble
Dump of assembler code for function _start:
=> 0x0000000000401000 <+0>:      mov     $0x3c,%rax
   0x0000000000401007 <+7>:      mov     $0x3,%rdi
   0x000000000040100e <+14>:     syscall
End of assembler dump.
(gdb) _
```

The arrow (=>) points to the current instruction. The long hexadecimal number (0x0000000000401000) is the address of the instruction. The number next to it (<+0>) is the *offset* from the start of the nearest previous label or function (_start). To the right of that is the next instruction it will execute, which is the first instruction in our program. Also note that the value that we will store in the register is given in hexadecimal. Remember, the computer has no idea that you originally typed that value in decimal, so it can't know to tell it to you in decimal.

To see the value of your registers, you can simply type the following:

```
info registers
```

This will provide a complete dump of all your registers. Notice at the present moment that most of our registers are initialized to zero. Since the first instruction has not executed yet, %rax is also zero.

The register values are given in two columns. The left column is the raw value. The right column is the debugger's attempt to interpret your value. Ultimately, the left column is the "official" value, but the right column may give additional important context. It may translate a value into an offset from an address, translate a hexadecimal number into a decimal, etc.

To go to the next instruction, simply type the following:

```
stepi
```

This will step to the next machine instruction. If you issue the disassemble command again, it will put the arrow on the next line of code. If you issue an info registers command, you will see that %rax is now set to 0x3c.

Running stepi again will take you to the next line. Running stepi again will have it issue the system call. Since the system call exits the program, the debugger will report the following:

```
[Inferior 1 (process 152) exited with code 03]
```

"Inferior 1" is simply GDB's internal name for our process. The exit code is the value that it would have given back to the shell.

C.3 Managing Breakpoints

In addition to stepping through the code, you can also just set breakpoints wherever you wish. If you have a symbol that the debugger knows about (because it is declared with .globl), you can add breakpoints directly to these locations just like we did for _start. You can add as many breakpoints as you wish.

To get a list of all of your defined breakpoints, use the command `info break`. This will give a list of your breakpoints, each with a number that the debugger uses to reference it. To remove a breakpoint, do `delete NUMBER`, where `NUMBER` is the number of the breakpoint you wish to remove (as revealed by `info break`). Note that this does *not* renumber the breakpoints. Even if you add a breakpoint back, it will be created with a new number.

Additionally, you can throw in breakpoints at any point within an assembly language function. When you ran the `disassemble` command, the debugger gave all of the addresses of each instruction. You can add a breakpoint to any instruction you want just by doing `break *ADDRESS`, where `ADDRESS` is the memory address of the instruction (as given by GDB) that you want to break before. Alternatively, you can use the offsets GDB gives you from the start of the function. When we disassembled `myexit.s`, the second instruction was listed as having an offset of +7. Therefore, I can add a breakpoint to that instruction by saying `break *_start+7`.

If I want to add a breakpoint to the interior of a function I haven't arrived at yet, I can disassemble that particular function by giving GDB the command `disassemble MYFUNCTION`, where `MYFUNCTION` is the label of the code I want to disassemble. You can also give an address instead of the name of a function (but don't prefix it with * like you did in the `break` command).

C.4 Printing Values

In addition to displaying all of the register values, you can also display them individually with the `print` command. However, in GDB, to print out a register, it has to be prefixed with a $ instead of a %. Therefore, to print the contents of `%rax`, you would issue `print $rax`. Now, you can specify what format you want this value to be displayed in by adding in a format code. `print/d` prints the value as a decimal, `print/x` prints the value as hexadecimal, `print/t` prints the value as a binary, `print/c` prints the value as a character, and `print/f` prints the value as a floating-point value.

While printing out register values is useful, we often want to print out values in memory as well. For this, we will need to tell the computer what kind of value it needs to print. However, the GNU debugger was actually primarily built around the C programming language. Therefore, you will need to "cast" the value into a type understood by GDB.

So, if there is a memory location that contains a quadword, called `myQuadword`, I could print it out by saying: `print/d (long long)myQuadword`. Here `(long long)` is the name of the C type that represents quadwords. So, `(long long)myQuadword` casts the value into the given type. Basic C types include:

- `char` (single byte)

- `short` (2 bytes)

- `int` or `long` (4 bytes)

- `long long` (8 bytes)

- `float` (4-byte floating-point value)

- `double` (8-byte floating-point value)

- `int *` (8-byte pointer to an int type)

- `void *` (8-byte pointer to an undetermined type)

- `void **` (8-byte pointer to an eight-byte pointer to an undetermined type)

You can also add in a * to *dereference* (look up the value for) a pointer. Let's say that `%rax` contained a pointer to an integer. We could look up that value by doing

```
print/d *(int *)$rax
```

For more information on using the GNU debugger, you can check the manual out at: `https://sourceware.org/gdb/current/onlinedocs/gdb/`.

APPENDIX D

Nasm (Intel) Assembly Language Syntax

This book has focused on the assembly language syntax used by the GNU Assembler, known as AT&T syntax, because it originated on Unix which was, at the time, developed by AT&T (the phone company). The reason for this is that it is the "native" syntax used in the Linux kernel and output by the GNU Compiler Collection. However, there is another syntax that is commonly used, which is known as "Nasm" Syntax (named after the popular assembler that uses it) or "Intel" syntax (because this is the syntax used in Intel's manuals on their chips). If you want to learn new instructions from Intel's manuals, you need to know Intel syntax, and this short guide should help you with most differences.

D.1 Capitalization

This is not a real difference per se, but, conventionally, in AT&T syntax instruction, names and register names are written in lowercase. In Nasm Syntax, the convention is to use all uppercase. Therefore, the `mul` instruction is actually `MUL` in Nasm Syntax. Again, this is a convention, not a requirement, but I've also found that following this convention helps you realize which syntax you should be thinking about.

D.2 Register Naming and Immediate-Mode Prefixes

While register names are prefixed in AT&T syntax with a % sign, registers in Nasm Syntax are not prefixed at all. Therefore, you would refer to `%rax` as just RAX.

Additionally, immediate-mode values do not have the $ prefixes in Nasm Syntax. The number 1 is just 1, not $1.

© Jonathan Bartlett 2021
J. Bartlett, *Learn to Program with Assembly*, https://doi.org/10.1007/978-1-4842-7437-8_23

D.3 Operand Order

The most difficult difference to overcome is the difference in operator order. Basically, in every instruction, Intel syntax reverses the order of its operands. The destination is placed first, and the remaining arguments, if any, are after. So, for instance, the instruction `mov %rax, %rdx` in AT&T syntax would be `MOV RDX, RAX` in Nasm Syntax.

D.4 Specifying Memory Addressing Modes

Addressing modes in Nasm Syntax are also different from AT&T syntax. Just like AT&T syntax, in Nasm Syntax, you can leave off any part of the addressing mode, and it will assume it is zero (or 1 for the multiplier). If you remember from Chapter 6, the full format for a memory address reference in AT&T syntax is

```
VALUE(BASEREG, IDXREG, MULTIPLIER)
```

The formula to compute the final address is

```
address = VALUE + BASEREG + IDXREG * MULTIPLIER
```

For Nasm Syntax, memory references are always enclosed in brackets and look like this:

```
[BASEREG + IDXREG*MULTIPLIER + VALUE]
```

Interestingly, this literally tells you how to compute the address as well. You can also reorder the values in the brackets as desired for clarity.

D.5 Specifying Operand Sizes

In AT&T syntax, we normally add a suffix to the instruction indicating what "size" of data we are using: q for quadword (64-bit) values, l for 32-bit values, w for 16-bit values, and b for single-byte values.

In Nasm Syntax, the size is applied to the *operand* not the *instruction*. Additionally, since the place where size is unknown is on pointers (register sizes are pretty obvious and immediate-mode sizes are inferable from context), these operands are prefixed with `SIZE PTR` where `SIZE` is one of `QWORD`, `DWORD`, `WORD`, or `BYTE`.[1]

So, to move the number 1 to a byte of memory specified by the label `myvalue`, you would do `MOV BYTE PTR [myvalue], 1`.

---

[1] On vector extensions, these can also be XMMWORD, YMMWORD, and ZMMWORD. See Appendix F for more information on what XMM, YMM, and ZMM refers to.

APPENDIX E

Common x86-64 Instructions

The following commands are given by their instruction family name. For instance, movq, movl, etc. are simply referred to by their family name, mov. Since registers often need to be referred to in the description, we will refer to their 64-bit version, but if you are using a smaller version of the command, you will usually be using the smaller version of the register. For instance, on the mul command, the table describes its function as working with %rax, but mull would be working with %eax instead, and mulw would be working with %ax.

Note that when %rax and %rdx are combined to act as a larger value, %rax contains the low-order bits and %rdx contains the high-order bits.

To keep the table abbreviated, many caveats for using each instruction are ignored. For a full description of the full functionality of each instruction, AMD and Intel each have instruction manuals clocking in at well over 600 pages each (which is why this appendix aims to simplify). The AMD manual is the *AMD64 Architecture Programmer's Manual Volume 3* and the Intel manual is the *Intel 64 and IA-32 Architectures Software Developer's Manual Volume 2.*

E.1 Data Moving Instructions

Instruction	Meaning	Chapter
mov SRC, DST	Moves the value stored in SRC into the location designated by DST.	3
lea SRC, DST	Moves the address indicated by SRC into the location designated by DST.	6
xchg SRC, DST	Swaps the values in SRC and DST.	7
bswap DST	Reverses the bytes of a destination register (32-bit or 64-bit registers only).	7

© Jonathan Bartlett 2021
J. Bartlett, *Learn to Program with Assembly*, https://doi.org/10.1007/978-1-4842-7437-8_24

E.2 Arithmetic Instructions

Instruction	Meaning	Chapter
add SRC, DST	Adds the contents of SRC to DST and stores the result in DST.	4
sub SRC, DST	Subtracts the contents of SRC from DST and stores the result in DST.	4
mul SRC	Multiplies %rax by SRC and stores the result in the combined registers %rax and %rdx. Treats all values as unsigned.	4
div SRC	Divides the combined %rax and %rdx by SRC and stores the result in %rax and the remainder in %rdx. If just using %rax to store the dividend, it is wise to explicitly set %rdx to zero. Treats all values as unsigned.	4
inc DST	Increments the value (adds one) at the location designated by DST.	4
dec DST	Decrements the value (subtracts one) at the location designated by DST.	4
idiv SRC	Similar to div but performs a signed integer division.	8
imul SRC	Similar to mul but performs a signed integer multiplication.	8
adc SRC, DST	Add with carry. Similar to add, but also adds one if the carry flag is set.	8

E.3 Stack Instructions

Instruction	Meaning	Chapter
push SRC	Pushes the given value onto the stack. Decrements %rsp by the size of the value in SRC and then moves the value stored in SRC into the location specified by the new value of %rsp.	11
pop DST	Pops off the value from the current location of the stack. Moves the value stored in the location specified by %rsp into DST and then adds the size of DST to %rsp.	11

E.4 Comparison, Branching, and Looping Instructions

Instruction	Meaning	Chapter
cmp SRC, DST	Compares SRC to DST by performing a virtual subtraction (subtracting SRC from DST), but only sets flags.	5
test SRC, DST	Performs a logical AND to the two arguments and then sets flags according to the result.	8
jmp DST	Jumps to the value specified by DST.	5
jmp (DST)	Jumps (sets the program counter) to the address specified by the register DST.	9
jmp *DST	Indirect jump. Looks up the value in the address specified by DST and sets the program counter to that address.	9
jCC DST	Conditional jump. CC is the condition code which tells which conditions (based on the %eflags register) it should jump on.	5
loop DST	Decrements %rcx and then jumps to DST if %rcx is not zero.	5
loopne DST	Similar to loop, but also will not jump if the zero flag (ZF) is set.	5
loope DST	Similar to loop, but also will not jump if the zero flag (ZF) is not set.	5

E.5 Status Flag Manipulation Instructions

Instruction	Meaning	Chapter
sahf	Stores the contents of %ah into %eflags.	9
lahf	Stores the contents of %eflags into %ah.	9
clc	Clears the carry flag (CF).	9
setc	Sets the carry flag (CF).	9
cld	Clears the direction flag (DF).	9
setd	Sets the direction flag (DF).	9

E.6 Bit Operations

Instruction	Meaning	Chapter
and SRC, DST	Does a logical AND of each bit in both SRC and DST and stores the resulting value in DST.	9
or SRC, DST	Does a logical OR of each bit in both SRC and DST and stores the resulting value in DST.	9
xor SRC, DST	Does a logical XOR of each bit in both SRC and DST and stores the resulting value in DST.	9
nor SRC, DST	Does a logical NOR of each bit in both SRC and DST and stores the resulting value in DST.	9
not DST	Does a logical NOT of each bit in DST and stores the result in DST.	9
shl DST	Shifts the bits of DST to the left (toward the most significant bit). Bits that are shifted off are discarded, and "new" bits shifted in from the right are zero.	9
shr DST	Shifts the bits of DST to the right (toward the least significant bit). Bits that are shifted off are discarded, and "new" bits shifted in from the left are zero.	9
rol DST	Rotates (shifts) the bits of DST to the left (toward the most significant bit). Bits that are shifted off to the left are used as the "new" bits shifted in from the right.	9
ror DST	Rotates (shifts) the bits of DST to the right (toward the least significant bit). Bits that are shifted off to the right are used as the "new" bits shifted in from the left.	9
bsf SRC, DST	Searches SRC for the first nonzero bit it finds (starting at the least significant bit as bit 0) and stores the index of that bit in DST. DST must be a register.	9
bsr SRC, DST	Searches SRC for the first nonzero bit it finds (starting at the most significant bit) and stores the index of that bit in DST. DST must be a register.	9
lzcnt SRC, DST	Counts the number of leading zeroes of the value in SRC and stores that count in DST. DST must be a register.	9

E.7 Invocation-Oriented Instructions

Instruction	Meaning	Chapter
syscall	Invokes a "system call"—transfers control to the operating system.	3, 10
call DST	Calls a function. This pushes the address of the next instruction (the return address) onto the stack and transfers control to DST.	11
enter $SIZE, $0	Sets up a stack frame by (a) pushing %rbp onto the stack, (b) copying %rsp to %rbp, and (c) subtracting SIZE bytes from %rsp to make room for local variables on the stack.	11
leave	Tears down a stack frame by (a) copying %rbp to %rsp and (b) popping %rbp from the stack.	11
ret	Returns from a function call. Pops the return address off of the stack and transfers control to that address.	11

E.8 String and Memory Block Instructions

Instruction	Meaning	Chapter
movs	Loads a value from the address specified in %rsi and stores the value in the address specified in %rdi. It then moves both %rsi and %rdi to the "next" address based on the direction flag (DF).	9
cmps	Loads values from the addresses in %rsi and %rdi and compares them, setting %eflags. It then moves both %rsi and %rdi to the "next" address based on the direction flag (DF).	9
scas	Loads a value from the address specified by %rdi and compares that value with %rax (modifying %eflags) and moves %rdi to the "next" address based on the direction flag (DF). This instruction can be prefixed with repne to repeat as long as the value is not equal.	9

(continued)

Instruction	Meaning	Chapter
rep	This can be used as a prefix for the preceding instructions. Adding this as a prefix causes the given instruction to repeat, each time decrementing %rcx. The repetition ceases when %rcx is zero.	9
repe	This is similar to rep but also will terminate if the zero flag (ZF) is set.	9
repne	This is similar to rep but also will terminate if the zero flag (ZF) is not set.	9

E.9 SSE Instructions

These instructions generally use an XMM register as at least one of the parameters, usually implied by the operation. When these operations refer to *types*, available types are

- Single-value single-precision floating point (ss)
- Single-value double-precision floating point (sd)
- Single-value double-word integer (si)
- Single-value double quadword integer (dq)
- Packed single-precision floating point (ps)
- Packed double-precision floating point (pd)
- Packed double-word integer (pi or sometimes pd)
- Packed quadword integer (pq)
- Packed byte integer (pb)
- Packed word integer (pw)

Note that in the parallel integer adding instructions, the p and the size (i.e., b, w, d, and q) are separated by the instruction name itself. In other words, instead of addpq, the instruction is actually paddq.

Instruction	Meaning	Chapter
movsd SRC, DST	Moves SRC into the low-order 8 bytes of DST without affecting the high-order 8 bytes.	F
movss SRC, DST	Moves SRC into the low-order 4 bytes of DST without affecting the higher-order bytes.	F
movaps SRC, DST	Moves a 128-bit value into DST. Causes an exception if the value is not aligned. Optimized for floating-point values.	F
movups SRC, DST	Moves a 128-bit value into DST. Does not cause an exception if the value is not aligned. Optimized for floating-point values.	F
movdqa SRC, DST	Moves a 128-bit value into DST. Causes an exception if the value is not aligned. Optimized for integer values.	F
movdqu SRC, DST	Moves a 128-bit value into DST. Does not cause an exception if the value is not aligned. Optimized for integer values.	F
pslldq VAL, DST	Shifts the value in SRC to the left by VAL bytes.	F
psrldq VAL, DST	Shifts the value in SRC to the right by VAL bytes.	F
addXX SRC, DST	Does a parallel add of SRC to DST and stores the result in DST (only valid for floating-point values).	F
subXX SRC, DST	Does a parallel subtract of SRC from DST and stores the result in DST (only valid for floating-point values).	F
mulXX SRC, DST	Does a parallel multiply of SRC and DST and stores the result in DST (only valid for floating-point values).	F
divXX SRC, DST	Does a parallel divide of DST by SRC and stores the result in DST (only valid for floating-point values)	F
paddX SRC, DST	Does a parallel add of SRC to DST and stores the result in DST (only valid for integer values).	F
psubX SRC, DST	Does a parallel subtract of SRC from DST and stores the result in DST (only valid for integer values).	F
pmulX SRC, DST	Does a parallel multiply of SRC and DST and stores the result in DST (only valid for integer values).	F

(continued)

281

Instruction	Meaning	Chapter
pdivX SRC, DST	Does a parallel divide of DST by SRC and stores the result in DST (only valid for integer values)	F
cvtXX2YY SRC, DST	Converts the low-order bytes of SRC from a type given by XX into the low-order bytes of DST with a type given by YY. Not available for all types and combinations.	F

E.10 Miscellaneous Instructions

Instruction	Meaning	Chapter
lock	This is a prefix that can be tied to memory-oriented instructions that guarantee that we have exclusive access to the cache for that address.	K
nop	Performs a "no-operation" operation.	9

APPENDIX F

Floating-Point Numbers

So far, the only numbers we've dealt with are integers—numbers with no decimal point. Computers have a general problem with numbers with decimal points, because computers can only store fixed-size, finite values. Decimal numbers can be any length, including infinite length (think of a repeating decimal, like the result of 1/3).

The way a computer handles decimals is by storing them at a fixed **precision** (number of significant bits). A computer stores decimal numbers in three parts—the sign bit, the **exponent**, and the **mantissa**. The mantissa contains the actual digits that will be used, and the exponent is what magnitude the number is. For example, 12345.2 can be represented as 1.23452 * 10^4. The mantissa is 1.23452 and the exponent is 4 with a base of 10. Computers, however, use a base of 2. All numbers are stored as X.XXXXX * 2^XXXX. The number 1, for example, is stored as 1.00000 * 2^0. This way of storing numbers is known as a **floating-point** representation, because the position of the significant digits with respect to the decimal point can vary based on the exponent.

Now, the mantissa and the exponent are only so long, which leads to some interesting problems. For example, when a computer stores an integer, if you add 1 to it, the resulting number is one larger. This does not necessarily happen with floating-point numbers. If the number is sufficiently big, adding 1 to it might not even register in the mantissa (remember, both parts are only so long). This affects several things, especially order of operations. If you add 1.0 to a given floating-point number, it might not even affect the number if it is large enough. For example, on x86 platforms, a 4-byte floating-point number, although it can represent very large numbers, cannot have 1.0 added to it past 16777216.0, because it is no longer significant. The number no longer changes when 1.0 is added to it. So, if there is a multiplication of two numbers that are added together, doing the addition first may give different results than if the multiplication were distributed. For instance, `1000.0 * (16777216.0 + 1.0)` gives a different result than `1000.0 * 16777216.0 + 1000.0 * 1.0`. The former yields `16777216000.0` while the latter yields `16777217024.0` (which is still not exactly correct).

© Jonathan Bartlett 2021
J. Bartlett, *Learn to Program with Assembly*, https://doi.org/10.1007/978-1-4842-7437-8_25

The way that these are stored in memory is in a format known as IEEE 754. The details are a little weird (and outside the scope of this book), but, in general, for double-precision (64-bit) values, 1 bit is reserved for the sign, 11 bits are reserved for the exponent, and 52 bits are reserved for the mantissa. For single-precision (32-bit) values, 1 bit is reserved for the sign, 8 bits are reserved for the exponent, and 23 bits are reserved for the mantissa.

You should note that it takes most computers a lot longer to do floating-point arithmetic than it does integer arithmetic. So, for programs that really need speed, integers are mostly used.

There are a lot of features/considerations available for floating-point and vector (multiple value simultaneously) operations on x86-64. This appendix is simply to introduce the topic, not provide a complete reference.

F.1 History

The floating-point unit for x86 architectures has been through several iterations. The original 8086 chip had no support for floating point, and everything had to be done manually. Floating-point support was initially added with a co-processor, the 8087, where the processor deferred relevant instructions to the co-processor. The 8087 had an 80-bit floating-point value. It had eight registers arranged as a stack, known as the FPU (floating-point unit) stack, and operations mostly revolved around the "top" value of the stack. By the time the 80486 rolled around, the floating-point unit was integrated into the chip.

Then, to extend floating-point support (and add parallel operations), Intel and AMD each added additional instructions, where Intel's was known as "MMX" and AMD's was known as "3DNow!". Intel's MMX added eight special registers for floating point, naming them %mm0 through %mm7. These registers can be accessed directly, rather than having to go through a stack.

For the Pentium III, Intel added a set of instructions similar to 3DNow! known as SSE (Streaming SIMD Extensions) which uses a set of eight registers known as XMM registers (%xmm0 through %xmm7), which are 128 bits wide, but can only be used to store four 32-bit values simultaneously. The next iteration, SSE2, was introduced on the Pentium IV and expanded the number of registers to 16 (%xmm0 through %xmm15) and made it so that they could be accessed in a variety of ways (as integer or floating-point values of various sizes). SSE2 is required to be available for the x86-64 instruction set on both AMD and Intel.

Some chips support additional extensions, such as later versions of SSE and various versions of AVX (advanced vector extensions) which, depending on the version, can support additional registers which are sized at up to 512 bits. However, we will not cover these additional extensions.

F.2 Working with SSE2 Registers

SSE2 registers are 128 bits long. However, they do not use 128-bit values. The register can be treated as two 64-bit values, four 32-bit values, eight 16-bit values, or sixteen 8-bit values. Operations on these registers, unless otherwise specified, occur for all values simultaneously. However, if you are only interested in one value, then the lowest-order bits are the ones considered (the instructions still operate on everything, but you can ignore the other values).

We will start considering only using the XMM registers for holding a solitary double-precision (64-bit) floating-point value.

You can use the standard movq instruction to move a quadword into or out of one of the XMM registers. If the destination register is an XMM register, then the high-order quadword is zeroed out. This is generally fine, especially if you are only working with one value at a time in the XMM registers. This is an easy way to move data back and forth from/to memory or from/to a general-purpose register.

We can load values one of two ways. We can either encode them in memory as floating-point values, or we can load them in as integers and convert them.

In the data section, just like there is the .quad directive for 64-bit integers, there is a .double directive for 64-bit floating-point values. We can encode these and load them just like normal. For instance:

```
myval:
    .double 57.2

.section .text

_start:
    movq myval, %xmm0
```

Note that there is no immediate-mode instructions for loading values.

Alternatively, we may be starting with integers and want to convert them to floating point. To do this, we can use cvtsi2sd, which means convert (cvt) a single value (s) that is an integer (i) to (2) a scalar (s) double-precision floating-point value (d). This takes a source register (which *cannot* be an XMM register) and a destination register (which *must* be an XMM register).

So, if we wanted the number 5 as a floating-point value, we can load it in to %xmm0 as follows:

```
movq $5, %rax           # Put the integer 5 in %rax
cvtsi2sd %rax, %xmm0    # Convert it to a double in %xmm0
```

F.3 Moving Whole Registers

To move a whole 128 bits, there are actually *numerous* instructions for doing so! There are two general classes of instructions—*aligned* instructions and *unaligned* instructions (see Appendix I for more details on alignment). The unaligned instructions are slower, but you can do them on any register or memory location. The aligned instructions are faster, but, if done using a value that is not 16 byte aligned, will trigger an exception.

The other difference between the instructions is that, on *some* processors, the instructions make slight speed differences if used on integer or floating-point values. The instructions are

- movdqu: This instruction is for unaligned moves optimized for integers.

- movdqa: This instruction is for aligned moves optimized for integers.

- movups: This instruction is for unaligned moves optimized for floating-point values.

- movaps: This instruction is for aligned moves optimized for integers.

So, if you are using registers or you know the memory you are loading from is aligned, use the aligned version of the instruction. Otherwise, use the unaligned version.[1]

---

[1] Strangely, there are actually *two more* instructions as well! movupd and movapd are equivalent to movups and movaps, but use more space and are therefore generally slightly less optimized.

F.4 Floating-Point Numbers and Function Calls

When making function calls that use floating-point numbers, there are several considerations. For parameters which are floating-point values, the registers %xmm0 through %xmm7 are used to pass the values. If a function takes both floating-point and non-floating-point values, the non-floating-point values are passed in the ordinary way (using %rdi, %rsi, %rdx, %r8, and %r9), while floating-point values are passed using the XMM registers.

Additionally, for functions (like fprintf) which take a variable number of arguments, the number of XMM registers used should be put into %rax. The reason for this is so that the called function knows how many vector registers it needs to preserve.

If the return value is a floating-point value, it is returned in %xmm0.

So, if we had a function with the call signature double myfunc(int a, double b, int c, double d), we would pass a in %rdi, b in %xmm0, c in %rsi, and d in %xmm1. The return value would be in %xmm0. If this was a variadic function (i.e., it took a variable number of arguments), then we would set %rax to 2 in order to signify that only two XMM registers have contents of interest.

F.5 Floating-Point Arithmetic Operations

Now that the value is in the register, we can do standard operations with slightly different instructions. Adding an sd suffix to the end of the arithmetic instructions makes them operate on scalar (single-value), double-precision values. So, if %xmm0 and %xmm1 both have double-precision values loaded, I can do addsd %xmm0, %xmm1 to add them together and store the result in %xmm1.

Multiply (mulsd) and divide (divsd) now take both a source and destination operand. For division, the first operand is the divisor, and the second operand is the dividend and the destination for the resulting quotient.

When you are done with your floating-point operations, you have several options:

- Convert it back to an integer with cvtsd2si.

- movq it back to %xmm0 to be returned as the return value for your function.

- movq it to a register to pass as a parameter.

The following program will divide 1 by 3 and then print out the result using `fprintf`:

fpdiv.s

```
.globl main
output:
    .ascii "The result is %f\n\0"

.section .text
main:
    enter $0, $0

    movq $1, %rax
    movq $3, %rbx

    cvtsi2sd %rax, %xmm0
    cvtsi2sd %rbx, %xmm1

    divsd %xmm1, %xmm0

    movq stdout, %rdi
    movq $output, %rsi
    call fprintf

    leave
    ret
```

All of these operations can also be done using single-precision (32-bit) floating-point values as well. Simply modify the `sd` suffix to be `ss` (scalar single precision). This will give you the instructions `addss`, `subss`, `mulss`, `divss`, `cvtss2si`, and `cvtsi2ss`.

However, when passing it to a function (such as `fprintf`) that requires a double-precision value, you will need to change the "size" of the value to match. If you have a single-precision floating-point value and want to convert it to a double-precision floating-point value, you can use `cvtss2sd`, which you can call as `cvtss2sd SRC, DEST`. Or, if you need, you can go the other way with the similar instruction `cvtsd2ss`.

F.6 Vector Operations

In addition to handling individual values, SSE2 can also handle multiple values at the same time.

Since the XMM registers are 128 bits long, they can be used to store two double-precision values or four single-precision values. These are known as "packed" values, because you are packing more than one value into the register.

To move a value into a different part of the register, you can load directly into the low-order bytes of the register and then shift the register to the left to make room for the next one. However, the typical movq instruction will zero out the higher-order bytes when moving in a 64-bit value. Therefore, a different instruction, movsd, will move in a quadword but keep the higher-order bytes of the register intact.

However, to shift an XMM register to the left, we have to use SSE-specific instructions. The instruction pslldq will shift an XMM register to the left by a specific number of *bytes*. So, pslldq $8, %xmm5 will shift the contents of the %xmm5 register to the left by 8 bytes, allowing for another quadword to be inserted.

The following is a snippet of how to take a double-precision value that is in memory and copy it to both quadwords of an XMM register:

```
mydata:
    .double 1.5

.section .text
    # ... previous code ...
    movq mydata, %xmm6     # movq zeroes out upper bytes
    pslldq $8, %xmm6       # shift this value to higher-order bytes
    movsd mydata, %xmm6    # load the value into lower bytes
                           # without affecting upper bytes
```

Likewise, to extract values, you can just do an ordinary movq to move data out of the register and then shift the source register to the right with psrldq (which works the same way) to get at the next value.

You can use this same technique to load smaller values as well, though you will need to use the movss instruction to move 4 bytes (instead of eight) without affecting the others. While SSE can operate on word-sized and byte-sized values as well, you are probably best to *load* them either 4 or 8 bytes at a time.

Loading values in this way allows you to perform operations in parallel. For floating-point values, the instruction looks like the normal arithmetic instruction, but with a p added (for packed) and then d for double precision and s for single precision. Therefore, `mulpd %xmm0, %xmm1` would multiply together the low-order double-precision values of `%xmm0` and `%xmm1` and store it in the low-order double-precision location of `%xmm1`. Simultaneously, it would do the same for the high-order double-precision values. So you would actually be doing two parallel multiplies with the same instruction. If you are doing single-precision floating point, you can do four parallel multiplies with the same instruction.

The following program will multiply the value 2.1 by 5.0, 6.0, 7.0, and 8.0 simultaneously and then display the results using `fprintf`. In order to do all four at a time, the values will be stored as single-precision floats. However, the `fprintf` function requires that they be passed in separate registers as double-precision floating-point values. The majority of the code is dedicated to managing this transition—extracting values to individual XMM registers and converting them to double-precision floating-point values.

vectormultiply.s

```
.globl main

.balign 16
starting_value:
    .single 2.1, 2.1, 2.1, 2.1
multiply_by:
    .single 5.0, 6.0, 7.0, 8.0
output:
    .ascii "Results: %f, %f, %f, %f\n\0"

.section .text
main:
    enter $0, $0

    # Load the values a whole 128-bits at a time
    movaps starting_value, %xmm4
    movaps multiply_by, %xmm5

    # Multiply
```

```
mulps %xmm4, %xmm5

# Extract into parameters for fprintf
movss %xmm5, %xmm0        # Extract the first value to %xmm0
cvtss2sd %xmm0, %xmm0     # Upgrade from a float to a double
psrldq $4, %xmm5          # Shift the next value into position
movss %xmm5, %xmm1        # Extract the next value to %xmm1
cvtss2sd %xmm1, %xmm1     # Upgrade from a float to a double
psrldq $4, %xmm5          # Shift the next value into position
movss %xmm5, %xmm2        # Extract the next value to %xmm2
cvtss2sd %xmm2, %xmm2     # Upgrade from a float to a double
psrldq $4, %xmm5          # Shift the next value into position
movss %xmm5, %xmm3        # Extract the next value to %xmm3
cvtss2sd %xmm3, %xmm3     # Upgrade from a float to a double

movq $4, %rax # Protect 4 XMM registers

# Invoke function
movq stdout, %rdi
movq $output, %rsi
call fprintf

leave
ret
```

As you can see, although the marshalling of the values into parameters took some doing, the actual multiplication was done with a single instruction! If you have a lot of mathematics to do, this is a fast way to get it done.

SSE can also perform vector operations with integers as well. For those, the instructions are *prefixed* with a p (for packed), then the name of the operation, and then the size of the operands (b for bytes, w for words, d for double-words, and q for quadwords). So, paddw %xmm0, %xmm1 adds each byte of %xmm0 to %xmm1.

In any case, this has been an extremely short (and simplified) introduction to a huge topic. For more, the official reference manuals from Intel and AMD have a lot of good information. Additionally, Daniel Kusswurm's *Modern x86 Assembly Language* has a lot of detail about SSE programming as well as other vector extensions such as AVX, AVX2, and AVX-512.

APPENDIX G

The Starting State of the Stack

The stack starts off with the following values already in place (from high memory to low):

- Null pointer

- Pointer to the nth environment variable (if present)

- Pointer to the second environment variable (if present)

- Pointer to the first environment variable (if present)

- Null pointer

- Pointer to the nth program argument (if present)

- Pointer to the second program argument (if present)

- Pointer to the first program argument (if present)

- Pointer to the program filename

- Command line argument count (including the command itself)

Therefore, if you are in the `_start` entry point, you can walk through stack offsets to load this information into your program. The environment variables are stored as single strings, such as `MYVAR=MYVAL`, which, if you were interested in, you would need to separate into the key (`MYVAR`) and the value (`MYVAL`).

So, for instance, the following code loads the argument count into `%rax` and the pointer to the filename into `%rbx`:

```
_start:
    movq 0(%rsp), %rax
    movq 8(%rsp), %rbx
```

293

© Jonathan Bartlett 2021
J. Bartlett, *Learn to Program with Assembly*, https://doi.org/10.1007/978-1-4842-7437-8_26

If you are using the C library (and starting with main instead of _start), then the C library has done this for you. The first parameter to main is the command line argument count (and therefore will be available in %rdi). The second parameter to main is a pointer to the array of pointers to the command line argument strings, and this pointer will be in %rsi. Finally, you can get environment variables individually by calling the getenv function or get all of them by calling the environ function.

Note that while the beginning of the stack (growing downward in memory) is *near* 0x00007ffffffffffff, Linux implements some randomization to this to prevent hackers from being able to guess where in memory the stack actually lives.

ASCII, Unicode, and UTF-8

This book focuses on using ASCII codes for character data. As mentioned, the reason for this is that ASCII is fairly straightforward and is also compatible with the more advanced international standard, Unicode, to some degree.

H.1 Unicode

The core problem that Unicode attempts to solve is that, prior to Unicode, a whole hosts of ad hoc solutions had been implemented to add additional characters to strings, and none of them had a big picture in mind. In most of these systems, you could choose a set of characters, often known as a **code page**, and that essentially mapped a set of numbers to how they were displayed on-screen.

The problem with the code page approach becomes apparent (a) when you want to mix code pages and (b) when different groups come up with different code pages. What if you want to write a paper in Kanji (a Japanese writing system) about Sanskrit and its development into Hebrew? All of a sudden, code pages start looking pretty limited.

However, there is a problem with expanding the character sets, whether standardized or not. All *existing* documents generally used ASCII. Moving to a new standard would be difficult if all of your old documents (and old programs) were now defunct.

The solution that the Unicode Consortium came up with is to separate out the *list of characters* from *how they are represented*. Unicode assigns each character, in any language, a 32-bit number. Thirty-two bits gives them over four billion possibilities, so they are unlikely to run out. The current version of Unicode (Unicode 13.0) has 143,859 characters. This is much more than can be represented in 8 or 16 bits, but is a tiny fraction of what is available on inside 32 bits.

© Jonathan Bartlett 2021
J. Bartlett, *Learn to Program with Assembly*, https://doi.org/10.1007/978-1-4842-7437-8_27

When talking about Unicode characters, they are referenced as U+XXXX, where XXXX is a hexadecimal value. This is known as the character's **code point**. Since most values for most languages are in the first 16 bits, Unicode code points are usually referenced using 16-bit hexadecimal values, though any length hexadecimal value (up to 32 bits) can be used. For common ASCII characters, the code point and the ASCII code are the same.

H.2 Unicode Encodings and UTF-8

Even though every character has a unique code point, that doesn't mean that it has a unique representation on the computer. These representations are known as **character encodings**. A very simple character encoding for Unicode is **UTF-32**. In this encoding, each character is 32 bits wide, and the value is simply the Unicode value. This is a straightforward encoding and can be treated in code fairly simply. The problem is that it isn't compatible with hardly anything.

Therefore, the encoding of choice is usually UTF-8. UTF-8 utilizes *different* lengths of characters. Therefore, if I want to find the 13th character in a string, I can't just do an indexed lookup. Instead, I have to go through each character individually (figuring out its length along the way) in order to find the 13th character. The advantage, however, is that if you are using an old program that doesn't read UTF-8, if you just use standard English characters, it looks like ASCII.

The way that UTF-8 encodes characters of different length is by using the first bit of the first byte to specify if the character is multibyte or not. In traditional ASCII, the first bit is always zero, so this doesn't cause any problems with ASCII.

The way that UTF-8 is encoded is as follows:

- **Code points U+0000 to U+007F**: Encoded as 1 byte, 0xxxxxxx (7 bits)

- **Code points U+0080 to U+07FF**: Encoded as 2 bytes, 110xxxxx 10xxxxxx (11 bits)

- **Code points U+0800 to U+FFFF**: Encoded as 3 bytes, 1110xxxx 10xxxxxx 10xxxxxx (16 bits)

- **Code points U+10000 to U+10FFFF**: Encoded as 4 bytes, 11110xxx 10xxxxxx 10xxxxxx 10xxxxxx (21 bits)

Here, each x represents a bit from the Unicode code point value. For example, the Greek lowercase beta (β) is the code point U+03B2. In binary, this is 1110110010, which is ten bits long. In UTF-8, this gets encoded as 2 bytes, which allows for 11 bits, so the value gets extended to 01110110010. This gets encoded into the format specified previously as 11001110 10110010 or, in hexadecimal, 0xCEB2.

If you were to try to find the *n*th character of a string, you would use the initial bits of each character to know how long the character should be.

H.3 Some Weird Bits of UTF-8

Also, in UTF-8, some documents start with a byte-order mark (BOM), which is based on another Unicode encoding, UTF-16. When translated to UTF-8, this value is 0xEFBBBF. If this value occurs at the start of a UTF-8 file, it can be basically ignored.

One important issue that I've had some (bad) experience with is the Unicode character U+FFFD, the "Unicode Replacement Character." This character is sometimes used by systems which are doing text processing but encounter invalid characters. It simply replaces them with this character. In UTF-8, this is encoded as 0xEFBFBD.

If a binary file or data stream gets processed by a system expecting text, you can sometimes tell this has happened by the proliferation of 0xEFBFBD bytes in the output.

H.4 Final Thoughts on Unicode

Unicode has a lot of additional terminology to deal with technical aspects of character representation and display, which is out of scope for this book. Just know that displaying characters from a wide variety of languages, some of which the concept of "character" doesn't quite match up, has a lot of problems which people have spent a lot of time trying to solve. This explains most of the weird terminology and intricate details that Unicode provides.

H.5 An ASCII Table

ASCII is sufficiently important that I would be remiss if I did not provide you with a standard table of ASCII characters. To use Table H-1, find the character of interest, and add the number on the top row to the number in the left column.

Table H-1. *Table of ASCII codes in decimal*

	+0	+1	+2	+3	+4	+5	+6	+7
0	NULL	SOH	STX	ETX	EOT	ENQ	ACK	BEL
8	BS	HTAB	LF	VTAB	FF	CR	SO	SI
16	DLE	DC1	DC2	DC3	DC4	NAK	SYN	ETB
24	CAN	EM	SUB	ESC	FS	GS	RS	US
32		!	"	#	$	%	&	'
40	(	)	*	+	,	-	.	/
48	0	1	2	3	4	5	6	7
56	8	9	:	;	<	=	>	?
64	@	A	B	C	D	E	F	G
72	H	I	J	K	L	M	N	O
80	P	Q	R	S	T	U	V	W
88	X	Y	Z	[	\	]	^	_
96	`	a	b	c	d	e	f	g
104	h	i	j	k	l	m	n	o
112	p	q	r	s	t	u	v	w
120	x	y	z	{			}		DEL

However, even ASCII is not as standard as we might wish. For instance, the way that computers encode the end of line varies. On Windows, the standard is to have two characters encode the end of the line, a **carriage return** (CR), which brings you back horizontally to the beginning of the line, and a **line feed** (LF), which takes you vertically to the next line. On Unix-based machines, a single LF (also called a **newline**) was used to mark the end of the line and performed both the horizontal and vertical activities. Finally, on extremely old Macintoshes, the standard was to use a single carriage return! Added to this mess is the question of how many spaces should a horizontal tab represent, and that can lead to many arguments and disputes which I will leave to others.[1]

---

[1] My own opinion, should anyone care, is that tabs should generally be preferred to spaces for leading spacing, but that the specific number of spaces they represent should not be fixed, but represent a preference set by the user.

APPENDIX I

Optimization

While this isn't a book on optimizing assembly language, I did feel I should include a few basic optimization ideas, if only so that you will understand what other people are talking about when they talk about optimization. The code in this book is not intended to be optimal; it is intended to be explanatory. Therefore, in most cases, I opted to use code that was clear to the reader rather than optimal for the processor.

There are many reasons to learn assembly. The one that I have focused on in this book is learning assembly to better understand how programming works under the hood, so that the choices, limitations, and trade-offs made by various programming languages make more sense. Other people write in assembly language because, for certain platforms (like embedded processors), assembly language is actually best suited to what they are trying to do. However, some people gravitate to assembly language because they want to write code that executes really fast.

Optimizing assembly language code is a bit of a black art, as it requires fairly intricate knowledge about how the CPU's instruction-processing architecture works. Modern processors are complex beasts with the goal of maximizing every nanosecond of operation. Historically, processors listed how many clock cycles each instruction took to complete, and if you wanted to optimize your code, the goal would be to simply find out how to minimize the number of clock cycles that your code would run. Today, it's not that clock cycles are irrelevant; it's just that there is a lot more going on in a processor that is even more likely to affect your code. This appendix will give you a brief introduction to some of the common background ideas that will help you understand assembly language code optimization.

© Jonathan Bartlett 2021
J. Bartlett, *Learn to Program with Assembly*, https://doi.org/10.1007/978-1-4842-7437-8_28

I.1 Alignment

We will start our discussion with the concept of **alignment** because it tends to seep into a lot of the other pieces of optimization. The processor tends to work with data in chunks. Even if you are dealing with individual values, behind the scenes, the processor and other parts of the computer are doing things in larger sizes.

For instance, from your code's perspective, every byte in memory has a separate address. I can just as easily load a quadword from memory location 17 as 18 or 19. However, for the actual hardware RAM, that is not the case.

The RAM itself actually has a lower resolution than that. For x86-64 systems, data is usually grouped in quadword chunks (matching the word size of the processor). Practically, this means that if you try to load a quadword from memory, but the quadword does not have an address that is divisible by 8 (the number of bytes in a quadword), then the processor will actually have to load data from two different physical RAM locations and stitch together the result.

What this means is that you will want to pay attention to the data addresses so that the address that you want to load values from matches how it is physically stored in RAM.

The `.balign` directive (see Chapter 13) controls data alignment. So, to make sure that a value in the `.data` section is aligned on an 8-byte boundary, you would simply do `.balign 8` before marking the address with a label and adding your data.

Note that, as we will see, aligning with the data bus is not the only alignment worth worrying about!

I.2 Data Caching

Now let's take a look at the presence of data caches. When you access main memory, your processor puts a request on the data bus for the desired memory. It then has to *wait* for that request to be fulfilled. However, it is often the case that memory that is used once will be used again shortly. Therefore, the processor will store the value in one or more small caches that are on the processor itself. Then, when that memory is requested again, if it finds it in the cache (a **cache hit**), then it doesn't need to wait on the memory bus to fulfill its memory needs.

Data is transferred from memory to cache in chunks, called **cache lines** or **cache blocks.** Most x86-64 processors have 64-byte cache lines. Usually what happens is that, when you ask for memory, the processor assumes that you are going to want more than just the data you asked for eventually, so it goes ahead and requests more than the data needed to fulfill your request. It loads a full cache block from memory and then takes that data and adds it to the cache. These cache blocks are aligned to 64 bytes, so it won't necessarily just take the *next* 64 bytes, but all of the ones that are *within* the aligned block.

Therefore, if you are going to work several values from memory, having that memory all near each other helps the processor speed. If you have a large struct you are working with, for instance, the parts of the struct that are more likely to be accessed together should be stored near each other. This will improve cache performance. Additionally, you may even want to align some of your data to the nearest cache block using the directive `.balign 64`.

Cache management is a complex topic because of the sophisticated means that processors use to decide what and when to cache. However, the basics of keeping data together that is used together generally applies.

I.3 Pipelining

One of the ways that processors have given themselves a speed boost is by **pipelining** instructions. Modern CPU instructions are complex beasts, requiring a variety of operations from the processor, such as instruction fetching, instruction decoding, memory access, register access, arithmetic operations, floating-point operations, and writing the results of the operation to registers or memory.

Therefore, what modern processors do is divide the instruction up into phases. This allows the processor to execute multiple instructions at once. While one instruction is being decoded, another instruction is having memory fetched for it. The goal is to keep all of the individual "compartments" of the processor busy with different instructions.

In order to do this, the processor has to be able to detect when instructions can and can't be pipelined. If an instruction can't be pipelined with another instruction, that leads to what is known as a **pipeline stall**. For instance, if the first instruction ends by writing to %rax, but the next instruction has to read from %rax, the processor can't pipeline those instructions because the second is dependent on the first finishing. As a programmer, you don't have to worry about this—it's the processor's job to keep all this straight and not affect the *meaning* of your code. However, if you program with pipelining in mind, it allows you to help the processor execute your code optimally.

Essentially, the goal is to keep all parts of the processor busy, and not force it to wait around on the results of previous instructions as much as possible.

A **superscalar** processor takes this a step further and can even start two instructions simultaneously, or even execute them out of order (but only if the processor determines that this won't affect the meaning of the code).

I.4 Instruction Caching and Branch Prediction

In your processor, your code also lives in memory. Just like caching data, the processor can also cache the memory for your code, which makes it faster to load the next instruction. The processor is also very good at predicting where your program will be in the future, so it can prefetch upcoming instructions so that, when it comes time to execute them, you aren't waiting around on memory.

This all works fine until you hit a branch (i.e., a `jmp`, `call`, or especially a conditional `jmp`). At a branch, your code is not necessarily going to the next instruction. At a conditional branch, the processor isn't even capable of determining ahead of time which branch will be taken for certain. With an indirect jump, even the target of the branch may not be known ahead of time. This affects both caching and pipelining, because both require the processor to know which instructions is coming next.

Branch prediction allows processors to *guess* which branch of a conditional branch the code is likely to take. It doesn't need to be correct—it is just faster if it is correct. Otherwise, it will cache the wrong instructions and start the pipeline on them (known as **speculative execution**). Then, when the branch doesn't follow the processor's predictions, the pipeline will stall while the pipeline is cleared and the actual instructions are read from memory.

Branch prediction can be done in a variety of ways, from simple (always guess the same way) to more sophisticated (keeping track of how often different branches are or aren't taken). The x86 instruction set even allows you to hint to the processor whether you think the branch is more likely to be taken or not, though modern processors no longer use these hints.

Additionally, when doing indirect jumps, the processor has to do an even tougher feat—predict even where the jump might go! Again, modern processors can do this to some extent, but it does rely on putting the value into the register sufficiently far before the jump that the processor can predict the destination ahead of time and prepare accordingly.

Another point is that it is sometimes helpful for branch targets to be aligned to cache lines. This allows more efficient movement of code into your instruction cache when the branch is predicted. You can use the `.balign` directive in the `.text` section in order to have your branch targets be properly aligned. While `.balign` pads data with zeroes when in data sections, it pads instructions with `nop` (or equivalent) instructions when in the `.text` section.

I.5 Choosing Instructions and Registers

Instruction choice is also an important subject. Different instructions have a different physical size in bytes (see Appendix K), which affects caching. Additionally, different instructions can affect pipelining in different ways. For instance, the SSE instructions `movaps` and `movapd` (see Appendix F) actually perform identical operations, but `movaps` is encoded using fewer bytes and therefore fits better in the instruction cache. As noted in Chapter 11, despite the fact that the `enter` instruction is specifically for setting up stack frames, it tends to be slower than just setting them up by hand, despite it taking more instructions.

Register choice is also important. Sometimes, for instance, it is better to use a new register for a result than reuse and existing register, as it allows better pipelining.

I.6 Further Resources

There is much more that can be considered when thinking about optimizing assembly language. The goal of this chapter is to give a few broad strokes of the kinds of things that expert assembly language programmers think about when doing optimization. If this is something you find interesting, pursuing it further usually requires simply knowing more about the internals of how processors are architected and details about how exactly various instructions operate. Much of that is found in reference form from Intel and AMD, but also a great collection of resources for understanding optimized assembly language has been collected by Agner Fog, available at `https://agner.org/`.

Additionally, for a book on optimized techniques for programming x86-64 assembly language, see Daniel Kusswurm's *Modern x86 Assembly Language*.

APPENDIX J

A Simplified Garbage Collector

In Chapter 17, we discussed garbage collection. However, the code for the garbage collector was a little too long for inclusion in the chapter. This appendix has the complete code for the garbage collector.

This collector has a lot of limitations, and its primary purpose is to give you an idea of how garbage collection works in general. It is unlikely that this particular collector would be useful for anything other than demonstration purposes.

Some limitations include

- You have to explicitly initialize the collector at the start of your program by calling gc_init.

- You have to explicitly request collection by calling gc_scan.

- All pointers have to be 16 byte aligned.

- All pointers have to exist in the stack or on the heap to be scanned properly.

- All pointers have to be pointers to the *start* of a section of memory to be scanned properly.

- This only works with a single stack (and therefore only single-threaded code).

- This doesn't work with any other allocator.

- During the scan, this implementation temporarily doubles allocated memory.

© Jonathan Bartlett 2021
J. Bartlett, *Learn to Program with Assembly*, https://doi.org/10.1007/978-1-4842-7437-8_29

The code is organized as follows:

- `gc_defs.s` contains the `.equ` directives needed for the rest of the program.

- `gc_globals.s` contains the global variables shared by all the garbage collection code.

- `gc_init.s` contains the code for the `gc_init` function, which initializes the garbage collector. This saves the location of the beginning of the stack and initializes the beginning/end of the heap.

- `gc_allocate.s` contains the allocator function, `gc_allocate`, which works pretty much like the rest of the allocator functions we have encountered in this book. It also zeroes out the memory so that we don't have any accidental pointers being referenced.

- `gc_scan.s` contains the garbage collection function, `gc_scan`. The details of this function are further divided into other files:

  - `gc_scan_init.s` contains the code to initialize the scan. It records the current stack position and then allocates enough memory to store the potential pointer list.

  - `gc_unmark_all.s` this marks all allocations as being "unused." They will then be remarked as used when pointers to them are detected.

  - `gc_scan_memory.s` this takes a location in memory and the size of that memory and scans it for potential pointers to the heap.

  - `gc_scan_base_objects.s` scans the base objects—the stack and the data sections (`.data`, `.rodata`, and `.bss`)—for potentially valid pointers.

  - `gc_walk_pointers.s` walks through the pointer list and checks each pointer to see if the pointer points to memory that is (a) a valid heap allocation and (b) is currently unmarked. If so, it marks the memory as being in use and then scans the memory for more pointers.

  - `gc_is_valid_ptr.s` contains code for determining if a given pointer actually points to the start of a heap memory allocation.

- gc_scan_cleanup.s returns the memory that was allocated for list keeping.

- gc_test.c does a short test showing the usage of the garbage collector in C code.

Again, this is not meant to be optimal in any way, or even ready for production (or even non-production) use. It is merely meant to give you a concrete feeling for the way that garbage collectors can operate.

gc_defs.s

```
.globl BRK_SYSCALL
.globl HEADER_SIZE, HDR_IN_USE_OFFSET, HDR_SIZE_OFFSET

.equ BRK_SYSCALL, 12
.equ HEADER_SIZE, 16
.equ HDR_IN_USE_OFFSET, 0
.equ HDR_SIZE_OFFSET, 8
```

gc_globals.s

```
.include "gc_defs.s"
.globl heap_start, heap_end, stack_start, stack_end
.globl pointer_list_start, pointer_list_end, pointer_list_current

.section .data
heap_start:
    .quad 0
heap_end:
    .quad 0
stack_start:
    .quad 0
stack_end:
    .quad 0
.equ pointer_list_start, heap_end # These are the same
pointer_list_end:
    .quad 0
pointer_list_current:
    .quad 0
```

gc_init.s

.globl gc_init

.section .text
gc_init:

```
    # Assume %rbp has the previous stack frame,
    # and is properly aligned
    movq %rbp, stack_start

    # Save the location of the heap
    movq $BRK_SYSCALL, %rax
    movq $0, %rdi
    syscall

    movq %rax, heap_start
    movq %rax, heap_end

    ret
```

gc_allocate.s

.include "gc_defs.s"
.globl gc_allocate

.section .text

```
# Register usage:
#  - %rdx - size requested
#  - %rsi - pointer to current memory being examined
#  - %rcx - copy of heap_end
```

allocate_move_break:

```
    # Old break is saved in %r8 to return to user
    movq %rcx, %r8

    # Calculate where we want the new break to be
    # (old break + size)
    movq %rcx, %rdi
    addq %rdx, %rdi
    # Save this value
    movq %rdi, heap_end
```

```
    # Tell Linux where the new break is
    movq $BRK_SYSCALL, %rax
    syscall

    # Address is in %r8 - mark size and availability
    movq $1, HDR_IN_USE_OFFSET(%r8)
    movq %rdx, HDR_SIZE_OFFSET(%r8)

    # Actual return value is beyond our header
    addq $HEADER_SIZE, %r8
    movq %r8, %rax
    ret

gc_allocate:
    enter $0, $0

    pushq $0    # Keep stack aligned
    pushq %rdi # Save for later
    call gc_allocate_internal

    # Zero out the block to eliminate false pointers
    movq %rax, %rdx # Save original pointer
    popq %rcx        # Get the size of the block
zeroloop:
    movb $0, (%rdx)
    incq %rdx
    loop zeroloop

    leave
    ret

gc_allocate_internal:
    # Save the amount requested into %rdx
    movq %rdi, %rdx
    # Actual amount needed is actually larger
    addq $HEADER_SIZE, %rdx
    # Align %rdx to a 16-byte boundary
    addq $16, %rdx                      # Advance 16 bytes
    andq $0xfffffffffffffff0, %rdx   # Clear last bits
```

```
    # Put heap start/end in %rsi/%rcx
    movq heap_start, %rsi
    movq heap_end, %rcx

allocate_loop:
    # If we have reached the end of memory
    # we have to allocate new memory by
    # moving the break.
    cmpq %rsi, %rcx
    je allocate_move_break

    # is the next block available?
    cmpq $0, HDR_IN_USE_OFFSET(%rsi)
    jne try_next_block

    # is the next block big enough?
    cmpq %rdx, HDR_SIZE_OFFSET(%rsi)
    jb try_next_block

    # This block is great!
    # Mark it as unavailable
    movq $1, HDR_IN_USE_OFFSET(%rsi)
    # Move beyond the header
    addq $HEADER_SIZE, %rsi
    # Return the value
    movq %rsi, %rax
    ret

try_next_block:
    # This block didn't work, move to the next one
    addq HDR_SIZE_OFFSET(%rsi), %rsi
    jmp allocate_loop
```

gc_scan.s

.globl gc_scan
.section .text

```
# Parameters - none
```

```
# Registers - none
gc_scan:
    enter $0, $0

    # Setup space for pointer list
    call gc_scan_init
    # Unmark all objects
    call gc_unmark_all
    # Get initial set of pointers from base objects
    # (stack, data)
    call gc_scan_base_objects
    # Walk pointer list
    call gc_walk_pointers
    # Give back space from pointer list
    call gc_scan_cleanup

    leave
    ret
```

gc_scan_init.s

```
.globl gc_scan_init

# Make sure we *have* an rodata section, even if nothing is in there
.section .rodata

.section .text
gc_scan_init:
    enter $0, $0

    # Mark end of stack
    movq %rsp, stack_end

    # Calculate max memory we could need for pointer storage into %rdi
    # - Stack size
    movq stack_start, %rdi
    subq %rsp, %rdi
    # - Data section size
    movq $.rodata, %rdx
```

```
    andq $0xfffffffffffffff8, %rdi    # Align to 8-byte boundary

    movq $_end, %rcx
    subq %rdx, %rcx
    addq %rcx, %rdi
    # - Heap size
    movq heap_end, %rdx
    subq heap_start, %rdx
    addq %rdx, %rdi

    # The pointer space will be that many bytes
    # beyond the current heap end.
    movq pointer_list_start, %rdx
    addq %rdx, %rdi
    movq %rdi, pointer_list_end

    # pointer_list_start and _current start the same
    movq %rdx, pointer_list_current

    # Move the current break to this point
    # (new break already in %rdi)
    movq $BRK_SYSCALL, %rax
    syscall

    leave
    ret
```

gc_unmark_all.s

.include "gc_defs.s"

.globl gc_unmark_all
.section .text
gc_unmark_all:
```
    enter $0, $0

    movq heap_start, %rcx
    movq heap_end, %rdx
```

```
loop:
    cmpq %rcx, %rdx
    je finish

    movq $0, HDR_IN_USE_OFFSET(%rcx)
    addq HDR_SIZE_OFFSET(%rcx), %rcx
    jmp loop

finish:
    leave
    ret
```

gc_scan_base_objects.s

```
.globl gc_scan_base_objects
.section .rodata
.section .text
gc_scan_base_objects:
    enter $0, $0

    # the 'end' of the stack is the beginning
    # of the memory of the stack
    movq stack_end, %rdi
    # size is in %rsi
    movq stack_start, %rsi
    subq %rdi, %rsi
    call gc_scan_memory

    # .rodata is the first data segment
    movq $.rodata, %rdi
    andq $0xfffffffffffffff8, %rdi    # Align to an 8-byte boundary
    # _end marks the end of data
    movq $_end, %rsi
    subq %rdi, %rsi
    call gc_scan_memory

    leave
    ret
```

gc_walk_pointers.s

```
.include "gc_defs.s"
.globl gc_walk_pointers

.equ LCL_SAVED_RBX, -16
gc_walk_pointers:
    enter $16, $0

    # %rbx is supposed to be preserved - save it
    movq %rbx, LCL_SAVED_RBX(%rbp)

    # get initial value of `current' pointer
    movq pointer_list_start, %rbx

loop:
    # End of the list?
    cmpq %rbx, pointer_list_current
    je finished

    # Get the next potential pointer
    movq (%rbx), %rdi

    # Skip if already checked/marked
    cmpq $1, HDR_IN_USE_OFFSET - HEADER_SIZE(%rdi)
    je continue

    # Is it valid?
    call gc_is_valid_ptr
    cmpq $1, %rax
    jne continue

    # Valid pointer

    # Mark as valid
    movq (%rbx), %rdi
    movq $1, HDR_IN_USE_OFFSET - HEADER_SIZE(%rdi)

    # Scan contents of memory area for other pointers
    movq HDR_SIZE_OFFSET - HEADER_SIZE(%rdi), %rsi
```

```
    subq $HEADER_SIZE, %rsi
    call gc_scan_memory
```

continue:
```
    # Next pointer
    addq $8, %rbx
    jmp loop
```

finished:
```
    # Restore %rbx
    movq LCL_SAVED_RBX(%rbp), %rbx

    leave
    ret
```

gc_is_valid_ptr.s

```
.include "gc_defs.s"
.globl gc_is_valid_ptr
.section .text
gc_is_valid_ptr:
    enter $0, $0
    # %rdi has the pointer to check

    # Set %rcx to the first embedded pointer
    movq heap_start, %rcx
```

loop:
```
    leaq HEADER_SIZE(%rcx), %rax
    cmpq %rax, %rdi
    # It is the address - yay!
    je valid_ptr
    # We passed the address without finding it - boo!
    jb invalid_ptr

    # haven't gotten there yet - keep going

    # Find the location of the next pointer and loop
    addq HDR_SIZE_OFFSET(%rcx), %rcx
    jmp loop
```

invalid_ptr:
```
    movq $0, %rax
    leave
    ret
```

valid_ptr:
```
    movq $1, %rax
    leave
    ret
```

gc_scan_cleanup.s

```
.globl gc_scan_cleanup
gc_scan_cleanup:
    # Done with the pointer list - move break back to where it was
    movq $BRK_SYSCALL, %rax
    movq heap_end, %rdi
    syscall
```

A short example program which shows the garbage collector in action is here:

gc_test.c

```c
#include <stdio.h>

void *gc_allocate(int);
void gc_scan();
void gc_init();

volatile void **foo;
volatile void **goo;

int main() {
    gc_init();

    foo = gc_allocate(500);
    fprintf(stdout, "Allocation 1: %x\n", foo);
    goo = gc_allocate(200);
    foo[0] = goo; // Hold reference to goo so it won't go away
    fprintf(stdout, "Allocation 2: %x\n", goo);
```

```
    gc_scan();
    goo = gc_allocate(300);
    fprintf(stdout, "Allocation 3: %x\n", goo);
    gc_scan();

    goo = gc_allocate(200);
    fprintf(stdout, "Allocation 4: %x\n", goo);
    gc_scan();

    // This will be put in  the same spot as allocation 3
    goo = gc_allocate(200);
    fprintf(stdout, "Allocation 5: %x\n", goo);
    gc_scan();

    foo = gc_allocate(500); // No longer holding reference to allocations 1
                            & 2
    fprintf(stdout, "Allocation 6: %x\n", foo);
    gc_scan();

    // This will be put in the same spot as allocation 1
    goo = gc_allocate(10);
    fprintf(stdout, "Allocation 7: %x\n", goo);
    // This will be put in the same spot as allocation 2
    foo = gc_allocate(10);
    fprintf(stdout, "Allocation 8: %x\n", foo);

}
```

You can compile all of this together and run it with

```
gcc gc_*.* -o gc_test
./gc_test
```

APPENDIX K

Going to an Even Lower Level

This book has been focused on assembly language programming. For most computer programmers, assembly language is really the lowest-level language they will ever need to deal with. Nonetheless, for those interested in going deeper, here we will give a small taste of what is beneath.

K.1 Instruction Formats

Remember that, in computers, everything is stored as a number. Everything. That includes the instructions that operate the computer. When you assemble your files, it is converting the operations you give (often called **mnemonics**) into numbers to represent those commands.

In the x86-64 instruction set architecture, these instructions have a variable size. Some instructions are a single byte long, while others can be up to 15 bytes long. The format is a little strange due to the long history of the x86 platform, originating as a 16-bit platform, going through a stage as a 32-bit platform, and winding up today as a 64-bit platform, all while maintaining backward compatibility throughout.

Instructions are geared around **opcodes**, which are numbers that represent an instruction. The opcodes don't *exactly* match the mnemonics, but they are close. Occasionally, a mnemonic will encode multiple opcodes based on the operands.

The basic format is as follows:

1. Prefixes (1 byte for each prefix)

2. Opcode (1–3 bytes)

3. ModR/M (1 byte if required by the opcode)

© Jonathan Bartlett 2021
J. Bartlett, *Learn to Program with Assembly*, https://doi.org/10.1007/978-1-4842-7437-8_30

4. SIB (1 byte if required by the opcode)

5. Displacement (1, 2, 4, or 8 bytes if required by the opcode)

6. Immediate (1, 2, 4, or 8 bytes if required by the opcode)

Prefixes modify the operation of the instruction, though, in some cases, the prefix is considered more or less part of the instruction itself. We have already seen prefixes before with the rep family of prefixes. These are encoded before the block instructions to cause them to repeat (see Chapter 9). rep and repe are encoded as a prefix value of 0xf3 and repne is encoded as 0xf2. rep and repe share a prefix because they modify different instructions.

An important prefix that we have not covered in this book is the LOCK prefix (0xf0). This can be added to an instruction to tell the processor that it alone should have a cache line for the memory location referenced in the instruction. This is used to maintain synchronization among multiple CPUs. You can add the lock prefix in assembly language to any instruction dealing with memory to be sure that only you have access to that memory for the duration of the instruction.

The other set of prefixes is known as the REX family of prefixes, which causes legacy instructions (those that were available in the 32-bit platform) to work as 64-bit instructions. The assembler automatically adds the REX prefix to the instruction when needed. The format of the REX prefixes is somewhat complicated, so we won't go into the details. However, the REX prefix always goes immediately before the instruction.

After the prefixes comes the opcode. The opcode is 1–3 bytes long, and it tells the processor *which* instruction it should be doing. These don't exactly translate to the instructions we have been doing, but they do so loosely. For instance, the opcodes for the mov family of instructions vary depending on both the size and the arguments. For instance, the opcode for the movl instruction is 0x89 when the source is a register, but is 0x8b when the source is memory (either opcode can be used for register-to-register moves) and is 0xb8 when the source is an immediate-mode value. For the equivalent movq instructions, the same opcodes are used in those cases, but an appropriate REX prefix is added. However, if you were to be moving individual bytes, different opcodes are used entirely.

The ModR/M byte tells the processor which registers are being used and/or what addressing modes are being used. Its format is both tricky and variable, so we won't cover it here.

The SIB (scale-index-base) byte is used when doing indexed addressing modes. It encodes within it which register is the base register, which register is the index register, and which register is the base register.

You might have noticed that having single bytes to represent these attributes doesn't sound like enough to specify all the combinations of registers you might want to use. The variations of the REX prefix actually can extend these bytes further to express the larger set of registers available on x86-64 platforms.

After the ModR/M and SIB bytes is the displacement, which is only used if needed, and can be 1, 2, or 4 bytes long. The displacement is the fixed value used in the various addressing modes. It may encode an entire address (for direct addressing), or it may be a displacement to a base pointer address.

Last, if needed, is an immediate-mode value, which can be 1, 2, or 4 bytes long. For instance, if doing movq $7, %rax, the 7 would be encoded here.

Let us look at a simple instruction and see how it is encoded. The instruction is movb $8, %ah. In this instruction, there are actually different opcodes for each destination register, starting with 0xb0 for using %al. So this gets encoded as 0xb4 0x08.

A more complex instruction is movq $8, %rbx. This is encoded as

0x48 0xc7 0xc3 0x08 0x00 0x00 0x00

The first value (0x48) is the appropriate REX prefix (since we are dealing with 64-bit values). The second value is the opcode (0xc7), which is an even different opcode for moving values. This one allows for shorter values that then get sign extended into the full register, so that you can encode it in fewer bytes. The 0xc3 is the ModR/M byte which specifies (among other things) that the instruction is using the %rbx register. Finally, the 0x08 0x00 0x00 0x00 is the little-endian encoding of the value 8 as a 4-byte immediate value.

In any case, the details of how instructions are encoded are beyond the scope of this book, but I wanted to give you at least a feel for it.

K.2 Electronics

Down even lower, everything in computers is implemented with electrical signals. While I've rarely (if ever) had the need to understand the underlying electrical circuits behind the computer in order to program well, it is nonetheless a fascinating area to look into.

Everything on the computer is ultimately implemented through a series of microchips, which each hold a plethora of logic gates, which are each ultimately made up of transistors. The design of a computer, as you might have guessed, is very complicated. Nonetheless, if this is of interest to you, let me suggest some books to help you understand this part of computing (which is really electrical engineering) better:

- *Electronics for Beginners* by Jonathan Bartlett (yes, that's me!): This book is a straightforward introduction to working with electronic circuits for the absolute beginner. While it is for beginners, it actually has a significant amount of material that is targeted toward someone aiming to be a professional.

- *The Art of Electronics* by Paul Horowitz: This book essentially starts where *Electronics for Beginners* leaves off. Every professional I know of has a copy of this book. It details many important circuits, why they are useful, and caveats to their usage.

- *Build Your Own Computer: From Scratch* by David Whipple: This book actually shows you how to design your own simplified CPU. This uses a special piece of hardware, an FPGA (field programmable gate array), which is essentially like a microchip that is rewirable, to allow you to build a fully functioning processor from scratch! If you want to get even more into the messy details, Ben Eater has a YouTube video on how to make a simple 8-bit CPU using just components on breadboards at `https://eater.net/8bit/`. Another good book on this topic is *The Elements of Computing Systems: Building a Modern Computer from First Principles* by Noam Nissan and Shimon Schocken.

- *Computer Organization and Design* by David Patterson and John Hennessy or *Computer Architecture: A Quantitative Approach* by John Hennessy: These books are the standard for understanding how CPUs work at the organizational level. They discuss caching, parallelism, instruction set architectures, and a variety of other important topics in the design of CPU architecture. The former book is a more general approach, while the latter book contains many more technical details.

Index

A

abs function, 152

Accessing memory, 67

Addressing modes, 62–64, 67, 72, 272

Address of the memory, 61, 177

Address space, 111, 173, 174, 176, 184, 194

Advanced vector extensions (AVX), 285

Aligned instructions, 286

Allocator, 182, 183, 222, 226, 228

AND function, 107, 287

andq instruction, 114

Annotate, 170

Application binary interface, 138

Arguments, 30, 138

Arithmetic and logic unit (ALU), 18, 19

Arithmetic instructions, 33, 34, 50, 276

    commands, 36

    program, 35

Array, 16, 62, 63, 65

Artificial intelligence, 9, 10

ASCII codes, 295, 297

Assembly language, 1, 56, 112, 205

    tools, 2

    types, 5

Assembly language programming, 3, 25, 57, 249

AT&T syntax

    addressing modes, 272

    operand size, 272

    operator order, 272

    register names, 271

B

Base address, 194

Base case, 147

Base pointer indexed mode, 73

Base pointer mode, 72

Bigger integers, 104

Binary digit, 13, 37

Binary number, 39, 40, 99

Binary system, 13

Bitmask, 107

Bit operations, 108, 278

Block instructions, 279, 320

Blocks of memory, 117

    compare, 118

    copy, 117

    length of a string, 119

    scan, 118

Branching, 56

Branch prediction, 302

Breakpoint, 265–267

.bss section, 168, 171, 175, 206, 230

Buffer overflow, 179

Byte-order mark (BOM), 297

© Jonathan Bartlett 2021

J. Bartlett, *Learn to Program with Assembly*, https://doi.org/10.1007/978-1-4842-7437-8

Printed in the United States
by Baker & Taylor Publisher Services

Printed in the United States
by Baker & Taylor Publisher Services